Credits

Author

Vanesa S. Olsen

Reviewers

Don Davis

Els van Tol - Homan

Acquisition Editor

Sarah Cullington

Development Editor

Chris Rodrigues

Technical Editors

Gauri Iyer

Prashant Macha

Project Coordinator

Shubhanjan Chatterjee

Proofreader

Samantha Lyon

Indexer

Tejal Daruwale

Production Coordinator

Aparna Bhagat

Cover Work

Aparna Bhagat

About the Author

Vanesa S. Olsen is a Speech Therapist. She has been working for more than six years in therapeutic centers, schools, and hospitals. She has been applying modern technologies in language disorders and learning disabilities treatments, and in helping schools to keep the students in the least restrictive environment. Specifically, she has been working with Alice 3, Moodle as an e-Learning platform, and other tools. She combined this software with the usage of Web 2.0 and general purpose modern hardware as gamepads, pen sketches, touch screens, netbooks, tablets, smartphones, and joysticks. She enjoys helping children and teenagers to improve their skills.

She has written another book for Packt Publishing, Moodle 1.9 for Teaching Special Education Children (5-10): Beginner's Guide.

She lives with her husband, Gaston, and his little son, Kevin. When she is not working, she devotes her spare time to her family and hobbies. She enjoys modeling in cold porcelain, swimming, and researching about new technologies and techniques to apply in her treatments.

You can contact her at vanesaolsen@gmail.com and also at olsenvanesa@live.com.

Acknowledgement

While writing this book, I was fortunate enough to work with an excellent team at Packt Publishing Ltd, whose contributions vastly improved the presentation of this book. Sarah Cullington helped me to transform the idea in the final book and to shape this Cookbook. Shubhanjan Chatterjee helped me to follow an organized schedule. Chris Rodrigues provided many sensible suggestions regarding the text, the format, and the flow. The reader will notice his great work. Prashant Macha and Gauri Iyer made sure that all the recipes were accurate and added great value to the final drafts.

I would like to thank my reviewers, Don Davis and Els van Tol, for their thorough reviews and insightful comments. I was able to incorporate some of the knowledge and wisdom they have gained in their many years of experience with Alice in the classroom. The recipes and the pictures include their great feedback.

Special thanks go to my husband, Gaston Hillar, who suggested me to use new technologies in therapeutic environments a few years ago and motivated me to work on this new project. Moreover, I would like to thank my sister-in-law, Silvina Hillar, who also helped with her teaching expertise, my son Kevin and my nephew Nicolas, who enrich my life with their affect, my friends, and my fathers-in-law.

About the Reviewers

Don Davis has taught Alice in the classroom and discussed its use as a cognitive tool at state and international conferences. He is dedicated to researching and advocating the use of Free and Open Source Software in education. In his free time, he works to assist the Helios Project and `reglue.org` in providing refurbished GNU/Linux computers to students in need.

> I would like to thank Carnegie Mellon University for making Alice 3 available for GNU/Linux.

Els van Tol–Homan: is working as an informatics teacher in a High School (College Hageveld) at Heemstede/Netherlands. He has experience in teaching the following subjects: Hardware, Data communication, Programming (PHP, C++, Java, Alice, NXT), Project management, UML, and so on.

During the 15 years of his experience, he worked as a senior software engineer and developer in Research and Development areas for different institutes. He developed low-level software (such as device drivers) and high-level software (GUIs) for automation of science projects at different institutes, such as **ESRF (European Synchrotron Facility)**, European Molecular Biology Laboratory, and the University of Leiden.

Currently, he is working on a Dutch book about Alice 3.0 & Java.

Technical skills/experience: Java (J2SE, Java SE, J2EE, Java EE), JavaScript, SQL, PHP, XML, C, C++, Haskell, Python, Ruby, Open wonderland, Alice, OpenGL, 3D programming.

OS: MS Windows 9x/XP/NT,7, Linux

Databases: Oracle, MySQL

Web: J2EE, Java Security, JSP/Servlets, Java Applets, DHTML, JavaScript, CSS, PHP, Perl, XML, CGI, Apache, Zope

Alice 3 Cookbook

79 recipes to harness the power of Alice 3 for teaching students to build attractive and interactive 3D scenes and videos

Vanesa S. Olsen

[PACKT] open source
PUBLISHING
community experience distilled

BIRMINGHAM - MUMBAI

Alice 3 Cookbook

First published: April 2011

Production Reference: 1180411

Published by Packt Publishing Ltd.
32 Lincoln Road
Olton
Birmingham, B27 6PA, UK.

ISBN 978-1-849514-92-7

www.packtpub.com

Cover Image by Ed Maclean (edmaclean@gmail.com)

www.PacktPub.com

Support files, eBooks, discount offers, and more

You might want to visit www.PacktPub.com for support files and downloads related to your book.

Did you know that Packt offers eBook versions of every book published, with PDF and ePub files available? You can upgrade to the eBook version at www.PacktPub.com and as a print book customer, you are entitled to a discount on the eBook copy. Get in touch with us at service@packtpub.com for more details.

At www.PacktPub.com, you can also read a collection of free technical articles, sign up for a range of free newsletters, and receive exclusive discounts and offers on Packt books and eBooks.

http://PacktLib.PacktPub.com

Do you need instant solutions to your IT questions? PacktLib is Packt's online digital book library. Here, you can access, read, and search across Packt's entire library of books.

Why Subscribe?

- Fully searchable across every book published by Packt
- Copy and paste, print and bookmark content
- On demand and accessible via web browser

Free Access for Packt account holders

If you have an account with Packt at www.PacktPub.com, you can use this to access PacktLib today and view nine entirely free books. Simply use your login credentials for immediate access.

I would like to dedicate this book to my son Kevin and my husband Gaston

Table of Contents

Preface

Alice is a free and innovative 3D programming environment that makes it easy to create an animation for telling a story, playing an interactive game, or a video to share on the Web. Alice is a teaching tool designed as a revolutionary approach to teaching and learning introductory programming concepts.

Alice 3 Cookbook focuses on performing common tasks required in classrooms with Alice 3. The recipes target teachers who would like to take advantage of this exciting 3D environment in their classrooms and/or labs.

Alice 3 uses 3D graphics and a drag-and-drop interface to facilitate a more engaging, less frustrating programming experience. Each recipe provides step-by-step instructions that allow you to learn the most important Alice features by example. You will learn about everything from the addition of the initial actors, up to the advanced procedures to react to the keyboard and mouse input.

You will work with the different elements that compose a scene and learn how to change the values for properties and run simple methods. Discover how to create simple animations that will allow you to recognize the most important elements of the user interface and explore the models provided by Alice to use them in games.

A cookbook for teachers filled with practical recipes for showing students how to build scenes with animations and videos, using Alice 3

What this book covers

Chapter 1, Setting Scenes: This chapter provides many tasks that will allow us to start working with simple scenes in Alice 3. We will work with the different elements that compose a scene. We will change the values for properties and run simple methods. We will render simple animations that will allow us to recognize the most important elements of the user interface. In addition, by performing the different tasks, we will be able to explore the models provided by Alice and check their capabilities to use them in games and animations.

Chapter 2, Working with Actors: This chapter provides many tasks that will allow us to start making simple animations with many actors in the 3D environment provided by Alice. We will search for models of specific animals in the diverse galleries. We will locate and orient the actors in the 3D space. We will give some simple orders to the actors to create simple animations. We will learn to work with procedures with many required and optional parameters. We will move, rotate, resize, and orient actors. In addition, we will put a rabbit face to face with a dressed white rabbit.

Chapter 3, Organizing Statements: This chapter provides many tasks that will allow us to start controlling the behavior of animations with many actors performing different actions. We will execute many actions with a specific order. We will use counters to run one or more statements many times. We will execute actions for many actors of the same class. We will run code for different actors at the same time to render complex animations. In addition, we will create a new procedure that will allow us to make some flowers dance with the wind.

Chapter 4, Working with Functions and Conditions: This chapter provides many tasks that will allow us to decide whether to run certain statements according to the results of the evaluation of expressions. We will define many actions that will run when certain things happen. We will use counters to evaluate a group of expressions many times. We will work with logical operators to combine many sub-expressions into a complex expression. We will use relational operators to compare values between functions and sub-expressions. We will run many statements while a condition is true. In addition, we will create a new function that will allow us to detect whether a red bird has hit the ground.

Chapter 5, Working with Variables: This chapter provides many tasks that will allow us to use variables to control values for some parameters. We will make many birds fly towards a fence. We will make these birds run different races. We will use variables to hold simple numbers but we will also use arrays to hold many instances of diverse kinds of birds. We will run conditional code according to the values of certain variables. In addition, we will use variables to work with parts of a hawk to make it move his wings while it moves. We will write the code to make the hawk fly.

Chapter 6, Working with Properties: This chapter provides many tasks that will allow us to use properties and to combine them with local variables and mathematic operations. We will define new properties to allow many hawks to fly with their own speed values. We will use properties to call procedures, edit their initial values, and combine these properties with local variables and mathematic operations. In addition, we will request the user to enter values and we will assign these values to properties.

Chapter 7, Working with People: This chapter provides many tasks that will allow us to use people as actors in our scenes. We will create a random person but we will also customize its body and its head. We will call simple procedures to perform complex animations with the person's body and its head. We will organize statements in different kinds of blocks to make people interact between them. We will create animations that show people talking to each other while performing realistic gestures and we will make people interact with the environment.

Chapter 8, Working with Keyboard and Mouse Input: This chapter provides many tasks that will allow us to control actors and the camera view with the keyboard and the mouse. We will define mouse and keyboard listeners and we will learn to program code in response to certain events. We will combine properties and conditional code to make sure that the user performs one action at a time with the keystrokes. We will allow the user to drag and drop actors to new locations in the scene. In addition, we will control the camera with the keyboard to provide dozens of exciting points of view for our scenes.

Chapter 9, Creating Interactive Stories: This chapter provides many tasks that will provide examples of how to combine all the things learned in previous chapters with some good ideas and the capabilities of the 3D models included in the galleries. We will change a girl's outfit, build a house, make people talk at a cafeteria, and allow the user to customize the layout of an amusement park. We will make a medieval knight kneel before a princess, animate the coach to throw a basketball through a hoop, and show living animals at a farm. In addition, we will allow the user to customize the layout of a bedroom.

Chapter 10, Customizing the Output: This chapter provides many tasks that will allow us to control cameras and the output produced by the real-time rendering process that transforms a viewport of the 3D world into a 2D frame. We will change the properties that define the active viewport and we will animate the camera while the actors move. We will generate a video and we will share it on YouTube. In addition, we will use shortcut keys to switch between multiple cameras and we will use different cameras to follow characters while they change their position in the 3D world.

What you need for this book

Alice version 3.0 (version 3.0.0.2.10 or higher)

Who this book is for

This book is designed primarily for teachers developing education plans and willing to exploit 3D environments using Alice 3. Alice users who want to improve their Alice programming skills will also find this book useful as it offers innovative 3D models in action. Some basic knowledge of Alice and how it works is necessary, although you are not expected to have worked with version 3 before.

Conventions

In this book, you will find a number of styles of text that distinguish between different kinds of information. Here are some examples of these styles, and an explanation of their meaning.

Code words in text are shown as follows: "Search for the `WhiteRabbit` class in the gallery."

A block of code is set as follows:

```
for each (Model m in birds)
    while (m.getDistanceBehind(this.fence) ≤ 0.25) is true
        m.move(FORWARD, STEP_SLOW, duration: 0.5)
    loop
loop
```

When we wish to draw your attention to a particular part of a code block, the relevant lines or items are set in bold:

```
for each (Model m in birds)
    while (m.getDistanceBehind(this.fence) ≤ 0.25) is true
        m.move(FORWARD, STEP_SLOW, duration: 0.5)
    loop
loop
```

Any command-line input or output is written as follows:

```
# cp /usr/src/asterisk-addons/configs/cdr_mysql.conf.sample
    /etc/asterisk/cdr_mysql.conf
```

New terms and **important words** are shown in bold. Words that you see on the screen, in menus or dialog boxes for example, appear in the text like this: "Click on the **Procedures** tab on the panel located behind the aforementioned dropdown list".

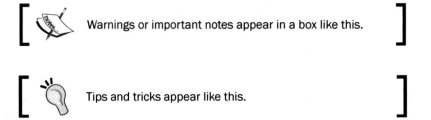

Warnings or important notes appear in a box like this.

Tips and tricks appear like this.

Reader feedback

Feedback from our readers is always welcome. Let us know what you think about this book—what you liked or may have disliked. Reader feedback is important for us to develop titles that you really get the most out of.

To send us general feedback, simply send an e-mail to feedback@packtpub.com, and mention the book title via the subject of your message.

If there is a book that you need and would like to see us publish, please send us a note in the **SUGGEST A TITLE** form on www.packtpub.com or e-mail suggest@packtpub.com.

If there is a topic that you have expertise in and you are interested in either writing or contributing to a book, see our author guide on `www.packtpub.com/authors`.

Customer support

Now that you are the proud owner of a Packt book, we have a number of things to help you to get the most from your purchase.

Downloading the example code for this book

You can download the example code files for all Packt books you have purchased from your account at `http://www.PacktPub.com`. If you purchased this book elsewhere, you can visit `http://www.PacktPub.com/support` and register to have the files e-mailed directly to you.

Errata

Although we have taken every care to ensure the accuracy of our content, mistakes do happen. If you find a mistake in one of our books—maybe a mistake in the text or the code—we would be grateful if you would report this to us. By doing so, you can save other readers from frustration and help us improve subsequent versions of this book. If you find any errata, please report them by visiting `http://www.packtpub.com/support`, selecting your book, clicking on the **errata submission form** link, and entering the details of your errata. Once your errata are verified, your submission will be accepted and the errata will be uploaded on our website, or added to any list of existing errata, under the Errata section of that title. Any existing errata can be viewed by selecting your title from `http://www.packtpub.com/support`.

Piracy

Piracy of copyright material on the Internet is an ongoing problem across all media. At Packt, we take the protection of our copyright and licenses very seriously. If you come across any illegal copies of our works, in any form, on the Internet, please provide us with the location address or website name immediately so that we can pursue a remedy.

Please contact us at `copyright@packtpub.com` with a link to the suspected pirated material.

We appreciate your help in protecting our authors, and our ability to bring you valuable content.

Questions

You can contact us at `questions@packtpub.com` if you are having a problem with any aspect of the book, and we will do our best to address it.

1

Setting Scenes

In this chapter, we will cover:

- ▸ Working with templates to create a new planet
- ▸ Checking the instances that compose a scene
- ▸ Inspecting the properties for each instance that composes a scene
- ▸ Defining a light's initial properties
- ▸ Animating light's properties
- ▸ Animating an instance's property
- ▸ Checking the procedures and functions for each instance
- ▸ Playing background music

Introduction

Alice 3 is the newest version of Alice. Alice is a teaching tool designed as a revolutionary approach to teaching and learning introductory programming concepts. Each recipe provides step-by-step instructions that allow you to learn the most important Alice 3 features by example. You will learn the most important concepts, from the addition of the initial actors to the advanced procedures to react to the keyboard and mouse input. The recipes allow you to harness the power of Alice 3 for teaching students to build attractive and interactive 3D scenes and videos.

Alice 3 uses 3D graphics and a drag-and-drop interface to facilitate a more engaging, less frustrating programming experience. This chapter provides many tasks that will allow us to start working with simple scenes in Alice 3.

We will work with the different elements that compose a scene. We will change the values for properties and run simple methods. We will render simple animations that will allow us to recognize the most important elements of the user interface. In addition, by performing the different tasks, we will be able to explore the models provided by Alice and check their capabilities to use them in games and animations.

Working with templates to create a new planet

In this recipe, we will make changes to an existing template. We will set a scene of a terrifying purple planet with a stormy sky. We will add statements to change the default color for a moon surface.

Getting ready

We have to make sure that Alice 3 has some specific preferences activated before running the steps to perform this recipe. Select **Window | Preferences | Gallery** and make sure that the following options are activated, as shown in the following screenshot:

- **Provided Initial Field Names In Prompt**
- **Include Type And Initializer Information In Prompt**
- **Include Preview In Prompt**

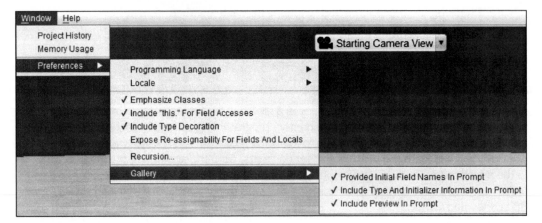

How to do it...

Follow these steps to set a scene of a terrifying purple planet with a stormy sky:

1. Click **Cancel** in the first dialog box that displays the templates for a new project. Alice will close this dialog box.

2. Select **File | New...** in the main menu to start a new project. A dialog box will display the six predefined templates with their thumbnail previews in the **Templates** tab.

3. Select `MoonProject.a3p` as the desired template for the new project and click **OK**. Alice will display a typical scene of the moon with a white marble surface and a black sky.

4. Click on **Edit Scene**, at the lower-right corner of the scene preview. Alice will show a bigger preview of the scene and will display the **Model Gallery** at the bottom.

5. Go to the **Model Gallery** and select **Generic Alice Models | Environments | Skies**. Use the horizontal scroll bar to find the `Stormsky` class, as shown in the next screenshot:

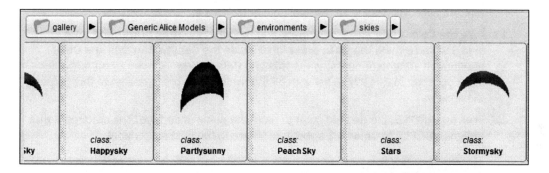

6. Click on the `Stormysky` thumbnail. Leave the default name, `stormysky`, for the new instance and click **OK** to add it to the existing scene. The scene preview will replace the black sky with a blue stormy sky.

7. Now, click on **Edit Code**, at the lower-right corner of the big scene preview. Alice will show a smaller preview of the scene and will display the **Code Editor** on a panel located at the right-hand side of the main window.

8. Click on the **class: MyScene** drop-down list and the list of classes that are part of the scene will appear.

9. Select **MyMoonSurface | Edit constructor**, as shown in the next screenshot:

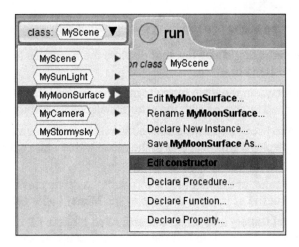

10. Click on the **Properties** tab on the panel, located at the left-hand side of the main window. Alice will display all the available properties for moonSurface.

11. Drag the **Color** assignment statement and drop it in the **Drop statement here** area, located behind the **do in order** label inside the **Constructor** tab. The **Color** assignment statement contains the **this** and **Color** labels followed by an arrow and three question marks **???**. A list with all the available colors to assign to this property will appear.

12. Click on **PURPLE**, the desired color to paint the planet's surface. The statement that assigns **PURPLE** to **Color** will appear as shown in the next screenshot:

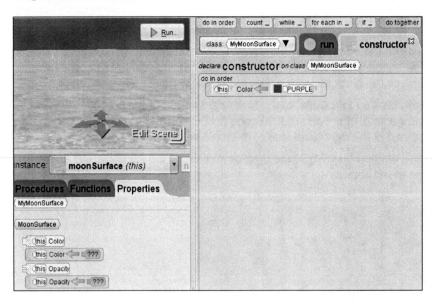

13. Select **File | Save as...** and give a name to the project, for example, `MyPurplePlanet`. Then you can use this new planet as a template for your next Alice project.

How it works...

When we create a new project, Alice provides six predefined templates. However, we wanted to customize the elements provided by the `MoonProject` template to set the scene of a purple planet.

The `Generic Alice Models` gallery provides dozens of skies that we can add as instances to our scenes. When we clicked on the thumbnail for the `Stormysky` class, the **Declare Property** dialog box provided information about what Alice was going to do, as shown in the following screenshot:

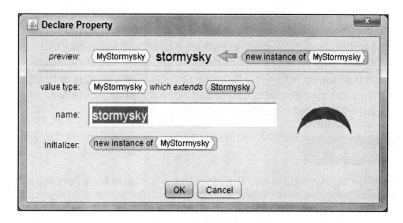

Alice defines a new class, `MyStormysky`, which extends `Stormysky`. `MyStormysky` is a new value type for the project, a subclass of `Stormysky`. A subclass is a class that is derived from another class or classes, and therefore, `MyStormysky` derives from `Stormysky`. The name for the new property that represents the new instance of `MyStormysky` is `stormysky`. This means that you can access this new element with the `stormysky` name and that this property is available for `scene`. Because the starting camera view is looking at the horizon, we see the new blue and stormy sky in the scene preview.

Alice creates each new object from a class and this object is called an **instance** of that class. When we add a new element or actor, we are adding a new object, known as an instance.

When you run the project, Alice shows a new window with the rendered scene. The planet's surface appears as a purple marble, as shown in the following screenshot:

The surface's color is different than the color shown in the scene preview. The MoonProject template defines a new class, `MyMoonSurface`, which extends `MoonSurface`. The name for the property that represents the instance of `MyMoonSurface` is `moonSurface`. We added a statement in the `MyMoonSurface` class constructor to set the value for its `Color` property to `PURPLE`. Alice doesn't run this statement at design-time, when you work design the scene and add your statement. However, when you run your project, Alice switches to run-time and runs the statements for each constructor to create each new instance. Therefore, the surface that was white appears with the color assigned to its `Color` property.

There's more...

Then, you can follow these steps to use the planet as a template for a new Alice project.

1. Select **File | New...** in the main menu to start a new project. A dialog box will display the six predefined templates with their thumbnail previews in the **Templates** tab. Click on **My Projects** to activate the tab that allows you to select from your projects.

2. Select `MyPurplePlanet.a3p` and click **OK**, as shown in the next screenshot:

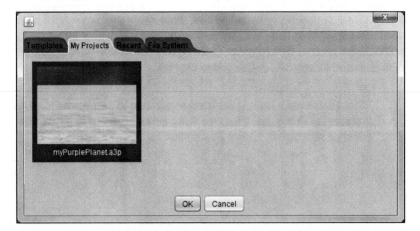

3. Select **File | Save as...** and give a new name to the project. Then, you can make changes to the project according to your needs.

See also

▶ *Checking the instances that compose a scene*, in this chapter

▶ *Inspecting the properties for each instance that composes a scene*, in this chapter

Checking the instances that compose a scene

In this task, we will learn to check the diverse elements that compose a scene. We will inspect their names and their classes. We will understand how Alice displays the information for each new instance added to the scene.

Getting ready

We have to be working on a project with some instances added to the virtual world. Therefore, we will use an existing project that has a stormy sky.

1. Open an existing project. You can open the **MyPurplePlanet** project saved in the *Working with templates to create a new planet* recipe.

2. Click on **Edit Scene**, at the lower-right corner of the scene preview. Alice will show a bigger preview of the scene and will display the names of all the elements that compose the scene at the upper-left corner, as shown in the following screenshot:

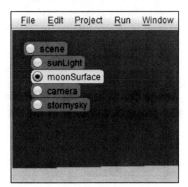

How to do it...

Follow these steps to inspect the instances that compose a scene:

1. Click on the `scene` element and then click on **Edit Code**, at the lower-right corner of the big scene preview. Alice will show a smaller preview of the scene and will display the **Code Editor** on a panel located at the right-hand side of the main window.

2. Click on the **class: MyScene** drop-down list and the list of classes that are part of the scene will appear.

3. Select **MyScene | Edit MyScene...**, as shown in the next screenshot:

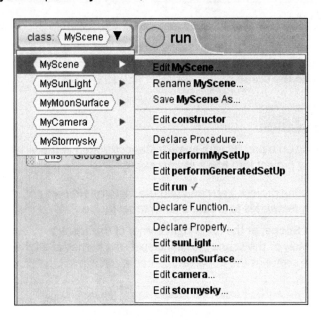

How it works...

When Alice displays the **Edit MyScene** dialog box, each element that composes the scene appears listed as a property. These properties appear in the **Properties** section, as shown in the next screenshot:

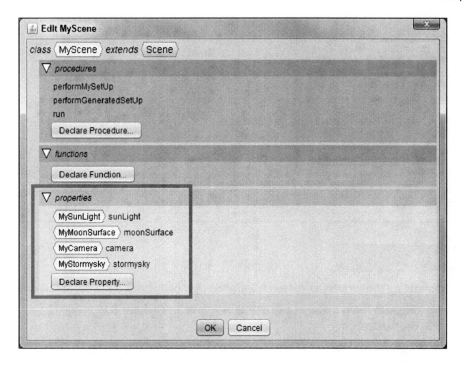

The dialog box shows the property type (the class name) followed by the property name. The following table summarizes the data presented in the previously shown dialog box:

Property type (Class name)	Property name
MySunLight	sunLight
MyMoonSurface	moonSurface
MyCamera	camera
MyStormysky	stormysky

There's more...

Double-click on one of the properties listed under **Properties** in the previous **Edit MyScene** dialog box and Alice will display the **Edit Field** dialog box. This dialog box allows you to rename the property name. For example, you can change the name of **moonSurface** to **purpleSurface**, as shown in the next screenshot:

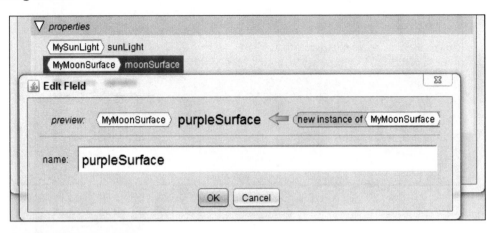

See also

▶ *Inspecting the properties for each instance that composes a scene*, in this chapter

▶ *Working with many instances of the same class*, in Chapter 6, *Working with Properties*

▶ *Working with templates to create a new planet*, in this chapter

Inspecting the properties for each instance that composes a scene

In this recipe, we will learn to inspect the diverse properties available for each instance that composes a scene. We will check their names and their types. We will be able to understand the purpose of each property because Alice uses very descriptive names for the properties.

Getting ready

We have to be working on a project with some instances added to the virtual world. Therefore, we will use an existing project that has a stormy sky.

1. Open an existing project. You can open the **MyPurplePlanet** project saved in the *Working with templates to create a new planet* recipe.

2. Click on **Edit Scene**, at the lower-right corner of the scene preview. Alice will show a bigger preview of the scene and will display the names of all the elements that compose the scene at the upper-left corner.

How to do it...

Follow these steps to inspect the properties for each instance that composes a scene:

1. Click on one of the elements displayed as part of the scene, such as **sunLight**, and then click on **Edit Code**, at the lower-right corner of the big scene preview. Alice will show a smaller preview of the scene. Below this preview, Alice will display a drop-down list with **sunLight** as the active instance and three tabs: **Procedures**, **Functions** and **Properties**.

2. Activate the **Properties** tab. Alice will display the properties for the **sunLight** instance, a property of **scene**, as shown in the next screenshot:

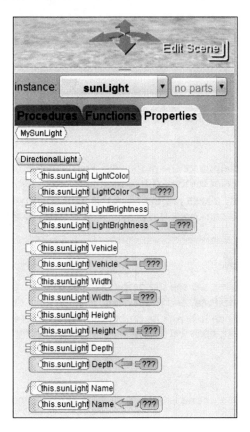

How it works...

When we click on the **Properties** tab, Alice displays all the properties for the instance selected in the drop-down list. sunLight is an instance of the MySunLight class. MySunLight is a subclass of DirectionalLight, and therefore the **Properties** tab displays the properties in two sections: MySunLight and DirectionalLight.

The MySunLight section is empty because there aren't specific properties defined for the MySunLight class. However, the sunLight instance has many properties inherited from the DirectionalLight superclass, and Alice shows them within the DirectionalLight section:

- ▶ LightColor
- ▶ LightBrightness
- ▶ Vehicle
- ▶ Width
- ▶ Height
- ▶ Depth
- ▶ Name

Alice uses very descriptive names for the properties. For example, the LightColor property allows you to assign a new color for the light generated by sunLight in the scene. The LightBrightness property allows you to adjust this light brightness value. By inspecting the available properties, you can check the possibilities offered by the element.

There's more...

Once you are in the code editor, we see the drop-down list with the active instance and the three tabs: **Procedures**, **Functions**, and **Properties**. You can click on the **Instance** drop-down list and select another instance to check its properties. For example, if you select **scene (this)** in the instance drop-down list, Alice will display all the properties for scene, as shown in the next screenshot:

 Because scene is the root element, it is referred to as this.

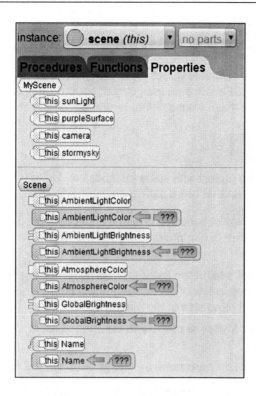

`scene` is an instance of the `MyScene` class. `MyScene` is a subclass of `Scene`; and therefore, the **Properties** tab displays the properties in two sections: `MyScene` and `Scene`.

The `MyScene` section displays the four properties that define the four instances added to this scene. These are the specific properties defined for the `MyScene` class in this project. The `scene` instance has many properties inherited from the `Scene` superclass, and Alice shows them within the `Scene` section:

- `AmbientLightColor`
- `AmbientLightBrightness`
- `AtmosphereColor`
- `GlobalBrightness`
- `Name`

See also

- *Defining a light's initial properties*, in this chapter
- *Animating light's properties*, in this chapter
- *Working with templates to create a new planet*, in this chapter

Defining a light's initial properties

In this task, we will learn to set initial values for two properties inherited from the `DirectionalLight` class. Because we are going to set the initial values for these properties, Alice will assign these values before rendering the directional light on the scene.

Getting ready

We have to be working on a project with some instances added to the virtual world. Therefore, we will use an existing project that has a stormy sky.

1. Open an existing project based on one of the six predefined Alice templates. You can open the `MyPurplePlanet` project saved in the *Working with templates to create a new planet* recipe.

2. Now, click on **Edit Code**, at the lower-right corner of the big scene preview. Alice will show a smaller preview of the scene and will display the **Code Editor** at a panel located at the right-hand side of the main window.

3. Click on the **class: MyScene** drop-down list and the list of classes that are part of the scene will appear.

4. Select **MyScene | Edit performMySetUp**, as shown in the next screenshot:

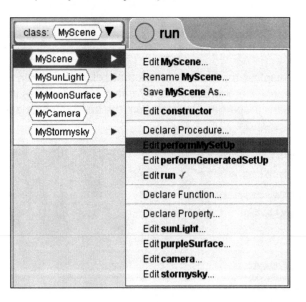

How to do it...

Follow these steps to set values for a light's initial properties:

1. Select `sunLight` in the instance drop-down list located at the left-hand side of the main window, behind the small scene preview.

2. Click on the **Properties** tab on the panel, located behind the aforementioned drop-down list. Alice will display all the available properties for `sunLight`.

3. Drag the **LightColor** assignment statement and drop it in the **Drop statement here** area located behind the **do in order** label, inside the **PerformMySetUp** tab. The **LightColor** assignment statement contains the **this.sunLight** and **LightColor** labels followed by an arrow and three question marks **???**. A list with all the available colors to assign to this property will appear.

4. Click on **RED**, the desired color to use for this directional light that represents a sun for the planet.

5. Drag the **LightBrightness** assignment statement and drop it behind the previously dropped assignment statement. A list with all the available brightness levels to assign to this property will appear.

6. Click on **10.0**, the desired brightness value to use for this directional light that represents a sun for the planet. The two statements that assign values to two properties of `sunLight`, RED to `LightColor` and `10.0` to `LightBrightness`, will appear as shown in the next screenshot:

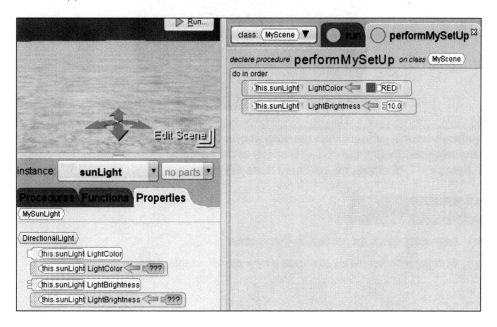

How it works...

By default, the constructor for the `MyScene` class runs the following two methods in order:

1. `performGeneratedSetUp`: This method run code is automatically generated by Alice. This method creates all the instances defined for your scene. You must not modify the contents of this method.

2. `performMySetUp`: This method allows you to add statements that you would like to run in the constructor and need access to the scene elements. It isn't convenient to make changes in the `MyScene` constructor. Instead, you can add the necessary statements in the `performMySetUp` method and you can be sure that the instances that compose the scene are going to be available. You need these instances to be created in order to access their properties.

We added two assignment statements to set values to properties of the `sunLight` instance in the `performMySetUp` method for the `MyScene` class.

When you run the project, Alice shows a new window with the rendered scene. Because there is an intense directional red light as the `sunLight` for the scene, the planet's surface appears as a bright red marble, as shown in the next screenshot:

The surface's color is different than the color shown in the scene preview and also different from the value assigned to the `Color` property of the `MoonSurface` instance. This happens because the red light affects the rendered surface's color.

See also

- ▶ *Animating light's properties*, in this chapter
- ▶ *Working with templates to create a new planet*, in this chapter

Animating light's properties

In this recipe, we will learn to change the value for the color of a light many times to animate the rendered colors of the scene. We will create a loop that runs three statements three times.

Getting ready

We have to be working on a project with some instances added to the virtual world. Therefore, we will use an existing project that has a stormy sky and a sun light.

1. Open an existing project based on one of the six predefined Alice templates. You can open the `MyPurplePlanet` project saved in the *Working with templates to create a new planet* recipe.

2. Now, click on **Edit Code**, at the lower-right corner of the big scene preview. Alice will show a smaller preview of the scene and will display the **Code Editor** on a panel located at the right-hand side of the main window.

3. Click on the **class: MyScene** drop-down list and the list of classes that are part of the scene will appear.

4. Select **MyScene | Edit run**.

How to do it...

Follow these steps to change the value for the color of the sun light many times:

1. Drag the **count** statement, located at the top, and drop it in the **Drop statement here** area located behind the **do in order** label, inside the **run** tab. A list with some predefined values to count up to it will appear.

2. Click on 3, the desired number of times that we want to repeat the statements grouped inside the **count up to** rectangle. The **count up to** statement will display a **drop statement here** placeholder as shown in the next screenshot:

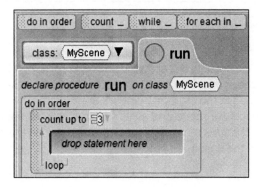

3. Select `sunLight` in the instance drop-down list located at the left-hand side of the main window, behind the small scene preview.

4. Click on the **Properties** tab on the panel located behind the aforementioned drop-down list. Alice will display all the available properties for `sunLight`.

5. Drag the **LightColor** assignment statement and drop it in the **drop statement here** area located behind the **count up to** label, inside the **run** tab. The **LightColor** assignment statement contains the **this.sunLight** and **LightColor** labels followed by an arrow and three question marks **???**. A list with all the available colors to assign to this property will appear.

6. Click on `RED`, the first desired color to use for this directional light that represents a sun for the planet.

7. Drag the **LightColor** assignment statement and drop it behind the previously dropped assignment statement again. In this case, click on `GREEN`, the second desired color to use for this directional light.

8. Drag the **LightColor** assignment statement and drop it behind the previously dropped assignment statement again. In this case, click on `BLUE`, the third color. The three statements that assign values to the `LightColor` property of `sunLight`, will appear as shown in the next picture:

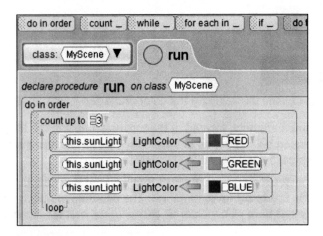

How it works...

When we run a project, Alice creates the scene instance, creates and initializes all the instances that compose the scene, and finally executes the `run` method defined in the `MyScene` class. This method is the starting point of our program. The statements included in the run method will run once the scene and all its visible elements are rendered. This means that each statement that changes a property that has an effect on the rendered scene will produce visual changes in the scene.

We added a `count` statement in the `run` method to execute a group of statements three times. The three statements change the color for the `sunLight` light to red, green and blue.

When you run the project, Alice shows a new window with the rendered animation. Because there is an intense directional red light as the `sunLight` for the scene and a purple marble surface, the animation will show the effects of the light combined with the planet's surface color. Thus, when the light is green, the combination of the green light with the purple surface generates a very dark surface. You will notice that the surface color changes many times, as shown in the next image with three screenshots of the rendered frames:

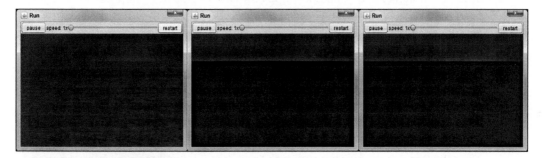

See also

▶ *Repeating statements*, in *Chapter 3, Organizing statements*
▶ *Working with templates to create a new planet*, in this chapter

Animating an instance's property

In this task, we will learn to change the value for the opacity of a stormy sky to generate the transition from evening to night in an unknown planet. We will use many statements to change the value of a property.

Getting ready

We have to be working on a project with some instances added to the virtual world. Therefore, we will use an existing project that has a stormy sky.

1. Open an existing project based on one of the six predefined Alice templates. You can open the `MyPurplePlanet` project saved in the *Working with templates to create a new planet* recipe.

2. Now, click on **Edit Code**, at the lower-right corner of the big scene preview. Alice will show a smaller preview of the scene and will display the **Code Editor** on a panel located at the right-hand side of the main window.

3. Click on the **class: MyScene** drop-down list and the list of classes that are part of the scene will appear.

4. Select **MyScene | Edit run**.

How to do it...

Follow these steps to change the value for the opacity of the stormy sky:

1. Select `stormysky` in the instance drop-down list located at the left-hand side of the main window, behind the small scene preview.

2. Click on the **Properties** tab on the panel located behind the aforementioned drop-down list. Alice will display all the available properties for `stormysky`.

3. Drag the **Opacity** assignment statement and drop it in the **drop statement here** area located behind the **do in order** label, inside the **run** tab. The **Opacity** assignment statement contains the **this.stormysky** and **Opacity** labels followed by an arrow and three question marks **???**. A list with all the predefined opacity values to assign to this property will appear. Click on **1.0**, the first desired opacity value to use for the sky.

4. Drag the **Opacity** assignment statement and drop it behind the previously dropped assignment statement. In this case, click on **0.9**, the second desired opacity level to use for the sky.

5. Repeat the aforementioned step nine times more, and assign a lower value to the opacity level each time. As a result, you will have 11 assignments, as shown in the next screenshot:

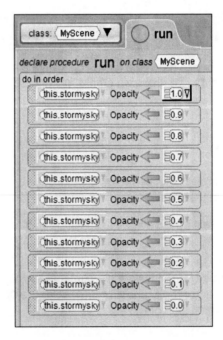

How it works...

When we run a project, Alice creates the scene instance, creates and initializes all the instances that compose the scene, and finally executes the `run` method defined in the `MyScene` class. The statements included in the run method will run once the scene and all its visible elements are rendered, including the sky that appears in the background.

When you run the project, the first statement that we added in the `run` method assigns `1.0` to the `Opacity` for the `stormysky`. This value means a 100% opacity level, which in fact is the default value for this property. Then, each statement reduces the opacity level by 10%, until the `stormysky` instance is completely transparent; and therefore, a completely black background appears as the sky for the planet.

You will notice that when the sky starts to fade away, there is a part of the surface that starts to appear, as shown in the next image with three screenshots of the rendered frames. This part of the surface was behind the stormy sky that was added to the scene.

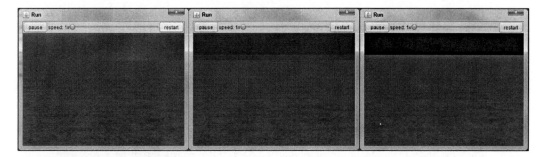

See also

- ▸ *Changing values for variables*, in *Chapter 5, Working with variables*
- ▸ *Running a loop while a condition is true*, in *Chapter 4, Working with functions and conditions*
- ▸ *Repeating statements*, in *Chapter 3, Organizing statements*
- ▸ *Working with templates to create a new planet*, in this chapter

Checking the procedures and functions for each instance

In this recipe, we will learn to inspect the diverse procedures and functions provided by each instance that composes a scene. We will check their names and their parameters. This way, we will recognize the procedures and functions that we can call and the parameters that we must pass to them.

Getting ready

We have to be working on a project with some instances added to the virtual world. Therefore, we will use an existing project that has a sun light.

1. Open an existing project. You can open the `MyPurplePlanet` project saved in the *Working with templates to create a new planet* recipe.

2. Click on **Edit Scene**, at the lower-right corner of the scene preview. Alice will show a bigger preview of the scene and will display the names of all the elements that compose the scene at the upper-left corner.

How to do it...

Follow these steps to inspect the diverse procedures and functions provided by each instance that composes a scene:

1. Click on one of the elements displayed as part of the scene, such as `sunLight`, and then click on **Edit Code**, at the lower-right corner of the big scene preview. Alice will show a smaller preview of the scene. Below this preview, Alice will display a drop-down list with `sunLight` as the active instance and three tabs: **Procedures**, **Functions**, and **Properties**.

2. Activate the **Procedures** tab. Alice will display the methods that don't return a value, known as **procedures**, for the sunLight instance, as shown in the next screenshot:

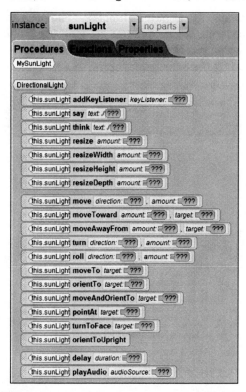

How it works...

When we click on the **Procedures** tab, Alice displays all the methods that don't return values for the instance selected in the drop-down list. sunLight is an instance of the MySunLight class. MySunLight is a subclass of DirectionalLight; and therefore, the **Procedures** tab displays the procedures in two sections: MySunLight and DirectionalLight.

The MySunLight section is empty because there aren't specific procedures defined for the MySunLight class. However, the sunLight instance has many procedures inherited from the DirectionalLight superclass, and Alice shows them within the DirectionalLight section.

As happens with properties, Alice uses very descriptive names for the procedures and their parameters. For example, the resizeWidth procedure allows you to pass an amount as a parameter to resize the width for the light source. The pointAt procedure allows you to pass a target instance as a parameter to make the light source point to it. By inspecting the available procedures and their parameters, you can check the possibilities offered by each instance.

There's more...

The methods that return a value are known as **functions** and Alice separates them from the previously introduced procedures. The procedures are methods that don't return a value. Once you are in the code editor, you can activate the **Functions** tab and Alice will display the methods that return a value for the selected instance, as shown in the next screenshot:

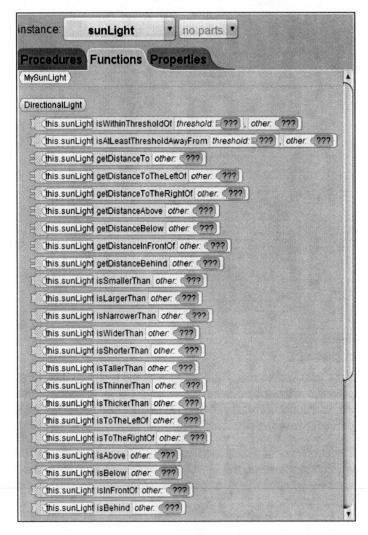

Because scene is the root element and it is referred to as this, the procedures and functions appear with the this. prefix, followed by the instance name (sunLight) and then the procedure or function name. Each new instance appears as a new property for scene. Thus, the instances that compose the virtual world appear as elements of scene.

See also

▶ *Declaring new procedures*, in *Chapter 3, Organizing statements*

▶ *Calling customized procedures*, in *Chapter 3, Organizing statements*

▶ *Running conditional code*, in *Chapter 4, Working with functions and conditions*

▶ *Defining new properties*, in *Chapter 6, Working with properties*

▶ *Working with templates to create a new planet*, in this chapter

Playing background music

In this recipe, we will learn to play background music while the code in the run method is executed. We will add many statements that will play music while Alice executes other statements.

Getting ready

We need an MP3 file to use as the background music for this task. In addition, make sure that you read the previous recipe, *Checking the procedures and functions for each instance*. You can also use a WAV file as the background sound. In fact, if you face problems when trying to play the MP3 file, try a WAV file. Alice has some incompatibilities with certain MP3 files.

1. Open an existing project based on one of the six predefined Alice templates. You can open the MyPurplePlanet project saved in the *Working with templates to create a new planet* recipe.

2. Now, click on **Edit Code**, at the lower-right corner of the big scene preview. Alice will show a smaller preview of the scene and will display the **Code Editor** on a panel located at the right-hand side of the main window.

3. Click on the **class: MyScene** drop-down list and the list of classes that are part of the scene will appear.

4. Select **MyScene Edit run**.

How to do it...

Follow these steps to play background music while other statements in the `run` method are executed:

1. Drag the **do in thread** statement, located at the top, and drop it in the **Drop statement here** area located behind the **do in order** label, inside the **run** tab. The **do in thread** statement will display a **drop statement here** placeholder as shown in the next screenshot:

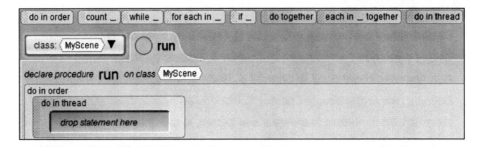

2. Select `scene (this)` in the instance drop-down list located at the left-hand side of the main window, behind the small scene preview.

3. Click on the **Procedures** tab on the panel located behind the aforementioned drop-down list. Alice will display all the available procedures for `scene`.

4. Drag the **playAudio** procedure, located within the **Scene** section, and drop it in the **drop statement here** area located behind the **do in thread** label, inside the **run** tab. The **playAudio** procedure contains the **this** and **playAudio** labels, followed by a parameter name, **audioSource**, and three question marks **???**. A context menu with an **Import new audio source...** option will appear. Click on this unique option and select an MP3 file with the background music to play. Then, click **Open** and the audio file name will appear. For example, if the audio file name is `distorted_velocity._1.mp3`, the following code will be displayed, as shown in the next screenshot:

    ```
    this.playAudio(new instance of AudioSource( distorted_velocity._
    1.mp3))
    ```

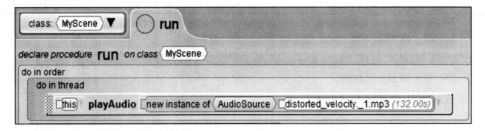

5. Follow the steps explained in the previously explained *Animating light's properties* recipe in this chapter. Add the `count up to` statement after the `do in thread` statement, as shown in the next screenshot:

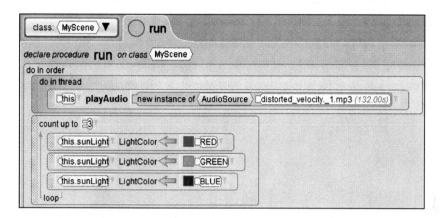

How it works...

The `playAudio` procedure receives an `AudioSource` instance as a parameter. When we dropped the `playAudio` method, Alice offered us the opportunity to specify an audio file and import a new audio source to the project. The MP3 file is now part of the audio resources included in the project. Thus, it included a statement that calls the `playAudio` method with a new `AudioSource` instance as a parameter. This new `AudioSource` instance receives the audio source name as a parameter, and therefore it references the previously imported MP3 file.

However, the `playAudio` procedure has a **synchronous execution**. This means that the procedure starts reproducing the `AudioSource` and it doesn't return the control to its caller until the audio file finishes. This means that the scene would keep its animation blocked until the music finishes. Therefore, we had to include this method within a `do in thread` statement. This statement encapsulates a group of statements with an **asynchronous execution**, because it generates a new independent **thread**. Thus, we could take advantage of the `do in thread` statement to call the `playAudio` procedure in an independent thread. This independent thread allowed us to have a background music being reproduced while other statements make visible changes to the scene.

The `count up to 3` statement that changes the color of the `sunLight` many times runs while the independent thread created with the do in thread statement is running the `playAudio` procedure. Therefore, we could create a scene with animations and music in the background.

See also

▶ *Speaking with other people*, in Chapter 7, *Working with People*

▶ *Exporting a video*, in Chapter 10, *Customizing the Output*

▶ *Animating light's properties*, in this chapter

▶ *Checking the procedures and functions for each instance*, in this chapter

▶ *Working with templates to create a new planet*, in this chapter

2
Working with Actors

In this chapter, we will cover:

- ▸ Browsing galleries to search for a specific class
- ▸ Creating a new instance from a class in a gallery
- ▸ Setting initial properties for an actor
- ▸ Moving an actor
- ▸ Resizing an actor
- ▸ Working with multiple actors
- ▸ Moving an actor with relative positions
- ▸ Orienting an actor to a target actor

Introduction

Once you set a nice scene, you need actors that perform actions. Alice 3 provides an extensive gallery with hundreds of customizable 3D models that you can easily incorporate as actors. This chapter provides many tasks that will allow us to start making simple animations with many actors in the 3D environment provided by Alice.

We will search for models of specific animals in the diverse galleries. We will locate and orient the actors in the 3D space. We will give some simple orders to the actors to create simple animations. We will learn to work with procedures with many required and optional parameters. We will move, rotate, resize, and orient actors. In addition, we will put a rabbit face to face with a dressed white rabbit.

Browsing galleries to search for a specific class

In this recipe, we will create a new project and set a simple scene. Then we will browse the different packages included in Alice to search for a specific class. We will visualize the thumbnail icons that represent each package and class.

Getting ready

We have to be working on a project in order to be able to browse the galleries. Therefore, we will create a new project and set a simple scene. Follow these steps:

1. Select **File | New...** in the main menu to start a new project. A dialog box will display the six predefined templates with their thumbnail previews in the **Templates** tab.

2. Select GrassyProject.a3p as the desired template for the new project and click **OK**. Alice will display a grassy ground with a light blue sky.

3. Click on **Edit Scene**, at the lower-right corner of the scene preview. Alice will show a bigger preview of the scene and will display the **Model Gallery** at the bottom.

4. Go to the **Model Gallery** and select **Generic Alice Models | Environments | Skies**. Use the horizontal scroll bar to find the ForestSky class.

5. Click on the ForestSky thumbnail. Leave the default name, forestSky, for the new instance and click **OK** to add it to the existing scene. The scene preview will replace the light blue sky with a violet one. Many trees will appear at the horizon, as shown in the next screenshot:

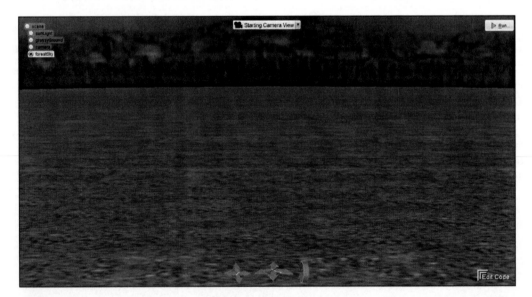

How to do it...

Follow these steps to browse the different packages included in Alice to search for a specific class:

1. Make sure that Alice is displaying the scene editor. If you see the **Edit Code** label at the lower-right corner of the big preview of the scene, it means that Alice is displaying the scene editor. If you see the **Edit Scene** label at the lower-right corner of a small scene preview, you should click on this label to switch to the scene editor. You will see the **Model Gallery** displayed at the bottom of the window. The initial view of the **Model Gallery** shows the following three packages located in the gallery root folder, as shown in the following screenshot:

    ❑ **Looking Glass Characters**: This package includes many characters that perform realistic animations for the characters. For example, you can make a person walk with a simple call to a procedure.

    ❑ **Looking Glass Scenery**: This package includes different kinds of scenery elements.

    ❑ **Generic Alice Models**: This package includes models that provide the basic and generic procedures. For example, you can move a person with a simple procedure call, but there isn't a procedure to make the person walk.

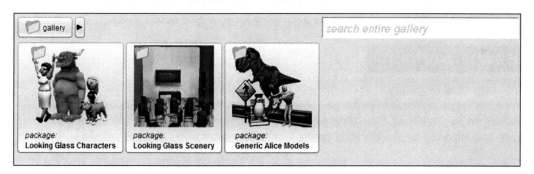

2. If you don't see the previously shown screenshot with the three packages, it means that you are browsing a subfolder of gallery and you need to go back to the gallery root folder. Click on the **gallery** button and Alice will display the thumbnails for the three packages. If you don't see the three packages, you should check your Alice installation.

3. Click on the **search entire gallery** textbox, located at the right-hand side of the **gallery** button.

4. Enter `rab` in the search entire gallery textbox. Alice will query for the classes and packages that contain the `rab` string and will display the thumbnails for the following classes, as shown in the next screenshot:

   ❑ `Rabbit`

   ❑ `Scarab`

   ❑ `WhiteRabbit`

   ❑ `Parabola`

5. Now you know that you have two different rabbits, `Rabbit` and `WhiteRabbit`. You can select your favorite rabbit and then add it as an actor in the scene.

6. Select **File | Save as...** and give a name to the project, for example, `MyForest`. Then, you can use this new scene as a template for your next Alice project.

How it works...

Alice organizes its gallery in packages with hierarchical folders. The previously mentioned three packages are located in the `gallery` root folder. We can browse each package by clicking on its thumbnail. Each time we click on a thumbnail, the related sub-folder will open and Alice will display the thumbnails for the new sub-folders and the classes.

The thumbnail that represents a folder, known as a package, displays a folder icon at the upper-left corner and includes the preview of some of the classes that it includes. The next screenshot shows the thumbnails for three packages, `amusementpark`, `animals`, and `beach`. These packages are sub-folders of the `Generic Alice Models` package:

The thumbnails for classes don't include the previously mentioned folder icon and they show a different background color. The next screenshot shows the thumbnails for three classes, Bird1, BirdBaby, and BlueBird:

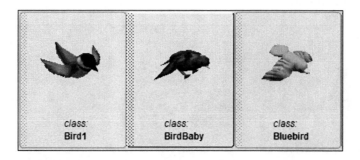

 The names for packages included within one of the three main packages use lowercase names, such as, aquarium, bedroom, and circus. The names for classes always start with an uppercase letter, such as, Monitor and Room. When a class name needs more than one word, it doesn't use spaces to separate them but it mixes lowercase with uppercase to mark the difference between words, such as, CatClock and OldBed.

The main packages contain hundreds of classes organized in dozens of folders. Therefore, we might spend hours browsing the galleries to find an appropriate rabbit for our scene. We took advantage of Alice query features to search the entire gallery for all the classes that contain a string. This way, we could find a simple rabbit, Rabbit, and a dressed rabbit, WhiteRabbit.

There's more...

While you type characters in the **search entire gallery** textbox, Alice will query all the packages and will display the results in real-time. You will notice that Alice changes the results displayed as you are editing the textbox. The results for your search will include both packages and classes that contain the entered string. For example, follow these steps:

1. Click on the **search entire gallery** textbox, located at the right-hand side of the **gallery** button.

2. Enter `bug` in the search entire gallery text box. Alice will query for the classes and packages that contain the `bug` string and will display two thumbnails. One thumbnail is the `bugs` package and the other thumbnail is the `Ladybug` class, as shown in the following screenshot:

If you think that `Ladybug` isn't the appropriate bug you want as an actor, you can click on the thumbnail for the `bugs` package and you will find many other bugs. When you click on the thumbnail, the text you entered in the **search entire gallery** textbox will disappear because there is no filter being applied to the gallery and you are browsing the contents of the **gallery | Generic Alice Models | animals | bugs** package.

You can add a `Beetle` or a `Catepillar`, as shown in the following screenshot:

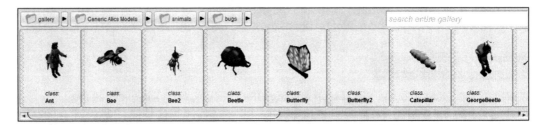

See also

▸ *Creating a new instance from a class in a gallery*, in this chapter

▸ *Creating a random person*, in *Chapter 7, Working with People*

Creating a new instance from a class in a gallery

In this task, we will add a new actor to an existing scene. We will drag and drop a thumbnail of a class from the gallery and then we will learn how Alice adds a new instance to the scene.

Getting ready

We want to add a new actor to an existing scene. Therefore, we will use an existing project that has a simple scene.

1. Open an existing project based on one of the six predefined Alice templates. You can open the `MyForest` project saved in the *Browsing galleries to search for a specific class* recipe in this chapter.

2. Select `Starting Camera View` in the drop-down list located at the top of the big scene preview.

How to do it...

Follow these steps to add a new instance of the `WhiteRabbit` class:

1. Search for the `WhiteRabbit` class in the gallery. You can browse **gallery | Generic Alice Models | animals** or enter `rab` in the search entire gallery textbox to visualize the `WhiteRabbit` thumbnail.

2. Drag the `WhiteRabbit` thumbnail from the gallery to the big scene preview. A bounding box that represents the 3D model in the 3D space will appear, as shown in the next screenshot:

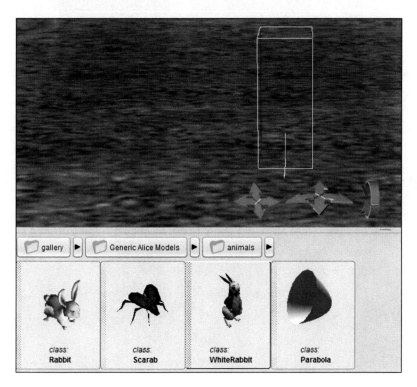

3. Keep the mouse button down and move the mouse to locate the bounding box in the desired initial position for the new element.

4. Once you have located the element in the desired position, release the mouse button and the **Declare Property** dialog box will appear.

5. Leave the default name, `whiteRabbit`, for the new instance and click **OK** to add it to the existing scene. The scene preview will perform an animation when Alice adds the new instance and then it will go back to the starting camera view to show how the new element appears on the scene. The next screenshot shows the new dressed white rabbit added to the scene, as seen by the starting camera:

6. Select **File | Save as...** from Alice's main menu and give a new name to the project. Then, you can make changes to the project according to your needs.

How it works...

When we dropped the thumbnail for the `WhiteRabbit` class, the **Declare Property** dialog box provided information about what Alice was going to do, as shown in the following screenshot:

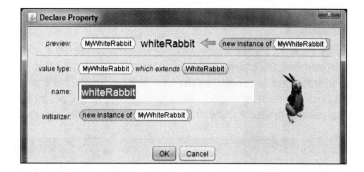

Alice defines a new class, MyWhiteRabbit, that extends WhiteRabbit. MyWhiteRabbit is a new value type for the project, a subclass of WhiteRabbit. The name for the new property that represents the new instance of MyWhiteRabbit is whiteRabbit. This means that you can access this new actor with the whiteRabbit name and that this property is available for scene. Because the starting camera view is looking at the horizon, we see the rabbit looking at the camera in the scene preview.

If you select TOP in the in the drop-down list located at the top of the big scene preview, you will see the rabbit on the grassy ground and how the camera is looking at the rabbit. The next screenshot shows the scene seen from the top and you can see the camera with a circle around it:

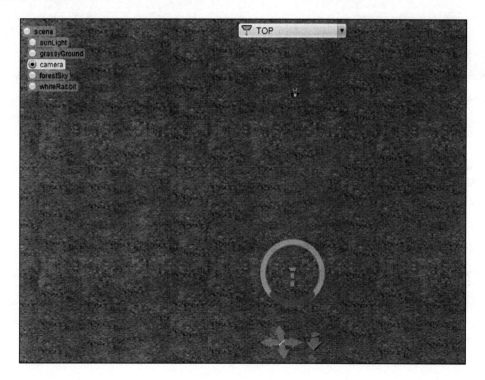

There's more...

When you run the project, Alice shows a new window with the rendered scene, as seen by the previously shown camera, the starting camera. The default window size is very small. You can resize the **Run** window and Alice will use the new size to render the scene with a higher resolution. The next time you run the project, Alice will use the new size, as shown in the next screenshot that displays the dressed white rabbit with a forest in the background:

See also

▶ *Browsing galleries to search for a specific class*, in this chapter

▶ *Setting initial properties for an actor*, in this chapter

▶ *Working with multiple cameras*, in *Chapter 10, Customizing the Output*

Setting initial properties for an actor

In this recipe, we will move, rotate and resize an actor that has already been added to the scene. We will learn some of the features provided by the Alice scene editor to change the location, rotation, and size of a 3D model in the 3D world.

Getting ready

We have to be working on a project with at least one actor. Therefore, we will use an existing project that has a rabbit.

1. Open the project saved in the *Creating a new instance from a class in a gallery* recipe in this chapter.

2. Click on **Edit Scene**, at the lower-right corner of the scene preview. Alice will show a bigger preview of the scene and will display the **Model Gallery** at the bottom.

How to do it...

Follow these steps to move, rotate, and resize an actor:

1. Click on the desired actor on the scene. If you have difficulties clicking on the actor, click on its instance name at the upper-left corner. Once the actor is selected, a circle will appear below it and the radio button with its instance name will be activated, as shown in the next screenshot:

2. Activate the **Rotation** radio button on the panel located at the right-hand side of the window, under **Handle Styles**.

3. Activate the **Use Snap** checkbox, located in the same panel. Make sure that the **Snap Rotation** checkbox is also activated and that the value for the **Angle Snap** textbox is 45, as in the next screenshot:

4. Now, hover the mouse pointer over the yellow circle located around the bottom of the actor and on top of the ground. The yellow circle will increase its brightness level when the mouse pointer is over it.

5. Press the mouse button and drag the mouse slowly towards the right-hand side until the actor rotates around itself 90 degrees, as shown in the next screenshot:

6. Activate the **Move** radio button on the panel located at the right-hand side of the window, under **Handle Styles**.

7. Hover the mouse pointer over the red arrow located at the left-hand side of the actor and on top of the ground. The red arrow will reduce its brightness level when the mouse pointer is over it.

8. Press the mouse button and drag the mouse slowly towards the left-hand side until the actor is located at the left-hand side of the scene, as shown in the following screenshot:

9. Activate the **Resize** radio button on the panel located at the right-hand side of the window, under **Handle Styles**.

10. Hover the mouse pointer over the gray arrow located at the top of the actor. Don't confuse the gray arrow with the yellow arrow that appears at the left-hand side of the gray arrow. The gray arrow will reduce its brightness level when the mouse pointer is over it.

10. Press the mouse button and drag the mouse slowly towards the top of the scene. The actor will increase its size while keeping its aspect ratio, as shown in the next screenshot:

11. Select **File | Save as...** from Alice's main menu and give a new name to the project. Then, you can make changes to the project according to your needs.

How it works...

By default, when you select an instance, Alice displays a circle that allows us to rotate the model around itself. We used the radio buttons on the panel located at the right-hand side of the window, under **Handle Styles**, and we were able to perform the following three actions for an actor:

- Rotation
- Move
- Resize

We activated the different snap options because they allow us to be more accurate when performing the aforementioned actions. For example, when we rotated the model around itself, each time we reached 45 degrees, the snap forced us to accelerate the mouse movement to leave the angle. In addition, a green arrow indicated to us that we reached an angle that was multiple of 45. This way, when we see a green arrow for the second time, it means we have rotated the model around itself 90 degrees to the right.

When we moved the actor horizontally, the **Show grid** option displayed a grid on top of the grassy ground. This grid is useful when you want to set the initial position for many elements on a scene. The cells that compose the grid allow us to align many models on the same row or column. In addition, the 3D perspective applied to the grid is also useful to understand how the models are going to change their size when you move them through the visible part of the scene.

We resized the actor while keeping the model's aspect ratio. The gray arrow allowed us to increase the model's width, height, and depth at the same time while we moved the mouse.

There's more...

When we activate each radio button to perform one of the three actions for an actor, **Rotation**, **Move**, or **Resize**, we can apply the action to the three axes (X, Y, and Z). For example, we can rotate three angles for a 3D model:

- ▸ X (horizontal)
- ▸ Y (vertical)
- ▸ Z (depth)

When we activate the **Rotation** radio button, three circles appear around the model. We can drag each circle to rotate each angle for the model. Alice does the rotation among the middle point of the 3D model. The next screenshot shows the dressed white rabbit being rotated horizontally:

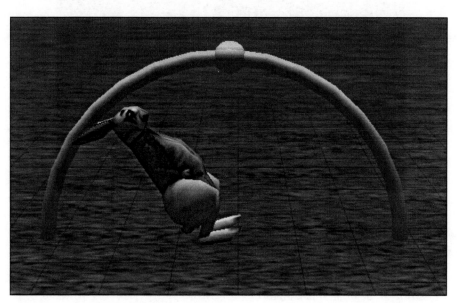

When we activate the **Move** radio button, three arrows appear around the model. We can drag each arrow to move the model in the following directions:

- ▸ **Red arrow**: horizontal
- ▸ **Green arrow**: vertical
- ▸ **Blue arrow**: depth

When we activate the **Resize** radio button, four arrows appear around the model. We can drag each arrow to resize the following parts of the model:

- ▸ **Gray arrow**: X, Y, and Z at the same time. It keeps the original model's aspect ratio values.
- ▸ **Cyan arrow**: horizontal
- ▸ **Yellow arrow**: vertical
- ▸ **Magenta arrow**: depth

The next screenshot shows the dressed white rabbit with its aspect ratio being modified because it is increasing only its horizontal size:

See also

- ▸ *Moving an actor*, in this chapter
- ▸ *Resizing an actor*, in this chapter
- ▸ *Creating a new instance from a class in a gallery*, in this chapter

Moving an actor

In this task, we will learn to add code to animate the movement of an actor through a scene. We will call a procedure and we will pass parameters to this procedure to specify the desired movement, the duration, and the animation's style.

Getting ready

We have to be working on a project with at least one actor. Therefore, we will use an existing project that has a rabbit.

1. Open the project saved in the _Setting initial properties for an actor_ recipe in this chapter.

2. Click on **Edit Code**, at the lower-right corner of the big scene preview. Alice will show a smaller preview of the scene and will display the **Code Editor** on a panel located at the right-hand side of the main window.

3. Click on the **class: MyScene** drop-down list and the list of classes that are part of the scene will appear.

4. Select **MyScene | Edit run**.

How to do it...

Follow these steps to make Alice move an actor:

1. Select the desired actor in the instance drop-down list located at the left-hand side of the main window, behind the small scene preview. For example, you can select `whiteRabbit`. Make sure that `part: none` is selected in the drop-down list located at the right-hand side of the chosen instance, as shown in the next screenshot. Otherwise, you would be adding code for one of the parts of this model.

2. Activate the **Procedures** tab. Alice will display the procedures for the previously selected actor.

3. Drag the **move** procedure and drop it in the **drop statement here** area located behind the **do in order** label, inside the **run** tab. If your instance name is `whiteRabbit`, the **move** assignment statement contains the **this.whiteRabbit** and **move** labels followed by the **direction** and **amount** parameters and their question marks **???**. A list with all the predefined direction values to pass to the first parameter will appear.

4. Click on FORWARD and then on 2.0 in the cascade menu that appears, as shown in the following screenshot:

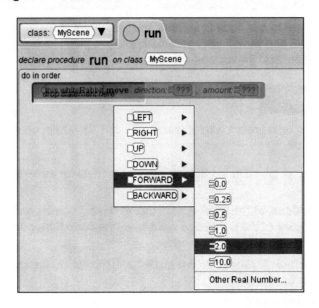

5. Click on the **more...** drop-down menu button that appears at the right-hand side of the recently dropped statement. Click on duration and then on 2.0 in the cascade menu that appears. If the instance name is whiteRabbit, the following code will be displayed, as shown in the following screenshot:

```
this.whiteRabbit.move(FORWARD, 2.0, duration: 2.0)
```

How it works...

When we run a project, Alice creates the scene instance, creates and initializes all the instances that compose the scene, and finally executes the run method defined in the MyScene class. The statements included in the run method will run once the scene and all its visible elements are rendered, including the actor with its initial properties.

When we run the project, the statement that we added in the `run` method calls the `move` procedure for the actor instance. This procedure requires at least two parameters:

1. `direction`: Specifies the desired direction in which the Actor has to be moved. There are six possible values for this parameter:

   ❑ LEFT

   ❑ RIGHT

   ❑ UP

   ❑ DOWN

   ❑ FORWARD

   ❑ BACKWARD

2. `amount`: This real number indicates the amount that the instance has to be moved in the specified direction.

When we added the call to the `move` procedure, we passed FORWARD to `direction` and 2.0 to `amount`.

 When you drop a statement in Alice code editor, Alice displays menus to allow you to specify the values for the **required parameters**. The required parameters cannot be left without values. If you don't specify the values for these parameters, Alice removes the statement.

After we specified the values for the required parameters, the **more...** drop-down menu button that appeared at the right-hand side of the statement allowed us to specify values for one of the **optional parameters**. The optional parameters can be left without values because they aren't required. However, they provide additional options for the procedure or function that we are calling. In this case, we passed 2.0 to duration and the procedure will animate the movement of the actor for 2.0 seconds, as shown in the next screenshot with three screenshots of the rendered frames:

There's more...

We can specify two additional optional parameters for the move procedure. By default, the optional asSeenBy parameter uses the instance that calls the move procedure as its value. For example, if this.whiteRabbit calls the move procedure, the default value for asSeenBy is this.whiteRabbit. The direction value has diverse effects on the movement of the actor in the scene according to the asSeenBy value. A FORWARD movement performed as seen by the actor is different than the same movement performed as seen by the camera (this.camera).

We can click the **more...** drop-down menu button again and specify a different value for the asSeenBy parameter and test the effect on the movement. When we want to write code that moves the actors according to a specific baseline, the asSeenBy is really useful. For example, we can set the same value for the asSeenBy parameter to many actors, to the ground instance (this.grassyGround) and program many movements as seen by the ground.

We can click the **more...** drop-down menu button again and specify a different value for the style parameter. This optional parameter defines the style of the movement animation and has four possible values:

▶ BEGIN_AND_END_ABRUPTLY: This value is useful when the user controls the movement of an actor by pressing certain keys

▶ BEGIN_GENTLY_AND_END_ABRUPTLY: The movement starts gently and increases the speed to end abruptly

▶ BEGIN_ABRUPTLY_AND_END_GENTLY: The movement starts immediately with a maximum speed but reduces the speed and ends gently

▶ BEGIN_AND_END_GENTLY: This is the default value and sometimes it won't look so good in the animation

The names for the aforementioned possible values are very easy to understand and define the way the animation begins and ends. We can change the value and check the effects on the rendered animation by running the project with each possible value.

See also

▶ *Running many statements at the same time*, in Chapter 3, Organizing Statements

▶ *Setting initial properties for an actor*, in this chapter

Resizing an actor

In this recipe, we will learn to add code to animate the resize of an actor through a scene. A rabbit will increase its size during a specific period of time.

Getting ready

We have to be working on a project with at least one actor. Therefore, we will use an existing project that has a rabbit.

1. Open the project saved in the _Setting initial properties for an actor_ recipe in this chapter.

2. Click on **Edit Code**, at the lower-right corner of the big scene preview. Alice will show a smaller preview of the scene and will display the **Code Editor** on a panel located at the right-hand side of the main window.

3. Click on the **class: MyScene** drop-down list and the list of classes that are part of the scene will appear.

4. Select **MyScene | Edit run**.

How to do it...

Follow these steps to make Alice resize an actor:

1. Select the desired actor in the instance drop-down list located at the left-hand side of the main window, behind the small scene preview. For example, you can select `whiteRabbit`.

2. Make sure that `part: none` is selected in the drop-down list located at the right-hand side of the chosen instance.

3. Activate the **Procedures** tab. Alice will display the procedures for the previously selected actor.

4. Drag the **resize** procedure and drop it in the **drop statement here** area located behind the **do in order** label, inside the **run** tab. If your instance name is `whiteRabbit`, the **resize** assignment statement contains the **this.whiteRabbit** and **resize** labels followed by the **amount** parameter and its question marks **???**. A list with predefined real numbers to pass to the first parameter will appear.

5. Select **Other Real Number...** and the **Enter custom real number** dialog box will appear. Enter 5 and click **OK**, as shown in the next screenshot:

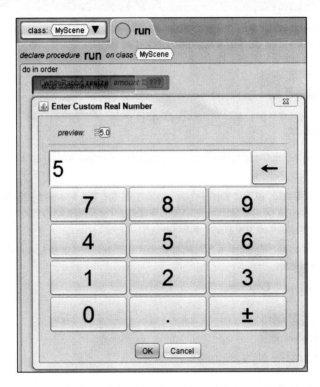

6. Click on the **more...** drop-down menu button that appears at the right-hand side of the recently dropped statement. Click on `duration` and then on **Other Real Number...**. The **Enter custom real number** dialog box will appear. Enter 3.5 and click **OK**. If the instance name is `whiteRabbit`, the following code will be displayed, as shown in the following screenshot:

```
this.whiteRabbit.resize(5.0, duration: 3.5)
```

How it works...

When we run the project, the statement that we added in the `run` method calls the `resize` procedure for the actor instance. This procedure requires at least one parameter, `amount`. This real number indicates the number of times that the instance has to be resized while keeping its original aspect ratio. A positive number increases the size and a negative number reduces the size. We used the **Enter custom real number** dialog box to specify 5 as the value for this parameter. This means that the actor is going to increase its size five times. You can specify a negative value when you want to decrease the size.

The **more...** drop-down menu button that appeared at the right-hand side of the statement allowed us to specify the value for one of the optional parameters, `duration`. In this case, we used the **Enter custom real number** dialog box again to specify 3.5 to `duration` and the procedure will animate the resizing of the actor for 3.5 seconds, as shown in the next screenshot with three screenshots of the rendered frames:

There's more...

We can also perform the resize action to only one of the three axes for an actor by using one of the following procedures:

- `resizeWidth`
- `resizeHeight`
- `resizeDepth`

We need to specify the value for the `amount` parameter when we call one of the aforementioned procedures. In addition, we can specify a value for the `duration` parameter. These procedures have the following three additional optional parameters:

1. `resizePolicy`: It has two possible values:
    - `PRESERVE_NOTHING`: It resizes the width, height, or depth according to the procedure that has been called.

❑ PRESERVE_VOLUME: It resizes the width, height, or depth according to the procedure that has been called, but the resize operation always preserves the volume of the 3D model. In order to preserve the volume, the resize operation might resize the other two axes that the method isn't supposed to alter.

2. howMuch: It has three possible values:

❑ DESCENDANT_PARTS_ONLY: It resizes only the parts that descend from the instance (this).

❑ THIS_AND_DESCENDANT_PARTS: This is the default value for this optional parameter. This value indicates that all the parts that compose the model must be resized at the same time.

❑ THIS_ONLY: It resizes only the main instance (this) but it doesn't change the size of its parts.

3. style: It defines the style of the movement animation and has four possible values. These values were explained in the *Moving an actor* recipe in this chapter.

See also

▶ *Working with parts of characters*, in *Chapter 5, Working with Variables*.

▶ *Setting initial properties for an actor*, in this chapter

▶ *Moving an actor*, in this chapter

Working with multiple actors

In this task, we will learn to add a second actor to a scene with an existing actor, and to use the snap features to define the new actor's initial location. This way, we will have a scene with multiple actors.

Getting ready

We have to be working on a project with at least one actor. Therefore, we will use an existing project that has a rabbit.

1. Open the project saved in the *Setting initial properties for an actor* recipe in this chapter.

2. Activate the scene editor.

3. Activate the **Use Snap** checkbox, located in the panel at the right-hand side of the window. Make sure that the **Show grid** checkbox is activated.

4. Select Starting Camera View in the drop-down list located at the top of the big scene preview.

How to do it...

Follow these steps to add a new actor to the scene and set the actor's initial location:

1. Search for the `Hare` class in the gallery. You can browse **gallery | Generic Alice Models | animals** or enter `har` in the **search entire gallery textbox** to visualize the `Hare` thumbnail. You can follow the steps explained in the *Browsing galleries to search for a specific class* recipe in this chapter.

2. Drag the `Hare` thumbnail from the gallery to the big scene preview. A bounding box that represents the 3D model in the 3D space will appear.

3. Keep the mouse button down and move the mouse to locate the bounding box in the desired initial position for the new element. When the center of the model is located on one of the lines defined by the grid, the line will appear with a light green color.

4. Keep the mouse button down and move the mouse to locate the bounding box in the same horizontal grid line than the existing actor. Make sure that the two lines of the grid appear highlighted with a light green color, as shown in the next screenshot:

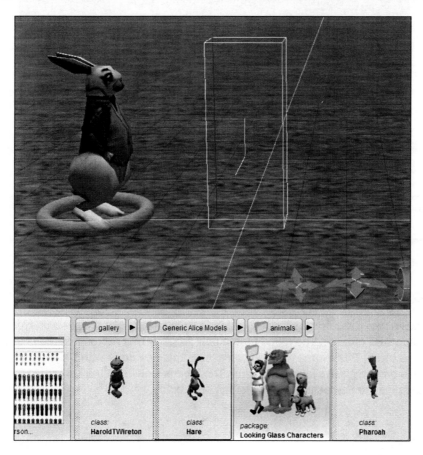

5. Once you have located the element in the desired position, snap to the lines of the grid, release the mouse button and the **Declare Property** dialog box will appear.

6. Leave the default name, hare, for the new instance and click **OK** to add it to the existing scene. The scene preview will perform an animation when Alice adds the new instance and then it will go back to the starting camera view to show how the new element appears on the scene. The following screenshot shows the new hare added to the scene and the other actor on its left-hand side, as seen by the starting camera:

7. Select **File | Save as...** and give a name to the project, for example, MyForest. Then, you can use this new scene as a template for your next Alice project.

How it works...

When we dropped the thumbnail for the Hare class, the **Declare Property** dialog box provided information about the new instance that represents a new actor for our scene.

Alice defines a new class, MyHare, which extends Hare. MyHare is a new value type for the project, a subclass of Hare. The name for the new property that represents the new instance of MyHare is hare. This means that you can access this new actor with the hare name and that this property is available for scene. The hare is looking at the camera in the scene preview because the new actor uses its default orientation.

If you select `Layout Scene View` in the in the drop-down list located at the top of the big scene preview, you will see the two actors on the grassy ground and how the camera is looking at them. The next screenshot shows the aforementioned view and you can see the hare with a circle around it because it is selected:

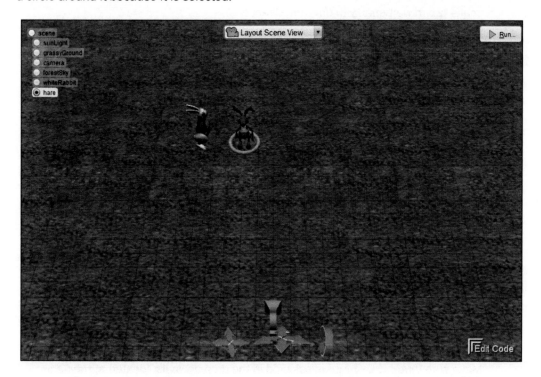

When we use the grid to locate the actors in their initial position, it is easy to organize the initial layout with great accuracy. In the previous screenshot, `whiteRabbit` identifies the first actor and `hare` the second one. We can call procedures and functions for each of these actors.

See also

- ▸ *Running statements for many actors*, in *Chapter 3, Organizing Statement*.
- ▸ *Browsing galleries to search for a specific class*, in this chapter
- ▸ *Setting initial properties for an actor*, in this chapter

Moving an actor with relative positions

In this recipe, we will learn to move an actor towards another actor. We will add code to make the hare make two movements with different directions.

Getting ready

We have to be working on a project with at least two actors. Therefore, we will use an existing project that has a rabbit and a hare.

1. Open the project saved in the *Working with multiple actors* recipe in this chapter.

2. Click on **Edit Code**, at the lower-right corner of the big scene preview. Alice will show a smaller preview of the scene and will display the **Code Editor** on a panel located at the right-hand side of the main window.

3. Click on the **class: MyScene** drop-down list and the list of classes that are part of the scene will appear.

4. Select **MyScene | Edit run**.

How to do it...

Follow these steps:

1. Select one of the actors in the instance drop-down list located at the left-hand side of the main window, behind the small scene preview. For example, you can select `hare`. Make sure that `part: none` is selected in the drop-down list located at the right-hand side of the chosen instance.

2. Activate the **Procedures** tab. Alice will display the procedures for the previously selected actor.

3. Drag the **move** procedure and drop it in the **drop statement here** area located behind the **do in order** label, inside the **run** tab. If your instance name is `hare`, the **move** assignment statement contains the **this.hare** and **move** labels followed by the **direction** and **amount** parameters and their question marks **???**. A list with all the predefined direction values to pass to the first parameter will appear.

4. Click on `LEFT` and then on `2.0` in the cascade menu that appears.

5. Click on the **more...** drop-down menu button that appears at the right-hand side of the recently dropped statement. Click on `duration` and then on `1.0` in the cascade menu that appears.

6. Click on the new **more...** drop-down menu that appears. Click on `asSeenBy` and then on `this.` followed by the other actor's name. For example, if the other actor's name is `whiteRabbit`, you must select `this.whiteRabbit`, as shown in the following screenshot:

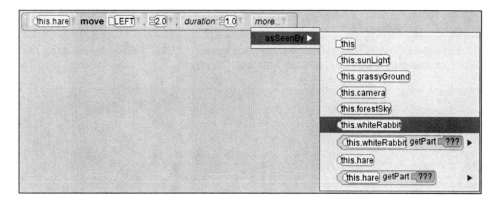

7. Click on the new **more...** drop-down menu that appears. Click on `style` and then on `BEGIN_AND_END_GENTLY`. For example, if the instance that calls the move procedure is hare and the value specified for the `asSeenBy` parameter is `whiteRabbit`, the following code will be displayed:

```
this.hare.move(LEFT, 2.0, duration: 2.0, asSeenBy: this.
whiteRabbit, style: BEGIN_AND_END_GENTLY)
```

Downloading the example code for this book

You can download the example code files for all Packt books you have purchased from your account at `http://www.PacktPub.com`. If you purchased this book elsewhere, you can visit `http://www.PacktPub.com/support` and register to have the files e-mailed directly to you.

8. Drag the **move** procedure again and drop it behind the previously dropped procedure call. A list with all the predefined direction values to pass to the first parameter will appear.

9. Click on `BACKWARD` and then on `1.0` in the cascade menu that appears.

10. Click on the **more...** drop-down menu button that appears at the right-hand side of the recently dropped statement. Click on `duration` and then on `1.0` in the cascade menu that appears.

11. Click on the new **more...** drop-down menu that appears. Click on `asSeenBy` and then on `this.` followed by the other actor's name. For example, if the other actor's name is `whiteRabbit`, you must select `this.whiteRabbit`.

12. Click on the new **more...** drop-down menu that appears. Click on `style` and then on `BEGIN_AND_END_GENTLY`. For example, if the instance that calls the move procedure is hare and the value specified for the `asSeenBy` parameter is `whiteRabbit`.

The following code will be displayed as the second statement, as shown in the following screenshot:

```
this.hare.move(BACKWARD, 1.0, duration: 1.0, asSeenBy: this.
whiteRabbit, style: BEGIN_AND_END_GENTLY)
```

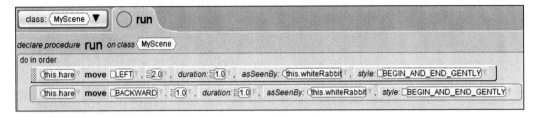

How it works...

When we run the project, Alice executes the two statements that we added in the `run` method one after the other. First, it calls the `move` procedure for the actor instance to move it left as seen by the other actor. The value for the `asSeenBy` parameter is the instance of the other actor. We want one of the actors to move 2 units to the left-hand side of the other actor.

Then, Alice calls another `move` procedure for the actor instance to move it backward as seen by the other actor. The two movements are relative to how the actor is seen by the other one. Imagine that the dressed white rabbit is watching the hare, as shown in the first frame in the following screenshot. The hare is the actor being moved and the white rabbit determines the relative position for the movements. First, the hare moves to the rabbit's left-hand side and then it goes towards the rabbit's location. The last movement is backward, as seen by the rabbit; and therefore, the hare moves away from the rabbit.

See also

▶ *Orienting an actor to a target actor*, in this chapter

▶ *Using variables to hold instances*, in *Chapter 7, Working with People*

▶ *Working with multiple actors*, in this chapter

Facing an actor to a target actor

In this task, we will learn to turn an actor to the face of another actor. We will make the hare turn to look at the rabbit's face. Thus, we will be able to leave the hare and the rabbit face to face.

Getting ready

We have to be working on a project with at least two actors. Therefore, we will use an existing project that has a rabbit and a hare.

1. Open the project saved in the *Working with multiple actors* recipe in this chapter.

2. Click on **Edit Code**, at the lower-right corner of the big scene preview. Alice will show a smaller preview of the scene and will display the **Code Editor** on a panel located at the right-hand side of the main window.

3. Click on the **class: MyScene** drop-down list and the list of classes that are part of the scene will appear.

4. Select **MyScene | Edit run**.

How to do it...

Follow these steps:

1. Select one of the actors in the instance drop-down list located at the left-hand side of the main window, behind the small scene preview. For example, you can select hare. Make sure that part: none is selected in the drop-down list located at the right-hand side of the chosen instance.

2. Activate the **Procedures** tab. Alice will display the procedures for the previously selected actor.

3. Drag the **turnToFace** procedure and drop it in the **drop statement here** area located behind the **do in order** label, inside the **run** tab. If your instance name is hare, the **turnToFace** assignment statement contains the **this.hare** and **move** labels followed by the **target** parameter and its question marks **???**. A list with all the possible instances to pass to the first parameter will appear.

4. Click on this. followed by the other actor's name. For example, if the other actor's name is whiteRabbit, you must select this.whiteRabbit.

5. Click on the **more...** drop-down menu that appears. Click on duration and then on 2.0.

6. Click on the new **more...** drop-down menu that appears. Click on `style` and then on `BEGIN_AND_END_GENTLY`. For example, if the instance that calls the move procedure is `hare` and the value specified for the `target` parameter is `whiteRabbit`, the following code will be displayed, as shown in the following screenshot:

```
this.hare.turnToFace(this.WhiteRabbit, duration: 2.0,
style: BEGIN_AND_END_GENTLY)
```

How it works...

When we run the project, Alice calls the `turnToFace` procedure for the specified actor instance. This procedure rotates the 3D model that represents the actor among its middle point until the actor looks at the face of the other actor. This way, the two actors will appear face to face. The value for the `target` parameter is the instance of the other actor. We want one of the actors to perform an animation of two seconds to turn to face the other actor.

Imagine that the dressed white rabbit is watching the camera and is looking at the hare, as shown in the first frame in the following screenshot. The hare is the actor that turns to face the white rabbit:

See also

▶   *Working with multiple actors*, in this chapter

3
Organizing Statements

In this chapter, we will cover:

- ▸ Performing many statements in order
- ▸ Using a counter to run statements many times
- ▸ Running statements for different actors
- ▸ Running statements for many actors
- ▸ Running many statements at the same time
- ▸ Repeating statements at the same time
- ▸ Declaring new procedures
- ▸ Calling customized procedures

Introduction

Once you set a nice scene and the main characters are ready to perform actions, you need to organize the statements that request the different actors to perform actions. Alice 3 provides blocks that allow us to configure the order in which many statements should be executed. This chapter provides many tasks that will allow us to start controlling the behavior of animations with many actors performing different actions.

We will execute many actions with a specific order. We will use counters to run one or more statements many times. We will execute actions for many actors of the same class. We will run code for different actors at the same time to render complex animations. In addition, we will create a new procedure that will allow us to make some flowers dance with the wind.

Performing many statements in order

In this recipe, we will execute many statements for an actor with a specific order. We will add eight statements to control a sequence of movements for a bee.

Getting ready

We have to be working on a project with at least one actor. Therefore, we will create a new project and set a simple scene with a few actors.

1. Select **File | New...** in the main menu to start a new project. A dialog box will display the six predefined templates with their thumbnail previews in the **Templates** tab.

2. Select `GrassyProject.a3p` as the desired template for the new project and click **OK**. Alice will display a grassy ground with a light blue sky.

3. Click on **Edit Scene**, at the lower right corner of the scene preview. Alice will show a bigger preview of the scene and will display the **Model Gallery** at the bottom.

4. Add an instance of the `Bee` class to the scene, and enter `bee` for the name of this new instance. First, Alice will create the `MyBee` class to extend `Bee`. Then, Alice will create an instance of `MyBee` named `bee`. Follow the steps explained in the *Creating a new instance from a class in a gallery* recipe, in *Chapter 2, Working with Actors*.

5. Add an instance of the `PurpleFlower` class, and enter `purpleFlower` for the name of this new instance.

6. Add another instance of the `PurpleFlower` class, and enter `purpleFlower2` for the name of this new instance. The additional flower may be placed on top of the previously added flower.

7. Add an instance of the `ForestSky` class to the scene.

8. Place the bee and the two flowers as shown in the next screenshot:

How to do it...

Follow these steps to execute many statements for the bee with a specific order:

1. Open an existing project with one actor added to the scene.

2. Click on **Edit Code**, at the lower-right corner of the big scene preview. Alice will show a smaller preview of the scene and will display the **Code Editor** on a panel located at the right-hand side of the main window.

3. Click on the **class: MyScene** drop-down list and the list of classes that are part of the scene will appear.

4. Select **MyScene | Edit run**.

5. Select the desired actor in the instance drop-down list located at the left-hand side of the main window, below the small scene preview. For example, you can select bee. Make sure that part: none is selected in the drop-down list located at the right-hand side of the chosen instance.

6. Activate the **Procedures** tab. Alice will display the procedures for the previously selected actor.

7. Drag the **pointAt** procedure and drop it in the **drop statement here** area located below the **do in order** label, inside the **run** tab. Because the instance name is bee, the **pointAt** statement contains the **this.bee** and **pointAt** labels followed by the **target** parameter and its question marks **???**. A list with all the possible instances to pass to the first parameter will appear.

8. Click on this.purpleFlower. The following code will be displayed, as shown in the next screenshot:

```
this.bee.pointAt(this.purpleFlower)
```

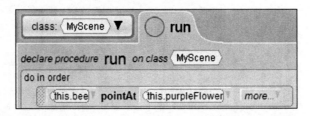

9. Drag the **moveTo** procedure and drop it below the previously dropped procedure call. A list with all the possible instances to pass to the first parameter will appear. Select **this.purpleFlower getPart ???** and then **lStemMiddle_lStemTop_lHPistil_ lHPetal01**, as shown in the following screenshot:

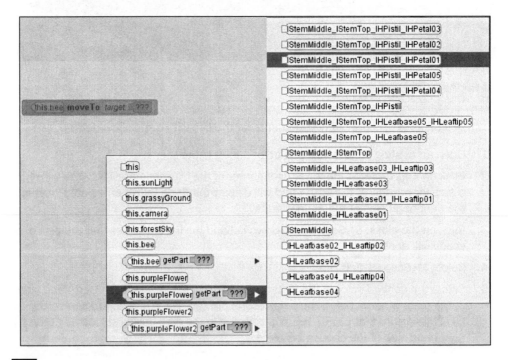

10. Click on the **more...** drop-down menu button that appears at the right-hand side of the recently dropped statement. Click on `duration` and then on `1.0` in the cascade menu that appears.

11. Click on the new **more...** drop-down menu that appears. Click on `style` and then on `BEGIN_AND_END_ABRUPTLY`. The following code will be displayed as the second statement:

```
this.bee.moveTo(this.purpleFlower.getPart(IStemMiddle_IStemTop_
IHPistil_IHPetal01), duration: 1.0, style: BEGIN_AND_END_ABRUPTLY)
```

12. Drag the **delay** procedure and drop it below the previously dropped procedure call. A list with all the predefined direction values to pass to the first parameter will appear. Select `2.0` and the following code will be displayed as the third statement:

```
this.bee.delay(2.0)
```

13. Drag the **moveAwayFrom** procedure and drop it below the previously dropped procedure call. Select `0.25` for the first parameter. Click on the **more...** drop-down menu button that appears and select **this.purpleFlower getPart ???** and then **IStemMiddle_IStemTop_IHPistil_IHPetal01**. Click on the additional **more...** drop-down menu button, on `duration` and then on `1.0` in the cascade menu that appears. Click on the new **more...** drop-down menu that appears, on `style` and then on `BEGIN_ABRUPTLY_AND_END_GENTLY`. The following code will be displayed as the fourth statement:

```
this.bee.moveAwayFrom(0.25, this.purpleFlower.getPart(IStemMiddle_
IStemTop_IHPistil_IHPetal01), duration: 1.0, style: BEGIN_
ABRUPTLY_AND_END_GENTLY)
```

14. Drag the **turnToFace** procedure and drop it below the previously dropped procedure call. Select **this.purpleFlower2 getPart ???** and then **IStemMiddle_IStemTop_IHPistil_IHPetal05**. Click on the additional **more...** drop-down menu button, on `duration` and then on `1.0` in the cascade menu that appears. Click on the new **more...** drop-down menu that appears, on `style` and then on `BEGIN_ABRUPTLY_AND_END_GENTLY`. The following code will be displayed as the fifth statement:

```
this.bee.turnToFace(this.purpleFlower2.getPart(IStemMiddle_
IStemTop_IHPistil_IHPetal05), duration: 1.0, style: BEGIN_
ABRUPTLY_AND_END_GENTLY)
```

15. Drag the **moveTo** procedure and drop it below the previously dropped procedure call. Select **this.purpleFlower2 getPart ???** and then **IStemMiddle_IStemTop_IHPistil_IHPetal05**. Click on the additional **more...** drop-down menu button, on `duration` and then on `1.0` in the cascade menu that appears. Click on the new **more...** drop-down menu that appears, on `style` and then on `BEGIN_AND_END_ABRUPTLY`. The following code will be displayed as the sixth statement:

```
this.bee.moveTo(this.purpleFlower2.getPart(IStemMiddle_IStemTop_
IHPistil_IHPetal05), duration: 1.0, style: BEGIN_AND_END_GENTLY)
```

16. Drag the **delay** procedure and drop it below the previously dropped procedure call. A list with all the predefined direction values to pass to the first parameter will appear. Select `2.0` and the following code will be displayed as the seventh statement:

```
this.bee.delay(2.0)
```

17. Drag the **move** procedure and drop it below the previously dropped procedure call. Select `FORWARD` and then `10.0`. Click on the **more...** drop-down menu button, on `duration` and then on `10.0` in the cascade menu that appears. Click on the additional **more...** drop-down menu that appears, on `asSeenBy` and then on **this. bee**. Click on the new **more...** drop-down menu that appears, on `style` and then on `BEGIN_AND_END_ABRUPTLY`. The following code will be displayed as the eighth and final statement. The following screenshot shows the eight statements that compose the `run` procedure:

```
this.bee.move(FORWARD, duration: 10.0, asSeenBy: this.bee, style:
BEGIN_ABRUPTLY_AND_END_GENTLY)
```

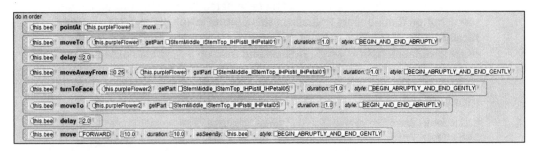

18. Select **File | Save as...** from Alice's main menu and give a new name to the project. Then you can make changes to the project according to your needs.

How it works...

When we run a project, Alice creates the scene instance, creates and initializes all the instances that compose the scene, and finally executes the `run` method defined in the `MyScene` class. By default, the statements we add to a procedure are included within the `do in order` block. We added eight statements to the `do in order` block, and therefore Alice will begin with the first statement:

```
this.bee.pointAt(this.purpleFlower)
```

Once the `bee` finishes executing the `pointAt` procedure, the execution flow goes on with the next statement specified in the `do in order` block. Thus, Alice will execute the following second statement after the first one finishes:

```
this.bee.moveTo(this.purpleFlower.getPart(IStemMiddle_IStemTop_
IHPistil_IHPetal01), duration: 1.0, style: BEGIN_AND_END_ABRUPTLY)
```

The do in order statement encapsulates a group of statements with a synchronous execution. Thus, when we add many statements within a do in order block, these statements will run one after the other. Each statement requires its previous statement to finish before starting its execution, and therefore we can use the do in order block to group statements that must run with a specific order.

The moveTo procedure moves the 3D model that represents the actor until it reaches the position of the other actor. The value for the target parameter is the instance of the other actor. We want the bee to move to one of the petals of the first flower, purpleFlower, and therefore we passed this value to the target parameter:

```
this.purpleFlower.getPart(IStemMiddle_IStemTop_IHPistil_IHPetal01)
```

We called the getPart function for purpleFlower with IStemMiddle_IStemTop_IHPistil_IHPetal01 as the name of the part to return. This function allows us to retrieve one petal from the flower as an instance. We used the resulting instance as the target parameter for the moveTo procedure and we could make the bee move to the specific petal of the flower.

Once the bee finishes executing the moveTo procedure, the execution flow goes on with the next statement specified in the do in order block. Thus, Alice will execute the following third statement after the second one finishes:

```
this.bee.delay(2.0)
```

The delay procedure puts the actor to sleep in its current position for the specified number of seconds. The next statement specified in the do in order block will run after waiting for two seconds.

The statements added to the run procedure will perform the following visible actions in the specified order:

1. Point the bee at purpleFlower.
2. Begin and end abruptly a movement for the bee from its position to the petal named IStemMiddle_IStemTop_IHPistil_IHPetal01 of purpleFlower. The total duration for the animation must be 1 second.
3. Make the bee stay in its position for 2 seconds.
4. Move the bee away 0.25 units from the position of the petal named IStemMiddle_IStemTop_IHPistil_IHPetal01 of purpleFlower. Begin the movement abruptly but end it gently. The total duration for the animation must be 1 second.

5. Turn the `bee` to the face of the petal named `IStemMiddle_IStemTop_IHPistil_IHPetal05` of `purpleFlower2`. Begin the movement abruptly but end it gently. The total duration for the animation must be 1 second.

6. Begin and end abruptly a movement for the `bee` from its position to the petal named `IStemMiddle_IStemTop_IHPistil_IHPetal05` of `purpleFlower2`. The total duration for the animation must be 1 second.

7. Make the `bee` stay in its position for 2 seconds.

8. Move the `bee` forward `10` units. Begin the movement abruptly but end it gently. The total duration for the animation must be `10` seconds. The bee will disappear from the scene.

The following screenshot shows six screenshots of the rendered frames:

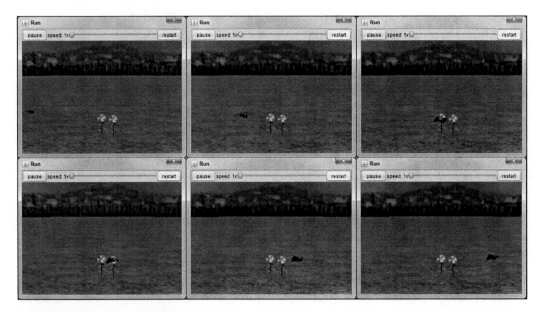

There's more...

When you work with the Alice code editor, you can temporarily disable statements. Alice doesn't execute the **disabled statements**. However, you can enable them again later. It is useful to disable one or more statements when you want to test the results of running the project without these statements, but you might want to enable them back to compare the results.

To disable a statement, right-click on it and deactivate the **IsEnabled** option, as shown in the following screenshot:

The disabled statements will appear with diagonal lines, as shown in the next screenshot, and won't be considered at run-time:

To enable a disabled statement, right-click on it and activate the **IsEnabled** option.

See also

- ▶ *Running many statements at the same time*, in this chapter
- ▶ *Working with parts of characters*, in *Chapter 5, Working with Variables*
- ▶ *Creating a new instance from a class in a gallery*, in this chapter

Using a counter to run statements many times

In this task, we will learn to group many statements into a block that repeats the execution of the code a specific number of times. We will create a loop that repeats the execution of a group of statements with a synchronous execution the number of times specified by its required integer parameter.

Getting ready

We have to be working on a project with many actors. Therefore, we will use an existing project that has two flowers and a bee.

1. Open the project saved in the *Performing many statements in order* recipe in this chapter.
2. Click on **Edit Code**, at the lower-right corner of the big scene preview. Alice will show a smaller preview of the scene and will display the **Code Editor** on a panel located at the right-hand side of the main window.

3. Click on the **class: MyScene** drop-down list and the list of classes that are part of the scene will appear.

4. Select **MyScene | Edit run**.

How to do it...

Follow these steps to create a loop that repeats the execution of a group of statements:

1. Drag the **count** statement, located at the top, and drop it below the first statement. Alice will display a green line indicating the position in which this new statement will be inserted, as shown in the following screenshot:

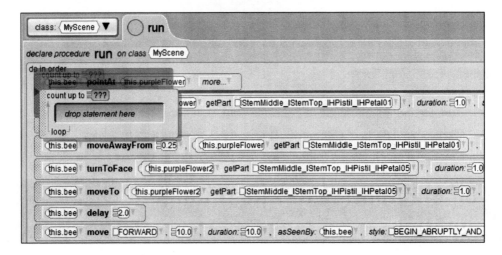

2. Select **Other Integer...** and the **Enter custom integer** dialog box will appear. Enter 5 and click **OK**. The count up to statement will display a **drop statement here** placeholder.

3. Place the mouse pointer over the light shade at the left-hand side of the statement below the count up to placeholder. The mouse pointer will appear as a link select hand.

4. Drag the statement and drop it in the **drop statement here** area located within the count up to block, as shown in the following screenshot:

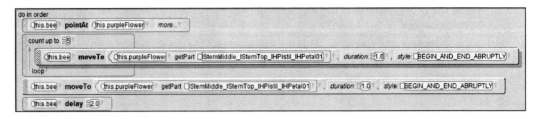

5. Place the mouse pointer over the light shade at the left-hand side of the statement below the count up to placeholder. Drag this statement and drop it after the last statement within the count up to block.

6. Repeat the aforementioned step for the next four statements. The count up to 5 statement will group the following block of code:

```
this.bee.moveTo(this.purpleFlower.getPart(IStemMiddle_IStemTop_
IHPistil_IHPetal01), duration: 1.0, style: BEGIN_AND_END_ABRUPTLY)
this.bee.delay(2.0)
this.bee.moveAwayFrom(0.25, this.purpleFlower.getPart(IStemMiddle_
IStemTop_IHPistil_IHPetal01), duration: 1.0, style: BEGIN_
ABRUPTLY_AND_END_GENTLY)
this.bee.turnToFace(this.purpleFlower2.getPart(IStemMiddle_
IStemTop_IHPistil_IHPetal05), duration: 1.0, style: BEGIN_
ABRUPTLY_AND_END_GENTLY)
this.bee.moveTo(this.purpleFlower2.getPart(IStemMiddle_IStemTop_
IHPistil_IHPetal05), duration: 1.0, style: BEGIN_AND_END_GENTLY)
this.bee.delay(2.0)
```

How it works...

We added a count up to 5 statement that allowed us to create a block of code that will be repeated 5 times. The count up to statement creates a loop that repeats the execution of a group of statements with a synchronous execution the number of times specified by its required integer parameter.

The statements added within the count up to block run one after the other. When the execution flow reaches the last statement within the count up to block, Alice checks the number of times that the block was executed. If the number of times hasn't reached the integer number specified as a parameter, the loop will start with the first statement in the block again. Once the number of times is reached, Alice goes on with the execution of the next statement after the count up to block.

We dragged and dropped many statements from the main do in order block to the count up to 5 block. The run procedure will perform the following visible actions in the specified order:

1. Point the bee at purpleFlower.

2. Set up a counter to 0.

3. Increase the counter.

4. Begin and abruptly end a movement for the bee from its position to the petal named IStemMiddle_IStemTop_IHPistil_IHPetal01 of purpleFlower. The total duration for the animation must be 1 second.

5. Make the bee stay in its position for 2 seconds.

6. Move the bee away 0.25 units from the position of the petal named IStemMiddle_ IStemTop_IHPistil_IHPetal01 of purpleFlower. Begin the movement abruptly but end it gently. The total duration for the animation must be 1 second.

7. Turn the bee to the face of the petal named IStemMiddle_IStemTop_IHPistil_ IHPetal05 of purpleFlower2. Begin the movement abruptly but end it gently. The total duration for the animation must be 1 second.

8. Begin and end abruptly a movement for the bee from its position to the petal named IStemMiddle_IStemTop_IHPistil_IHPetal05 of purpleFlower2. The total duration for the animation must be 1 second.

9. Make the bee stay in its position for 2 seconds.

10. If the counter hasn't reached 5, go back to step number 3. If the counter reached 5, go on with step number 11.

11. Move the bee forward 10 units. Begin the movement abruptly but end it gently. The total duration for the animation must be 10 seconds. The bee will disappear from the scene.

The following image shows six screenshots of the rendered frames:

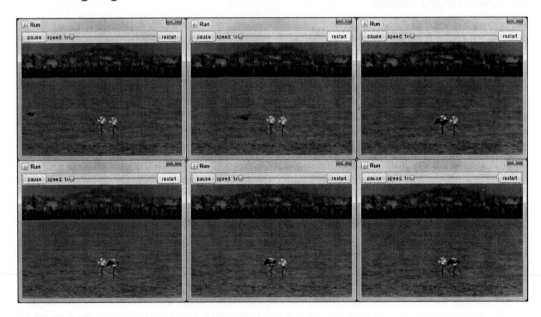

Once the bee reaches the first flower, it will move to and from the two flowers five times. Finally, the bee will leave the flowers.

See also

▶ *Running conditional code within a counter*, in *Chapter 4, Working with Functions and conditions*

▶ *Running a loop while a condition is true*, in *Chapter 4, Working with Functions and Conditions*

▶ *Performing many steps in order*, in this chapter

Running statements for different actors

In this recipe, we will run many statements to create an animation that calls procedures for many actors of the same class. We will coordinate the actions of many flowers available in our scene.

Getting ready

We have to be working on a project with at least two actors of the same class. Therefore, we will use an existing project that has two instances of `MyPurpleFlower`.

1. Open the project saved in the *Performing many statements in order* recipe.

2. Click on **Edit Code**, at the lower right corner of the big scene preview. Alice will show a smaller preview of the scene and will display the **Code Editor** on a panel located at the right-hand side of the main window.

3. Click on the **class: MyScene** drop-down list and the list of classes that are part of the scene will appear.

4. Select **MyScene | Edit run**.

5. Delete all the existing statements. Right-click on each statement and select **Delete Statement** in the context menu that appears.

How to do it...

Follow these steps to call procedures for many instances of the same class:

1. Drag the **each in _ together** statement, located at the top, and drop it in the **drop statement here** area located below the **do in order** label, inside the **run** tab.

2. Click **Other Array** and the **Enter custom array** dialog box will appear.

3. Click on the **type** drop-down list and a drop-down menu will appear. Select **MyTypes | MyPurpleFlower**, as shown in the following screenshot:

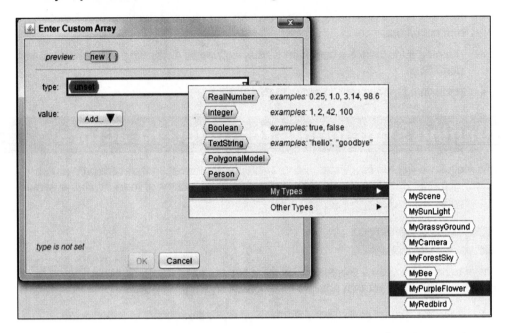

4. Click on the **Add...** drop-down menu button that appears at the right-hand side of **value**. Click on `this.purpleFlower` in the menu that appears.

5. Click on the **Add...** drop-down menu button that appears at the right-hand side of **value** and below **[0] this.purpleFlower**. Click on `this.purpleFlower2` in the menu that appears. The dialog box will display `this.purpleFlower` and `this.purpleFlower2` as the two values, as shown in the following screenshot:

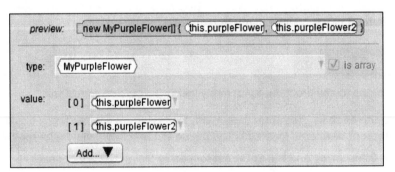

6. Click **OK**. The each in _ together statement will display a **drop statement here** placeholder, as shown in the following screenshot:

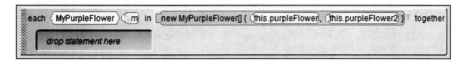

7. Select variable: m in the instance drop-down list located at the left-hand side of the main window, below the small scene preview. Make sure that part: none is selected in the drop-down list located at the right-hand side of the chosen instance.

8. Activate the **Procedures** tab. Alice will display the procedures for the local m variable that represents each MyPurpleFlower instance available in the scene.

9. Drag the **roll** procedure and drop it in the **drop statement here** area located within the each in _ together block. The **roll** assignment statement contains the **m** and **roll** labels followed by the **direction** and **amount** parameters and their question marks **???**. A list with all the predefined direction values to pass to the first parameter will appear.

10. Click on LEFT and then on 0.125 in the cascade menu that appears.

11. Click on the **more...** drop-down menu button that appears at the right-hand side of the recently dropped statement. Click on duration, select **Other Real Number...** and the **Enter custom real number** dialog box will appear. Enter 5 and click **OK**.

12. Click on the new **more...** drop-down menu that appears. Click on asSeenBy and then on m.

13. Click on the new **more...** drop-down menu that appears. Click on style and then on BEGIN_AND_END_ABRUPTLY. The following code will be displayed:

```
m.roll LEFT, 0.125, duration: 5.0, asSeenBy: m, style: BEGIN_AND_
END_ABRUPTLY
```

14. Drag the **roll** procedure and drop it below the previously dropped procedure call, within the each in _ together block. A list with all the predefined direction values to pass to the first parameter will appear.

15. Click on RIGHT and then on 0.125 in the cascade menu that appears.

16. Click on the **more...** drop-down menu button that appears at the right-hand side of the recently dropped statement. Click on duration, select **Other Real Number...** and the **Enter custom real number** dialog box will appear. Enter 5 and click **OK**.

17. Click on the new **more...** drop-down menu that appears. Click on asSeenBy and then on m.

18. Click on the new **more...** drop-down menu that appears. Click on `style` and then on `BEGIN_ABRUPTLY_AND_END_GENTLY`. The following code will be displayed and it will appear as the second statement for the `each in _ together` block, as shown in the following screenshot:

    ```
    m.roll RIGHT, 0.125, duration: 5.0, asSeenBy: m, style: BEGIN_
    ABRUPTLY_AND_END_GENTLY
    ```

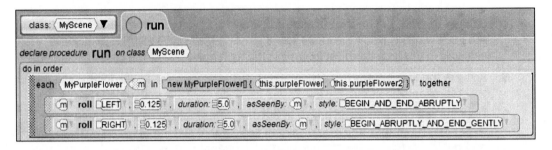

19. Select **File | Save as...** from Alice's main menu and give a new name to the project. Then you can make changes to the project according to your needs.

How it works...

We added an `each in _ together` statement that allowed us to create a block of code that executes statements for each instance of the specified class. There are two instances of the `MyPurpleFlower` class, `purpleFlower`, and `purpleFlower2`. We selected `MyPurpleFlower` as the type for a new array when we added the `each in _ together` statement. The following code defines the `each in _ together` block:

```
each (MyPurpleFlower m in new MyPurpleFlower[]{ this.purpleFlower,
this.purpleFlower2 }) together
```

We added two calls to the `roll` procedure for the m instance within the `each in _ together` block. The first `roll` procedure rolls the two `MyPurpleFlower` instances to the left. Because we called `m.roll` within the block, Alice calls the `roll` method for each of the `MyPurpleFlower` instances specified after the `in` keyword. Alice calls the `roll` method for each of these instances at the same time, together. Therefore, the wind rolls the two flowers to the right at the same time.

Once the first call to the `roll` procedure finishes for both flowers, the second call to this procedure also runs for the instances specified after the `in` keyword at the same time, together. However, this time, the two flowers roll to the left, back to their original angle.

The two calls to the `roll` procedure run with a synchronous execution. However, they run together for the instances specified in the array defined after the `in` keyword. Thus, you will see the two flowers rolling at the same time. The following screenshot shows three screenshots of the rendered frames:

See also

- ▸ *Repeating statements at the same time*, in this chapter
- ▸ *Working with a local variable*, in *Chapter 5, Working with Variables*
- ▸ *Using arrays*, in *Chapter 5, Working with Variables*
- ▸ *Performing many steps in order*, in this chapter

Running statements for many actors

In this task, we will learn to call procedures for different actors. We will see the results of animating two actors of different classes. Eight statements will call procedures for the `bee` instance and three statements will call procedures for the `redbird` instance.

Getting ready

We have to be working on a project with at least two actors of different classes. Therefore, we will use an existing project and we will add an actor to the scene.

1. Open the project saved in the *Performing many statements in order* recipe.

2. Click on **Edit Scene**, at the lower-right corner of the scene preview. Alice will show a bigger preview of the scene and will display the **Model Gallery** at the bottom.

3. Add an instance of the `Redbird` class to the scene, and enter `redbird` for the name of this new instance. First, Alice will create the `MyRedbird` class to extend `Redbird`. Then, Alice will create an instance of `MyRedbird` named `redbird`. Follow the steps explained in the *Creating a new instance from a class in a gallery* recipe, in *Chapter 2*.

4. Place the red bird as shown in the following screenshot:

How to do it...

Follow these steps to call procedures for the bee instance and the redbird instance:

1. Click on **Edit Code**, at the lower-right corner of the big scene preview. Alice will show a smaller preview of the scene and will display the **Code Editor** on a panel located at the right-hand side of the main window.

2. Click on the **class: MyScene** drop-down list and the list of classes that are part of the scene will appear.

3. Select **MyScene | Edit run**. The eight existing statements that control the movement of the bee will appear.

4. Select `redbird` in the instance drop-down list located at the left-hand side of the main window, below the small scene preview. Make sure that `part: none` is selected in the drop-down list located at the right-hand side of the chosen instance.

5. Activate the **Procedures** tab. Alice will display the procedures for the previously selected actor.

6. Drag the **moveTo** procedure and drop it below the second statement. Alice will display a green line indicating the position in which this new statement will be inserted. A list with all the possible instances to pass to the first parameter will appear. Select **this. purpleFlower2 getPart ???** and then **lStemMiddle_lStemTop_IHPistil_IHPetal03**.

7. Click on the **more...** drop-down menu button that appears at the right-hand side of the recently dropped statement. Click on `duration` and then on `10.0` in the cascade menu that appears.

8. Click on the new **more...** drop-down menu that appears. Click on `style` and then on `BEGIN_AND_END_GENTLY`. The following code will be displayed as the new third statement:

```
this.redbird.moveTo(this.purpleFlower2.getPart(IStemMiddle_
IStemTop_IHPistil_IHPetal03), duration: 10.0, style: BEGIN_AND_
END_GENTLY)
```

9. Drag the **delay** procedure and drop it below the fourth statement, `this.bee. delay(2.0)`. A list with all the predefined direction values to pass to the first parameter will appear. Select `1.0` and the following code will be displayed as the new fifth statement:

```
this.redbird.delay(2.0)
```

10. Drag the **move** procedure and drop it below the last statement. Select `FORWARD`, click on **Other Real Number...** and the **Enter custom real number** dialog box will appear. Enter 5 and click **OK**.

11. Click on the **more...** drop-down menu button, on `duration`, select **Other Real Number...** and the **Enter custom real number** dialog box will appear. Enter 6 and click **OK**.

12. Click on the additional **more...** drop-down menu that appears, on `asSeenBy` and then on **this.redbird**. Click on the new **more...** drop-down menu that appears, on `style` and then on `BEGIN_GENTLY_AND_END_ABRUPTLY`. The following code will be displayed as the last statement. The three procedure calls for the `redbird` instance mixed with calls for the `bee` instance:

```
this.redbird.move(FORWARD, duration: 6.0, asSeenBy: this.redbird,
style: BEGIN_GENTLY_AND_END_ABRUPTLY)
```

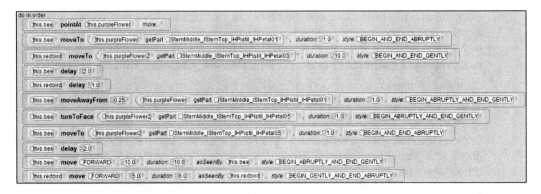

13. Select **File | Save as...** from Alice's main menu and give a new name to the project. Then you can make changes to the project according to your needs.

How it works...

The `run` procedure defined in the `MyScene` class executes 11 statements in order with a synchronous execution. Eight statements call procedures for the `bee` instance and three statements call procedures for the `redbird` instance. The three statements added to the `run` procedure that call procedures for the `redbird` instance will perform the following visible actions in the specified order:

1. Begin and abruptly end a movement for the `redbird` from its position to the petal named `IStemMiddle_IStemTop_IHPistil_IHPetal03` of `purpleFlower2`. The total duration for the animation must be `10` seconds.

2. Make the `redbird` stay in its position for `1` second.

3. Move the `bee` forward 5 units. Begin the movement gently but end it abruptly. The total duration for the animation must be `6` seconds. The `redbird` will disappear from the scene.

However, the scene will show only one actor performing actions at a time. For example, while the `redbird` flies towards one of the petals of `purpleFlower2`, the `bee` won't move. This happens because each statement is executed in order with a synchronous execution and there aren't two statements running at the same time, no matter the actor that calls the procedure. The following screenshot shows three screenshots of the rendered frames:

See also

▸ _Running many statements at the same time_, in this chapter

▸ _Controlling an actor with keystrokes_, in _Chapter 8, Working with Keyboard and Mouse Input_

▸ _Performing many steps in order_, in this chapter

Running many statements at the same time

In this recipe, we will learn to organize many calls to procedures for different actors to run them at the same time. We will see the results of animating two actors concurrently. We will make the `redbird` fly at the same time that the `bee` flies.

Getting ready

We have to be working on a project with at least two actors of different classes that must fly. Therefore, we will use an existing project with a `redbird` and a `bee`.

1. Open the project saved in the _Running statements for many actors_ recipe.

2. Click on **Edit Code**, at the lower-right corner of the big scene preview. Alice will show a smaller preview of the scene and will display the **Code Editor** on a panel located at the right-hand side of the main window.

3. Click on the **class: MyScene** drop-down list and the list of classes that are part of the scene will appear.

4. Select **MyScene | Edit run**. The 11 existing statements that control the movement of the bee and the red bird will appear.

How to do it...

Follow these steps to animate two actors concurrently:

1. Open the project saved in the *Running statements for many actors* recipe.

2. Drag the **do together** statement, located at the top, and drop it above the first statement. Alice will display a green line indicating the position in which this new statement will be inserted. The do together statement will display a **drop statement here** placeholder.

3. Drag the **do in order** statement, located at the top, and drop it in the **drop statement here** area located within the do together block. The do in order statement will display a **drop statement here** placeholder.

4. Drag another **do in order** statement, located at the top, and drop it below the previously dropped statement. Make sure that this do in order statement becomes part of the statements for the do together block. This do in order statement will also display a **drop statement here** placeholder, as shown in the following screenshot:

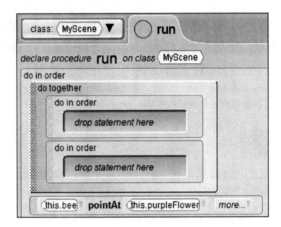

5. Place the mouse pointer over the light shade at the left-hand side of the statement below the do together placeholder. The mouse pointer will appear as a link select hand.

6. Drag the statement and drop it in the **drop statement here** area located within the first do in order block.

7. Place the mouse pointer over the light shade at the left-hand side of the statement below the do together placeholder. Drag this statement and drop it after the last statement within the first do in order block.

8. Repeat the aforementioned step for the remaining six statements that call procedures for `bee`. The first `do in order` statement will group the eight statements that call procedures for `bee`.

9. Place the mouse pointer over the light shade at the left-hand side of the statement below the `do together` placeholder that calls a procedure for `redbird`. The mouse pointer will appear as a link select hand.

10. Drag the statement and drop it in the **drop statement here** area located within the second `do in order` block.

11. Place the mouse pointer over the light shade at the left-hand side of the statement below the `do together` placeholder that calls a procedure for `redbird`. Drag this statement and drop it after the last statement within the second `do in order` block.

12. Repeat the aforementioned step for the remaining statement that calls a procedure for `redbird`. The second `do in order` statement will group the three statements that call procedures for `redbird`, as shown in the following screenshot:

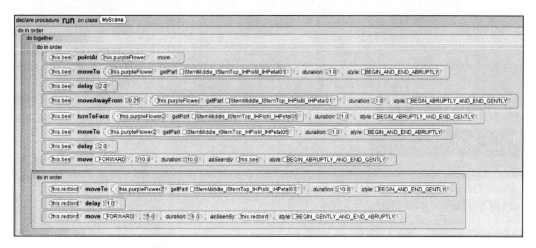

How it works...

We added a `do together` statement that allowed us to create a block of code that will run all the statements we add to the block at the same time. This means that all the statements added to this block will start their execution together.

We added two `do in order` statements within the `do together` block. Each of this `do in order` blocks will start their execution at the same time. We wanted to run an animation for the `bee` and to control the `redbird` at the same time. Thus, the first `do in order` block has the eight statements that control the `bee` and the second `do in order` block includes the three statements that control the `redbird`.

Alice allows us to group many statements in blocks to organize how the code has to be executed. In this case, we have three levels:

1. The first do in order block, defined by default for the run procedure
2. The do together block
3. Each do in order block within the do together block

The scene will show two actors performing actions at the same time, in parallel. For example, while the redbird flies towards one of the petals of purpleFlower2, the bee checks the pollen available in the two flowers. This happens because each group of statements is executed in order in two independent blocks that run together. The following image shows three screenshots of the rendered frames:

There's more...

When you work with the Alice code editor, you can convert or dissolve groups of statements included in a block. If you dissolve a block, the statements included in the block become part of the higher level block.

To dissolve a block, right-click on its label and select the **Disolve** option, followed by the block's description. For example, a do in order block shows a **Disolve DoInOrder** option, as shown in the following screenshot:

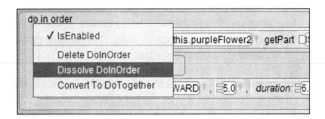

▶ *Working with the BOTH...AND operator*, in *Chapter 4, Working with Functions and Conditions*

▶ *Working with parts of characters*, in *Chapter 5, Working with Variables*

▶ *Running statements for many actors*, in this chapter

Repeating statements at the same time

In this task, we will repeat a group of statements for many actors of the same class. We will combine blocks that organize the code to animate two actors concurrently and to repeat this animation many times.

Getting ready

We have to be working on a project with at least two actors of the same class that must run animations concurrently. Therefore, we will use an existing project with two flowers.

1. Open the project saved in the *Running statements for different actors* recipe.

2. Click on **Edit Code**, at the lower-right corner of the big scene preview. Alice will show a smaller preview of the scene and will display the **Code Editor** on a panel located at the right-hand side of the main window.

3. Click on the **class: MyScene** drop-down list and the list of classes that are part of the scene will appear.

4. Select **MyScene | Edit run**. The each in _ together block with the two statements will appear.

How to do it...

Follow these steps to repeat a group of statements for many actors of the same class:

1. Drag the **count** statement, located at the top, and drop it on top of the first statement within the each in _ together block. Alice will display a green line indicating the position in which this new statement will be inserted.

2. Select **Other Integer...** and the **Enter custom integer** dialog box will appear. Enter 5 and click **OK**. The count up to statement will display a **drop statement here** placeholder.

3. Place the mouse pointer over the light shade at the left-hand side of the statement below the count up to block. The mouse pointer will appear as a link select hand.

4. Drag the statement and drop it in the **drop statement here** area located within the `count up to` block, as shown in the following screenshot:

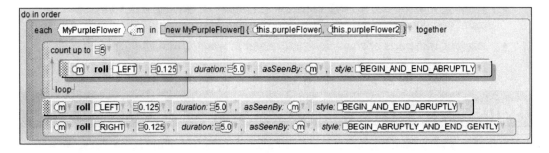

5. Place the mouse pointer over the light shade at the left-hand side of the statement below the `count up to` placeholder. Drag this statement and drop it after the last statement within the `count up to` block. The `count up to 5` statement will group the two calls to the `roll` procedure for the m variable, as shown in the following screenshot:

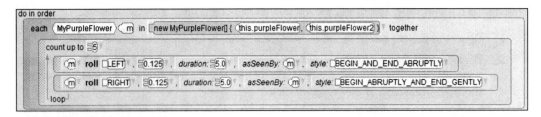

How it works...

We added a `count up to 5` statement that allowed us to create a block of code that executes two statements five times. The following two lines of code will run five times and they are also within the `each in _ together` block:

```
m.roll (LEFT, 0.125, duration: 5.0, asSeenBy: m, style: BEGIN_AND_END_
ABRUPTLY)
m.roll (RIGHT, 0.125, duration: 5.0, asSeenBy: m, style: BEGIN_
ABRUPTLY_AND_END_GENTLY)
```

The statements added within the `count up to` block run one after the other. However, each statement performs actions to many instances. In this case, each statement works with the two flowers at the same time. When the execution flow reaches the last statement within the `count up to` block, Alice checks the number of times that the block was executed. If the number of times hasn't reached the integer number specified as a parameter, the loop will start with the first statement in the block again. Once the number of times is reached, Alice goes on with the execution of the next statement after the `count up to` block.

We dragged and dropped two statements from the each in _ together block to the count up to 5 block. The combination of the two blocks allows us to repeat statements for many actors at the same time. You will see the two flowers rolling at the same time five times. The following screenshot shows six screenshots of the rendered frames:

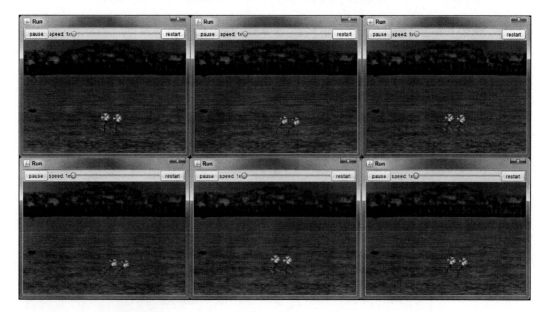

See also

1. *Using arrays*, in *Chapter 5, Working with Variables*
2. *Running statements for different actors*, in this chapter

Declaring new procedures

In this recipe, we will declare a new procedure for a class that will run many statements for the instance that calls this procedure. We will add a parameter and many statements for the new dance procedure. Then, we will be able to call the dance procedure for any instance of the class and pass a desired value for the parameter.

Getting ready

We have to be working on a project with at least two actors of the same class that must run animations concurrently. Therefore, we will use an existing project with two flowers.

1. Open the project saved in the *Performing many statements in order* recipe in this chapter.

2. Click on **Edit Code**, at the lower-right corner of the big scene preview. Alice will show a smaller preview of the scene and will display the **Code Editor** on a panel located at the right-hand side of the main window.

3. Click on the **class: MyScene** drop-down list and the list of classes that are part of the scene will appear.

4. Select **MyPurpleFlower | Declare procedure**.

How to do it...

Follow these steps to declare a new procedure:

1. Enter dance in name and click **OK**. The code editor will add a new tab with the name of the new procedure, **dance**, as shown in the following screenshot:

2. Click on the **Add Parameter...** button and the **Declare Parameter** dialog box will appear.

3. Click on the **type** drop-down list and a drop-down menu will appear. Select **RealNumber**.

4. Enter duration in name and click **OK**. The parameter will appear in the procedure declaration located at the top, below the tab, as shown in the following screenshot:

5. Select one of the instances of the `MyPurpleFlower` class that were added to the scene in the instance drop-down list located at the left-hand side of the main window, below the small scene preview. If you select another class, an out-of-scope label will appear and you won't be able to drag statements from the selected class. Make sure that `part: none` is selected in the drop-down list located at the right-hand side of the chosen instance.

6. Activate the **Procedures** tab.

7. Drag the **roll** procedure and drop it in the **drop statement here** area in the `dance` tab. The **roll** assignment statement contains the **this** and **roll** labels followed by the **direction** and **amount** parameters and their question marks **???**. A list with all the predefined direction values to pass to the first parameter will appear.

8. Click on `LEFT` and then on `0.125` in the cascade menu that appears.

9. Click on the **more...** drop-down menu button that appears at the right-hand side of the recently dropped statement. Click on `duration` and select **duration**.

10. Now, click on the **duration: duration** menu button that appears as a result of following the aforementioned step. Select **Math | duration / ??? | 2.0** in the menu that appears, as shown in the following screenshot:

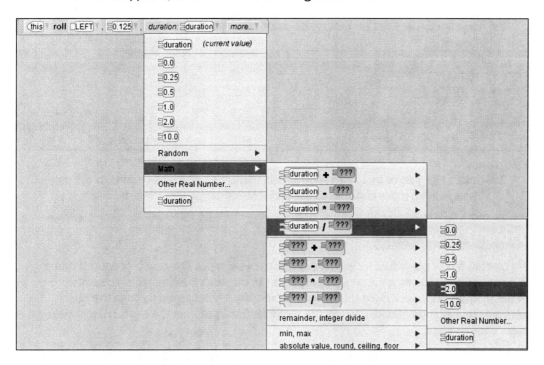

11. Click on the new **more...** drop-down menu that appears. Click on `asSeenBy` and then on `this`.

12. Click on the new **more...** drop-down menu that appears. Click on `style` and then on `BEGIN_AND_END_ABRUPTLY`. The following code will be displayed:

```
this.roll(LEFT, 0.125, duration: (duration / 2.0), asSeenBy: this,
style: BEGIN_AND_END_ABRUPTLY)
```

13. Drag the **roll** procedure and drop it below the previously dropped procedure call. A list with all the predefined direction values to pass to the first parameter will appear.

14. Click on `RIGHT` and then on `0.125` in the cascade menu that appears.

15. Click on the **more...** drop-down menu button that appears at the right-hand side of the recently dropped statement. Click on `duration` and select **duration**.

16. Click on the **duration: duration** menu button that appears as a result of following the aforementioned step. Select **Math | duration / ??? | 2.0** in the menu that appears.

17. Click on the new **more...** drop-down menu that appears. Click on `asSeenBy` and then on `this`.

18. Click on the new **more...** drop-down menu that appears. Click on `style` and then on `BEGIN_ABRUPTLY_AND_END_GENTLY`. The following code will be displayed, as shown in the following screenshot:

```
this.roll(RIGHT, 0.125, duration: (duration / 2.0), asSeenBy:
this, style: BEGIN_ABRUPTLY_AND_END_GENTLY)
```

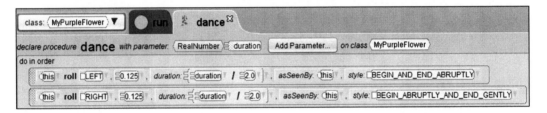

19. Select **File | Save as...** from Alice's main menu and give a new name to the project. Then you can make changes to the project according to your needs.

How it works...

We created a new procedure for the `MyPurpleFlower` class. The new procedure's name is `dance` and it receives a `duration` parameter of the `RealNumber` type. The instance of the `MyPurpleFlower` class that calls this procedure is accessed through the `this` keyword. Thus, the procedure can call the methods available from the `MyPurpleFlower` class through `this`.

The procedure makes two calls to the `this.roll` procedure and uses the value received in the `duration` parameter to calculate the duration for each call to the `roll` procedure. Each roll animation uses a value for the duration parameter of half the duration value received for the `dance` procedure.

- ▸ *Calling customized procedures*, in this chapter
- ▸ *Performing many steps in order*, in this chapter

Calling customized procedures

In this task, we will call the new procedure defined for a class in the previous recipe. We will call the `dance` procedure for the instances of the `MyPurpleFlower` class. The `dance` procedure will run statements that will make each flower dance.

Getting ready

We have to be working on a project with at least two actors of the same class. Therefore, we will use an existing project that has two instances of `MyPurpleFlower`.

1. Open the project saved in the *Declaring new procedures* recipe.
2. Click on **Edit Code**, at the lower-right corner of the big scene preview. Alice will show a smaller preview of the scene and will display the **Code Editor** on a panel located at the right-hand side of the main window.
3. Click on the **class: MyScene** drop-down list and the list of classes that are part of the scene will appear.
4. Select **MyScene | Edit run**.
5. Delete all the existing statements. Right-click on each statement and select **Delete Statement** in the context menu that appears.

How to do it...

Follow these steps to call the `dance` procedure for the instances of the `MyPurpleFlower` class:

1. Drag the **each in _ together** statement, located at the top, and drop it in the **drop statement here** area located below the **do in order** label, inside the **run** tab.
2. Click **Other Array** and the **Enter custom array** dialog box will appear.
3. Click on the **type** drop-down list and a drop-down menu will appear. Select **MyTypes | MyPurpleFlower**.
4. Click on the **Add...** drop-down menu button that appears at the right-hand side of **value**. Click on `this.purpleFlower` in the menu that appears.

5. Click on the **Add...** drop-down menu button that appears at the right-hand side of **value** and below **[0] this.purpleFlower**. Click on this.purpleFlower2 in the menu that appears. The dialog box will display this.purpleFlower and this. purpleFlower2 as the two values.

6. Click **OK**. The each in _ together statement will display a **drop statement here** placeholder.

7. Drag the **count** statement, located at the top, and drop it on the **drop statement here** area located within the each in _ together block. A list with some predefined values to count up to it will appear.

8. Select **Other Integer...** and the **Enter custom integer** dialog box will appear. Enter 5 and click **OK**. The count up to statement will display a **drop statement here** placeholder.

9. Select variable: m in the instance drop-down list located at the left-hand side of the main window, below the small scene preview. Make sure that part: none is selected in the drop-down list located at the right-hand side of the chosen instance.

10. Activate the **Procedures** tab. Alice will display the procedures for the local m variable that represents each MyPurpleFlower instance available in the scene. The previously declared dance procedure will appear under **MyPurpleFlower** with its duration parameter listed, as shown in the following screenshot:

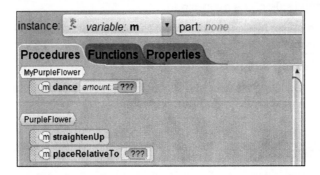

11. Drag the **dance** procedure and drop it in the **drop statement here** area located within the count up to 5 block. A list with all the predefined duration values to pass to the parameter will appear. Select 10.0 and the following code will be displayed and it will appear as the statement for the each in _ together block, as shown in the following screenshot:

```
m.dance(duration: 10.0)
```

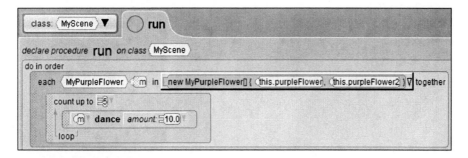

How it works...

We added an `each in _ together` statement that allowed us to create a block of code that executes statements for each instance of the specified class. There are two instances of the `MyPurpleFlower` class, `purpleFlower` and `purpleFlower2`. We selected `MyPurpleFlower` as the type for a new array when we added the `each in _ together` statement.

We added a single call to the previously defined `dance` procedure for the `m` instance within the `each in _ together` block. This dance procedure will run two rolls for the two `MyPurpleFlower` instances. When we call a procedure, Alice runs the code defined for this procedure for the instance. Thus, you will see the two flowers rolling at the same time. The following screenshot shows three screenshots of the rendered frames:

See also

> ▸ _Declaring and calling new functions_, in _Chapter 4, Working with Functions and Conditions_

> ▸ _Using properties to call procedures_, in _Chapter 6, Working with Properties_

> ▸ _Declaring new procedures_, in this chapter

4
Working with Functions and Conditions

In this chapter, we will cover:

- ▶ Running conditional code
- ▶ Running conditional code within a counter
- ▶ Working with the NOT operator
- ▶ Working with the BOTH...AND operator
- ▶ Working with the EITHER...OR operator
- ▶ Working with relational operators
- ▶ Running a loop while a condition is true
- ▶ Declaring and calling new functions

Introduction

Once you start organizing the statements that request the different actors to perform actions, you need to run groups of statements in response to those actions. Alice 3 allows you to evaluate expressions to determine whether you have to run certain blocks of code or not at run-time. This chapter provides many tasks that will allow us to decide whether to run certain statements according to the results of the evaluation of expressions.

We will define many actions that will run when certain things happen. We will use counters to evaluate a group of expressions many times. We will work with logical operators to combine many sub-expressions into a complex expression. We will use relational operators to compare values between functions and sub-expressions. We will run many statements while a condition is true. In addition, we will create a new function that will allow us to detect whether a red bird has hit the ground.

Running conditional code

In this recipe, we will run many statements according to the results of the evaluation of expressions. We will create blocks of code that will run when an expression evaluates to true or false. A bee and a red bird will respond to the evaluation of expressions.

Getting ready

We will be working on a project with at least two actors. Therefore, we will use an existing project that has a bee and a red bird. This project also has two purple flowers in the scene and a grassy ground.

1. Open the project saved in the *Performing many statements in order* recipe, in *Chapter 3, Organizing Statements*. In this project, there is some distance between the `redbird` and the `bee`.

2. Click on **Edit Code**, at the lower-right corner of the big scene preview. Alice will show a smaller preview of the scene and will display the **Code Editor** on a panel located at the right-hand side of the main window.

3. Click on the **class: MyScene** drop-down list and the list of classes that are part of the scene will appear.

4. Select **MyScene | Edit run**.

5. Delete all the existing statements. Right-click on each statement or block of statements and select **Delete Statement** in the context menu that appears.

How to do it...

Follow these steps to make the bee and the red bird respond to the evaluation of expressions:

1. Select `redbird` in the instance drop-down list located at the left-hand side of the main window, below the small scene preview. Make sure that `part: none` is selected in the drop-down list located at the right-hand side of the chosen instance.

2. Activate the **Procedures** tab. Alice will display the procedures for the previously selected actor.

3. Drag the **moveToward** procedure and drop it in the **drop statement here** area located below the **do in order** label, inside the **run** tab. Select 0.5 for the first parameter and then click on this.bee. Click on the **more...** drop-down menu button that appears, on duration and then on 1.0 in the cascade menu that appears. The following code will be displayed as the first statement:

```
this.redbird.moveToward(0.5, this.bee, duration: 1.0)
```

4. Drag the **think** procedure and drop it below the previously dropped procedure call. Click on **Other String...** and the **Enter Custom String** dialog box will appear. Enter Where is the bee? in the **value** textbox and click **OK**. Click on the **more...** drop-down menu button that appears, on duration and then on 1.0 in the cascade menu that appears. The following code will appear as a new statement:

```
this.redbird.think("Where is the bee?", duration: 1.0)
```

5. Drag the **if _** statement, located at the top, and drop it below the previously dropped procedure call. Click on **true** and two **drop statement here** placeholders will appear, as shown in the following screenshot:

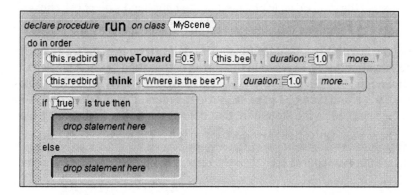

6. Activate the **Functions** tab. Alice will display the functions for the selected actor.

7. Drag the **isAbove** function and drop it on the first **true** expression that appears after the if keyword in the **if true is true then** block. A black rectangle will surround the true keyword when you start dragging the **isAbove** function. Select this.bee for the parameter in the menu that appears. The following code will be displayed as the statement that defines the conditional if block:

```
if this.redbird.isAbove(this.bee) is true then
```

8. Activate the **Procedures** tab. Alice will display the procedures for the selected actor.

9. Drag the **moveTo** procedure and drop it in the first **drop statement here** area located within the `if` block. Select `this.bee` as the target instance. Click on the **more...** drop-down menu button that appears, on `duration` and then on `2.0` in the cascade menu that appears. The following code will appear as a new statement:

```
this.redbird.moveTo(this.bee, duration: 2.0)
```

10. Drag the **moveAwayFrom** procedure and drop it in the **drop statement here** area located below the `else` keyword, within the `if` block. Select `2.0` for the first parameter and then click on `this.bee`. The following code will appear as a new statement:

```
this.redbird.moveAwayFrom(2.0, this.bee)
```

11. Drag another **if _** statement, located at the top, and drop it below the previously dropped `if` block. Click on **true** and two **drop statement here** placeholders will appear.

12. Now, select `bee` in the instance drop-down list located at the left-hand side of the main window, below the small scene preview. Make sure that `part: none` is selected in the drop-down list located at the right-hand side of the chosen instance.

13. Activate the **Functions** tab. Alice will display the functions for the selected actor.

14. Drag the **isWithinThresholdOf** function and drop it on the first **true** expression that appears after the `if` keyword in the **if true is true then** block. A black rectangle will surround the true keyword when you start dragging the **isWithinThresholdOf** function. Select `0.25` and then `this.redbird` in the menu that appears. The following code will be displayed as the statement that defines the new conditional `if` block:

```
if this.bee.isWithinThresholdOf(0.25, this.redbird) is true then
```

15. Activate the **Procedures** tab. Alice will display the procedures for the selected actor.

16. Drag the **moveAwayFrom** procedure and drop it on the first **drop statement here** area located within the second `if` block. Select `1.0` for the first parameter and then click on `this.redbird`. Click on the **more...** drop-down menu, on `duration` and then on `1.0` in the cascade menu. Click on the new **more...** drop-down menu that appears. Click on `style` and then on `BEGIN_AND_END_ABRUPTLY`. The following code will appear as a new statement, as shown in the following screenshot:

```
this.bee.moveAwayFrom(1.0, this.redbird, duration: 0.5, style:
BEGIN_AND_END_ABRUPTLY)
```

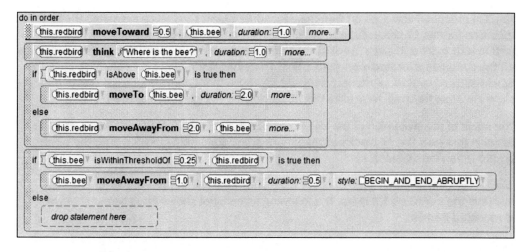

17. Select **File | Save as...** from Alice's main menu and give a new name to the project. Then you can make changes to the project according to your needs.

How it works...

We added two if _ statements that allowed us to create two blocks of code that execute statements according to the results of the evaluation of expressions. Once the redbird moves towards the bee and then thinks where the bee was, the execution flow goes on with the first if block. Thus, Alice evaluates the specified expression. If the result of calling the this.redbird.isAbove function with this.bee as a parameter is true, the execution flow goes on with the statements located after the if line. Therefore, if the result is true, Alice calls the this.redbird.moveTo procedure. Because there aren't additional statements before the else keyword, Alice exits the if block after the execution of this procedure.

If the result of the evaluation of the this.redbird.isAbove function is false, the execution flow goes on with the statements located after the else keyword. Alice doesn't execute the statements included after the else keyword if the evaluation of the function is true.

> The expression included between the if and then keywords is a **Boolean expression**, because it has two possible results, true or false.

If the redbird is above the bee, the redbird moves to the position of the bee. If the redbird isn't above the bee, the redbird moves away from the bee 2.0 units.

Then, the execution flow goes on with the second `if` block. Thus, Alice evaluates the specified expression for this `if` block. If the result of calling the `this.bee.isWithinThreshold` function with `0.25` and `this.redbird` as parameters is `true`, the execution flow continues with the statements located after the `if` line. Therefore, if the result is `true`, Alice calls the `this.redbird.moveAwayFrom` procedure. Because there aren't additional statements before the `else` keyword, Alice exits the `if` block after the execution of this procedure.

If the result of the evaluation of the `this.redbird.isAbove` function is `false`, the execution flow exits the `if` block because there aren't statements located after the `else` keyword within the `if` block.

If the `bee` is located within a threshold of 0.25 units near the `redbird`, the `bee` moves away from the `redbird` 1.0 units. The following screenshot shows three screenshots of the rendered frames:

There's more...

You can use blocks to group many statements within the two blocks of statements that could execute as a result of evaluating an expression in an `if` block. For example, you can add a `count up to` loop to repeat many statements a certain number of times within the block that runs code when the expression is `true`.

See also

  ▶ *Performing many statements in order*, in *Chapter 3, Organizing Statements*
  ▶ *Repeating statements at the same time*, in *Chapter 3, Organizing Statements*
  ▶ *Working with a local variable*, in *Chapter 5, Working with Variables*

Running conditional code within a counter

In this task, we will include many statements together with an `if` block into a loop that repeats the execution of the code a specific number of times. Thus, we will evaluate the result of an expression many times within a counter.

Getting ready

We will be working on a project with at least two actors. Therefore, we will use an existing project that has a bee and a red bird.

1. Open the project saved in the *Running conditional code* recipe in this chapter.

2. Click on **Edit code** and then on the **class: MyScene** drop-down list. The list of classes that are part of the scene will appear.

3. Select **MyScene | Edit run**.

4. Delete all the existing statements in the run procedure for the MyScene class.

How to do it...

Follow these steps to evaluate the result of an expression many times within a counter:

1. Drag the **count** statement, located at the top, and drop it on the **drop statement here** area located below the **do in order** label, inside the **run** tab. Select 3 from the context menu that appears. The count up to 3 statement will display a drop statement here placeholder:

2. Select redbird in the instance drop-down list located at the left-hand side of the main window, below the small scene preview. Make sure that part: none is selected in the drop-down list located at the right-hand side of the chosen instance.

3. Activate the **Procedures** tab. Alice will display the procedures for the previously selected actor.

4. Drag the **moveAndOrientTo** procedure and drop it in the **drop statement here** area located within the count up to 3 block. Select this.bee as the target instance. Click on the **more...** drop-down menu button that appears, on duration and then on 0.5 in the cascade menu that appears. The following code will be displayed as the first statement:

   ```
   this.redbird.moveAndOrientTo(this.bee, duration: 0.5)
   ```

5. Drag the **if _** statement, located at the top, and drop it below the previously dropped procedure call, within the count up to 3 block. Click on **true** and two **drop statement here** placeholders will appear.

6. Select bee in the instance drop-down list located at the left-hand side of the main window, below the small scene preview. Make sure that part: none is selected in the drop-down list located at the right-hand side of the chosen instance.

7. Activate the **Functions** tab. Alice will display the functions for the bee.

8. Drag the **isWithinThresholdOf** function and drop it on the first **true** expression that appears after the `if` keyword in the **if true is true then** block. A black rectangle will surround the true keyword when you start dragging the **isWithinThresholdOf** function. Select `0.5` and then `this.redbird` in the menu that appears. The following code will be displayed as the statement that defines the conditional `if` block:

```
if this.bee.isWithinThresholdOf(0.5, this.redbird) is true then
```

9. Now, activate the **Procedures** tab. Alice will display the procedures for the `bee`.

10. Drag the **moveAwayFrom** procedure and drop it on the first **drop statement here** area located within the `if` block. Select `0.25` for the first parameter and then click on `this.redbird`. Click on the **more...** drop-down menu button that appears, on `duration` and then on `0.25` in the cascade menu that appears. The following code will appear as a new statement, as shown in the following screenshot:

```
this.bee.moveAwayFrom(0.25, this.redbird, duration: 0.25)
```

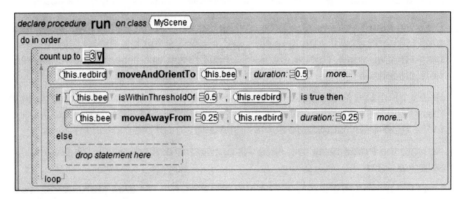

How it works...

We added a `count up to 3` statement that allowed us to create a block of code that will be repeated 3 times. The `run` procedure will perform the following visible actions in the specified order:

1. Create a counter and set it to `0`.

2. Increase the counter.

3. Move and orient the `redbird` towards the `bee` for `0.5` seconds.

4. If the `bee` is located within a threshold of `0.5` units near the `redbird`, the bee moves away from the `redbird` `0.25` units and the movement takes `0.25` seconds.

5. If the counter hasn't reached 3, go back to step number 2. If the counter reached 3, exit the loop.

The next screenshot shows three screenshots of the rendered frames:

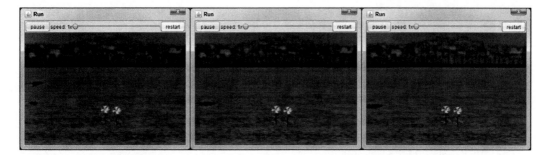

Each time the redbird reaches the `bee`, the `this.bee.isWithinThresholdOf` function will return `true`, and therefore, the code that makes the `bee` move away from the `redbird` will run.

See also

▶ *Running conditional code*, in this chapter

Working with the NOT operator

In this recipe, we will use the NOT operator to apply a logical negation to an expression. We will control the movement of a `bee`. If the `bee` is not located within a threshold of `0.25` units near a `purpleFlower`'s petal, the `bee` will continue moving towards this petal a random number of units.

Getting ready

We will be working on a project with at least two actors. Therefore, we will use an existing project that has a bee and a flower with petals. This project also has a red bird and another flower with petals.

1. Open the project saved in the *Running conditional code* recipe in this chapter.

2. Click on **Edit code** and then on the **class: MyScene** drop-down list. The list of classes that are part of the scene will appear.

3. Select **MyScene | Edit run**.

4. Delete all the existing statements in the `run` procedure for the `MyScene` class.

How to do it...

Follow these steps to control the movement of the bee:

1. Drag the **count** statement, located at the top, and drop it on the **drop statement here** area located below the **do in order** label, inside the **run** tab. Select **Other Integer...** and the **Enter Custom Integer** dialog box will appear. Enter 20 and click **OK**. The count up to 20 statement will display a **drop statement here** placeholder.

2. Drag the **if _** statement, located at the top, and drop it on the **drop statement here** area located within the count up to 20 block. Click on **true** and two **drop statement here** placeholders will appear.

3. Select bee in the instance drop-down list located at the left-hand side of the main window, below the small scene preview. Make sure that part : none is selected in the drop-down list located at the right-hand side of the chosen instance.

4. Activate the **Functions** tab. Alice will display the functions for the bee.

5. Drag the **isWithinThresholdOf** function and drop it on the first **true** expression that appears after the if keyword in the **if true is true then** block. A black rectangle will surround the true keyword when you start dragging the **isWithinThresholdOf** function. Select 0.25, **this.purpleFlower getPart ???** and then **IStemMiddle_IStemTop_IHPistil_IHPetal01** in the menu that appears. The following code will be displayed as the statement that defines the conditional if block:

```
if this.bee.isWithinThresholdOf(0.25, this.purpleFlower.
getPart(IStemMiddle_IStemTop_IHPistil_IHPetal01)) is true then
```

6. Now, click on the last down arrow that appears with a gray background at the right-hand side of the previously defined expression, before **is true then**. A drop-down menu will display different options to use to replace the current expression, as shown in the following screenshot:

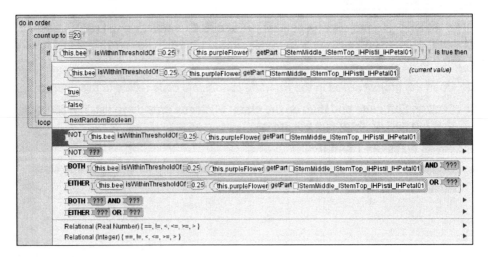

7. Select the fifth option that adds a NOT operator to the existing expression. The following code will be displayed as the new statement that defines the conditional if block:

```
if NOT(this.bee.isWithinThresholdOf(0.25, this.purpleFlower.
getPart(IStemMiddle_IStemTop_IHPistil_IHPetal01))) is true then
```

8. Activate the **Procedures** tab. Alice will display the procedures for the previously selected actor.

9. Drag the **moveToward** procedure and drop it on the first **drop statement here** area located within the if block. Select **1.00, this.purpleFlower getPart ???** and then **IStemMiddle_IStemTop_IHPistil_IHPetal01** in the menu that appears. Click on the **more...** drop-down menu button that appears, on duration and then on 0.25 in the cascade menu that appears. Click on the new **more...** drop-down menu that appears. Click on style and then on BEGIN_AND_END_GENTLY.

10. Now, click on the down arrow that appears with a gray background at the right-hand side of 1.0 on the previously defined statement, after **moveToward**. A drop-down menu will display different options to use to replace the current expression, as shown in the following screenshot:

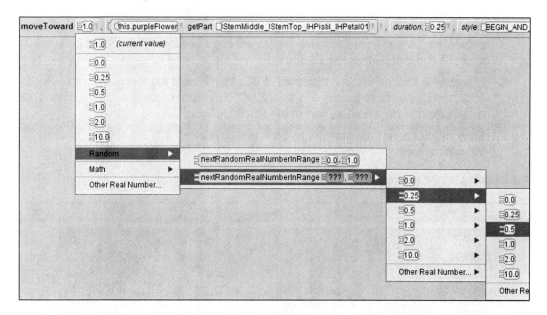

11. Select **Random | nextRandomRealNumberInRange ???, ??? | 0.25 | 0.5**. The following code includes the expression that generates a real random number to pass it as a parameter:

```
this.bee.moveToward(nextRandomRealNumberInRange(0.25, 0.5), this.
purpleFlower.getPart(IStemMiddle_IStemTop_IHPistil_IHPetal01),
duration: 0.25, style: BEGIN_AND_END_GENTLY)
```

12. Drag the **turn** procedure and drop it in the **drop statement here** area located below the `else` keyword, within the `if` block. Select `LEFT` for the first parameter and then click on `0.125`. Click on the **more...** drop-down menu button that appears, on `duration` and then on `0.25` in the cascade menu that appears. The following code will appear as a new statement:

```
this.bee.turn(LEFT, 0.125, duration: 0.25)
```

13. Select **File | Save as...** from Alice's main menu and give a new name to the project. Then you can make changes to the project according to your needs.

How it works...

We added a `count up to 20` statement that allowed us to create a block of code that will be repeated 20 times. The `run` procedure will perform the following visible actions in the specified order.

1. Set up a counter to `0`.

2. Increase the counter.

3. If the `bee` is not located within a threshold of `0.25` units near the first `purpleFlower`'s petal, the `bee` moves towards this petal a random number of units, between `0.25` and `0.5`. The movement takes `0.25` seconds. This code is included after the line that defines the `if` block.

4. If the `bee` is located within a threshold of `0.25` units near the first `purpleFlower`'s petal, the `bee` turns to the left `0.125` units. The movement takes `0.25` seconds. This code is included in the `else` part of the `if` block.

5. If the counter hasn't reached `20`, go back to step number 2. If the counter reached `20`, exit the loop.

The following image shows three screenshots of the rendered frames:

Each time you run the example, the movements of the `bee` are going to be different because the code is using random numbers.

The NOT operator allows us to negate the result of an expression, and therefore it is simpler to express the expression that we have to evaluate. If we want to take an action when something doesn't happen, we can apply the NOT operator and evaluate whether the result of the negated expression is true.

See also

▶ *Creating a random person*, in *Chapter 7, Working with People*

▶ *Working with relational operators*, in this chapter

▶ *Running conditional code*, in this chapter

Working with the BOTH...AND operator

In this recipe, we will use the BOTH...AND operator to create an expression that evaluates a logical conjunction between two sub-expressions. If a bee is smaller than a redbird and the bee is smaller than a purpleFlower, the bee will increase its size a random number of times.

Getting ready

We will be working on a project with at least three actors. Therefore, we will use an existing project that has a red bird, a bee, and a purple flower.

1. Open the project saved in the *Working with the NOT operator* recipe in this chapter.

2. Click on **Edit code** and then on the **class: MyScene** drop-down list. The list of classes that are part of the scene will appear.

3. Select **MyScene | Edit run**.

4. Delete all the existing statements in the run procedure for the MyScene class.

How to do it...

Follow these steps to use the BOTH...AND operator to create an expression that evaluates a logical conjunction between two sub-expressions:

1. Drag the **count** statement, located at the top, and drop it on the **drop statement here** area located below the **do in order** label, inside the **run** tab. Select **Other Integer...** and the **Enter Custom Integer** dialog box will appear. Enter 5 and click **OK**. The count up to 5 statement will display a **drop statement here** placeholder.

2. Drag the **if _** statement, located at the top, and drop it on the **drop statement here** area located within the count up to 5 block. Click on **true** and two **drop statement here** placeholders will appear.

3. Select bee in the instance drop-down list located at the left-hand side of the main window, below the small scene preview. Make sure that part: none is selected in the drop-down list located at the right-hand side of the chosen instance.

4. Activate the **Functions** tab. Alice will display the functions for the bee.

5. Drag the **isSmallerThan** function and drop it on the first **true** expression that appears after the if keyword in the **if true is true then** block. A black rectangle will surround the true keyword when you start dragging the **isSmallerThan** function. Select this. redbird in the menu that appears. The following code will be displayed as the statement that defines the conditional if block:

    ```
    if this.bee.isSmallerThan(this.redbird) is true then
    ```

6. Now, click on the last down arrow that appears with a gray background at the right-hand side of the previously defined expression, before **is true then**. A drop-down menu will display different options to use to replace the current expression. Select the seventh option that adds the BOTH keyword as a prefix to the existing expression and an AND keyword after the expression. Then, select true in the cascade menu that appears, as shown in the following screenshot. The following code will be displayed as the new statement that defines the conditional if block:

    ```
    if (BOTH this.bee.isSmallerThan(this.redbird) AND true) is true
    then
    ```

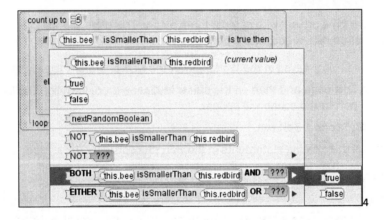

7. Drag the **isSmallerThan** function and drop it on the **true** expression that appears after the previously added AND keyword. A black rectangle will surround the true keyword when you start dragging the **isSmallerThan** function. Select this. purpleFlower in the menu that appears. The following code will be displayed as the statement that defines the definitive conditional if block:

    ```
    if (BOTH this.bee.isSmallerThan(this.redbird) AND this.bee.
    isSmallerThan(this.purpleFlower)) is true then
    ```

8. Activate the **Procedures** tab. Alice will display the procedures for the `bee`.

9. Drag the **resize** procedure and drop it on the first **drop statement here** area located within the `if` block. Select `1.00` as the value for the `amount` parameter. Click on the **more...** drop-down menu button that appears, on `duration` and then on `0.50` in the cascade menu that appears.

10. Now, click on the down arrow that appears with a gray background at the right-hand side of `1.0` on the previously defined statement, after **resize**. A drop-down menu will display different options to use to replace the current expression.

11. Select **Random | nextRandomRealNumberInRange ???, ??? | 1.0 | Other Real Number**. The Enter Custom Real Number dialog box will appear. Enter `1.1` and click **OK**. The following code includes the expression that generates a real random number to pass it as a parameter, as shown in the following screenshot:

```
this.bee.resize(nextRandomRealNumberInRange(1.0, 1.1), duration:
0.5)
```

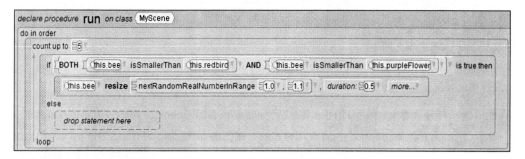

How it works...

We added a `count up to 5` statement that allowed us to create a block of code that will be repeated 5 times. The `run` procedure will perform the following visible actions in the specified order.

1. Set up a counter to `0`.

2. Increase the counter.

3. If the `bee` is smaller than `redbird` and the `bee` is smaller than `purpleFlower`, the bee increases its size a random number of times, between `1.0` (no change in the size) and `1.1`. The resize animation takes `0.5` seconds. The resize will run if and only if both subexpressions included in the `if` statement are `true`.

4. If the counter hasn't reached `5`, go back to step number 2. If the counter reached `5`, exit the loop.

The BOTH...AND operator allows us to combine two expressions to produce a single Boolean value, true or false. If we want to take an action when two things must happen, we can apply the BOTH...AND operator and evaluate whether the result of the logical conjunction is true.

See also

 ▸   *Working with the NOT operator*, in this chapter

Working with the EITHER...OR operator

In this task, we will use the EITHER...OR operator to create an expression that evaluates a logical disjunction between two sub-expressions.If a bee is located within a threshold of 0.25 units near the purpleFlower's petal or the bee is located within a threshold of 0.25 units near the fifth purpleFlower2's petal, the bee will turn to the left.

Getting ready

We will be working on a project with at least three actors. Therefore, we will use an existing project that has a bee and two purple flowers.

1.   Open the project saved in the *Working with the NOT operator* recipe in this chapter.

2.   Click on **Edit code** and then on the **class: MyScene** dropd-own list. The list of classes that are part of the scene will appear.

3.   Select **MyScene | Edit run**.

4.   Delete all the existing statements in the run procedure for the MyScene class.

How to do it...

Follow these steps to use the EITHER...OR operator to create an expression that evaluates a logical disjunction between two subexpressions:

1.   Drag the **count** statement, located at the top, and drop it on the **drop statement here** area located below the **do in order** label, inside the **run** tab. Select **Other Integer...** and the **Enter Custom Integer** dialog box will appear. Enter 20 and click **OK**. The count up to 20 statement will display a **drop statement here** placeholder.

2.   Drag the **if _** statement, located at the top, and drop it on the **drop statement here** area located within the count up to 20 block. Click on **true** and two **drop statement here** placeholders will appear.

3.   Select bee in the instance drop-down list located at the left-hand side of the main window, below the small scene preview. Make sure that part: none is selected in the drop-down list located at the right-hand side of the chosen instance.

4. Activate the **Functions** tab. Alice will display the functions for the `bee`.

5. Drag the **isWithinThresholdOf** function and drop it on the first **true** expression that appears after the `if` keyword in the **if true is true then** block. A black rectangle will surround the true keyword when you start dragging the **isWithinThresholdOf** function. Select `0.25`, **this.purpleFlower getPart ???** and then **IStemMiddle_IStemTop_ IHPistil_IHPetal01** in the menu that appears. The following code will be displayed as the statement that defines the conditional `if` block:

```
if this.bee.isWithinThresholdOf(0.25, this.purpleFlower.
getPart(IStemMiddle_IStemTop_IHPistil_IHPetal01)) is true then
```

6. Now, click on the last down arrow that appears with a gray background at the right-hand side of the previously defined expression, before **is true then**. A drop-down menu will display different options to use to replace the current expression. Select the ninth option that adds the `EITHER` keyword as a prefix to the existing expression and an `OR` keyword after the expression. Then, select `true` in the cascade menu that appears, as shown in the following screenshot. The following code will be displayed as the new statement that defines the conditional `if` block:

```
if (EITHER this.bee.isWithinThresholdOf(0.25, this.purpleFlower.
getPart(IStemMiddle_IStemTop_IHPistil_IHPetal01)) OR true) is true
then
```

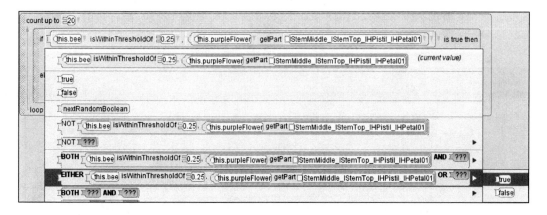

7. Drag the **isWithinThresholdOf** function and drop it on the **true** expression that appears after the previously added `OR` keyword. A black rectangle will surround the `true` keyword when you start dragging the **isWithinThresholdOf** function. Select `0.25`, **this.purpleFlower2 getPart ???** and then **IStemMiddle_IStemTop_IHPistil_ IHPetal02** in the menu that appears. The following code will be displayed as the statement that defines the definitive conditional `if` block:

```
if (EITHER this.bee.isWithinThresholdOf(0.25, this.purpleFlower.
getPart(IStemMiddle_IStemTop_IHPistil_IHPetal01)) OR this.bee.
isWithinThresholdOf(0.25, this.purpleFlower2.getPart(IStemMiddle_
IStemTop_IHPistil_IHPetal05))) is true then
```

8. Activate the **Procedures** tab. Alice will display the procedures for the `bee`.

9. Drag the **turn** procedure and drop it on the first **drop statement here** area located within the `if` block. Select `LEFT` for the first parameter and then click on `0.125`. Click on the **more...** drop-down menu button that appears, on `duration` and then on `0.25` in the cascade menu that appears. The following code will appear as a new statement:

```
this.bee.turn(LEFT, 0.125, duration: 0.25)
```

10. Drag the **moveToward** procedure and drop it in the **drop statement here** area located below the `else` keyword, within the `if` block. Select `1.00`, **this.purpleFlower2 getPart ???** and then **IStemMiddle_IStemTop_IHPistil_IHPetal05** in the menu that appears. Click on the **more...** drop-down menu button that appears, on `duration` and then on `0.25` in the cascade menu that appears. Click on the new **more...** drop-down menu that appears. Click on `style` and then on `BEGIN_AND_END_GENTLY`.

11. Now, click on the down arrow that appears with a gray background at the right-hand side of `1.0` on the previously defined statement, after **moveToward**. A drop-down menu will display different options to use to replace the current expression. Select **Random | nextRandomRealNumberInRange ???, ??? | 0.25 | 1.0**. The following code includes the expression that generates a real random number to pass it as a parameter, as shown in the following screenshot:

```
this.bee.moveToward(nextRandomRealNumberInRange(0.25, 1.0), this.
purpleFlower2.getPart(IStemMiddle_IStemTop_IHPistil_IHPetal05),
duration: 0.25, style: BEGIN_AND_END_GENTLY)
```

How it works...

We added a `count up to 20` statement that allowed us to create a block of code that will be repeated `20` times. The `run` procedure will perform the following visible actions in the specified order. The following screenshot shows three screenshots of the rendered frames.

1. Set up a counter to `0`.

2. Increase the counter.

3. If the `bee` is located within a threshold of `0.25` units near the first `purpleFlower`'s petal or the `bee` is located within a threshold of `0.25` units near the fifth `purpleFlower2`'s petal, the `bee` turns to the left `0.125` units. The movement takes `0.25` seconds. This code is included after the line that defines the `if` block. The `turn` procedure will run if any of the two subexpressions included in the `if` statement is `true`.

4. If both subexpressions included in the `if` statement are `false`, the `bee` moves towards the fifth `purpleFlower2`'s petal a random number of units, between `0.25` and `1.0`. The movement takes `0.25` seconds. This code is included in the `else` part of the `if` block.

5. If the counter hasn't reached `20`, go back to step number 2. If the counter reached `20`, exit the loop.

The `EITHER...OR` operator allows us to combine two expressions to produce a single Boolean value, `true` or `false`. If we want to take an action when only one of two things must happen, we can apply the `EITHER...OR` operator and evaluate whether the result of the logical disjunction is `true`.

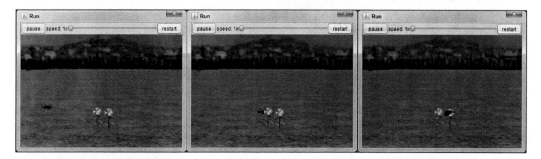

See also

▸ *Working with the NOT operator*, in this chapter

Working with relational operators

In this recipe, we will use the ≤ relational operator, also written as `<=`, to create an expression that evaluates whether the result of a subexpression is less than or equal to another subexpression.

Getting ready

We will be working on a project with at least two actors. Therefore, we will use an existing project that has a bee and a red bird.

1. Open the project saved in the *Running conditional code* recipe in this chapter.
2. Click on **Edit code** and then on the **class: MyScene** drop-down list. The list of classes that are part of the scene will appear.
3. Select **MyScene | Edit run**.
4. Delete all the existing statements in the run procedure for the MyScene class.

How to do it...

Follow these steps to use an expression that evaluates whether the result of a sub-expression is less than or equal to another sub-expression:

1. Select bee in the instance drop-down list located at the left-hand side of the main window, below the small scene preview. Make sure that part: none is selected in the drop-down list located at the right-hand side of the chosen instance.
2. Activate the **Procedures** tab. Alice will display the procedures for the bee.
3. Drag the **move** procedure and drop it on the **drop statement here** area located below the **do in order** label, inside the **run** tab. Click on FORWARD and then on 1.0 in the cascade menu that appears.
4. Now, click on the down arrow that appears with a gray background at the right-hand side of 1.0 on the previously defined statement, after **FORWARD**. A drop-down menu will display different options to use to replace the current expression.
5. Select **Random | nextRandomRealNumberInRange ???, ??? | 0.0 | 2.0**. The following code includes the expression that generates a real random number to pass it as a parameter:

   ```
   this.bee.move(FORWARD, nextRandomRealNumberInRange(0.0, 2.0))
   ```

6. Drag the **move** procedure and drop it below the previously dropped procedure call. Click on UP and then on 1.0 in the cascade menu that appears.
7. Click on the down arrow that appears with a gray background at the right-hand side of 1.0 on the previously defined statement, after **FORWARD**. A drop-down menu will display different options to use to replace the current expression.
8. Select **Random | nextRandomRealNumberInRange ???, ??? | 0.0 | 2.0**. The following code includes the expression that generates a real random number to pass it as a parameter:

   ```
   this.bee.move(UP, nextRandomRealNumberInRange(0.0, 2.0))
   ```

9. Drag the **if _** statement, located at the top, and drop it below the previously dropped procedure call. Click on **true** and two **drop statement here** placeholders will appear.

10. Now, click on the down arrow that appears with a gray background at the right-hand side of **true**, before **is true then**. A drop-down menu will display different options to use to replace the current expression. Select the eleventh option that provides a cascade menu with six relational operators to apply to real numbers. Then, select **??? ≤ ??? | 1.0 | 1.0** in the cascade menus that appear, as shown in the following screenshot:

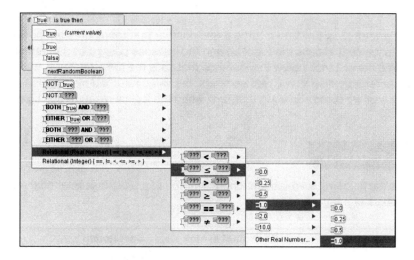

The following code will be displayed as the new statement that defines the conditional `if` block:

```
if (1.0 ≤ 1.0) is true then
```

11. Drag the **getDistanceBelow** function and drop it on the first **1.0** expression that appears before the ≤ operator. A black rectangle will surround the `1.0` value when you start dragging the **getDistanceBelow** function. Select `this.redbird` in the menu that appears. The following code will be displayed as the statement that defines the definitive conditional `if` block:

```
if (this.bee.getDistanceBelow(this.redbird) ≤ 1.0) is true then
```

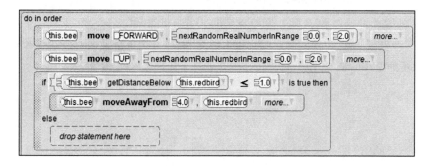

How it works...

First, the bee moves forward a random number of units, between 0.0 and 2.0. Then, the bee moves up a random number of units, between 0.0 and 2.0. According to the two generated random numbers, the bee might be located at different positions each time you run the project. The if statement evaluates whether the real number returned by the getDistanceBelow function, with this.redbird as a parameter, is less than or equal to 1.0. If the result of the evaluation of this expression is true, the bee moves away from the redbird.

The getDistanceBelow function returns a real number that represents the distance between the instance that calls the function and the instance passed as a parameter. The function returns the distance below the instance that calls the function. Thus, we used the ≤ relational operator applied to two real numbers, the value returned by getDistanceBelow and 1.0. This way, we could add code that runs when the logical result of this comparison is true.

There's more...

Alice provides the following six relational operators. You can use these relational operators with real numbers or integers:

Operator symbol	Equivalent syntax	Description
<	<	Less than
≤	<=	Less than or equal to
>	>	Greater than
≥	>=	Greater than or equal to
==	==	Equal to
≠	!=	Not equal to

See also

- ▶ *Running conditional code*, in this chapter
- ▶ *Running a loop while a condition is true*, in this chapter
- ▶ *Calculating new values for properties*, in *Chapter 6, Working with Properties*
- ▶ *Changing values for variables*, in *Chapter 5, Working with Variables*

Running a loop while a condition is true

In this recipe, we will use the ≥ relational operator to create an expression for a `while` loop. We will run a procedure many times while an expression evaluates to `true`. We will add many statements to a loop that will repeat its execution many times while a condition is satisfied. The condition will control the loop.

Getting ready

We will be working on a project with an actor and a ground. Therefore, we will use an existing project that has a red bird on the grassy ground.

1. Open the project saved in the *Running conditional code* recipe in this chapter.

2. Click on **Edit code** and then on the **class: MyScene** drop-down list. The list of classes that are part of the scene will appear.

3. Select **MyScene | Edit run**.

4. Delete all the existing statements in the `run` procedure for the `MyScene` class.

How to do it...

Follow these steps to run a procedure many times while an expression evaluates to `true`:

1. Drag the **while _** statement, located at the top, and drop it on the **drop statement here** area located below the **do in order** label, inside the **run** tab. Click on **true** and a **drop statement here** placeholder will appear within the `while true is true` block.

2. Click on the down arrow that appears with a gray background at the right-hand side of **true**, before **is true**. A drop-down menu will display different options to use to replace the current expression. Select the eleventh option that provides a cascade menu with six relational operators to apply to real numbers. Then, select **??? ≥ ??? | 1.0 | 1.0** in the cascade menus that appear. The following code will be displayed as the new statement that defines the `while` block:

   ```
   while (1.0 ≥ 1.0) is true
   ```

3. Select `redbird` in the instance drop-down list located at the left-hand side of the main window, below the small scene preview. Make sure that `part : none` is selected in the drop-down list located at the right-hand side of the chosen instance.

4. Activate the **Functions** tab. Alice will display the functions for the `redbird`.

5. Drag the **getDistanceAbove** function and drop it on the first **1.0** expression that appears before the ≥ operator. A black rectangle will surround the 1.0 value when you start dragging the **getDistanceAbove** function. Select this.grassyGround in the menu that appears. The following code will be displayed as the statement that defines the definitive while block:

```
while (this.redbird.getDistanceAbove(this.grassyGround) ≥ 1.0) is
true
```

6. Activate the **Procedures** tab. Alice will display the procedures for the redbird.

7. Drag the **move** procedure and drop it on the **drop statement here** area located within the **while** block. Click on DOWN and then on 0.25 in the cascade menu that appears. Click on the **more...** drop-down menu button, on duration and then on 1.0. Click on the additional **more...** drop-down menu that appears, on asSeenBy and then on this.grassyGround. Click on the new **more...** drop-down menu that appears, on style and then on BEGIN_AND_END_GENTLY. The following code will be displayed as the statement that will run while the previously specified condition is true, as shown in the following screenshot:

```
This.redbird.move(DOWN, 0.25, duration: 1.0, asSeenBy: this.
grassyGround, style: BEGIN_AND_END_GENTLY)
```

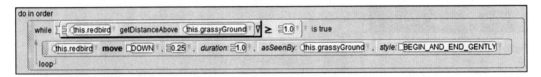

8. Select **File | Save as...** from Alice's main menu and give a new name to the project. Then you can make changes to the project according to your needs.

How it works...

The redbird will move down until it reaches the green grassyGround. Alice calls the move procedure for the redbird while the condition defined in the while loop is true. The while statement evaluates whether the real number returned by the getDistanceAbove function, with this.grassyGround as a parameter, is greater than or equal to 1.0.

The statement included within the while block will run as many times as the evaluation of the aforementioned expression is true. Thus, while the redbird has a relative distance above the grassyGround greater than or equal to 1.0, the redbird will go on moving down 0.25 units in each step.

The `getDistanceAbove` function returns a real number that represents the distance between the instance that calls the function and the instance passed as a parameter. The function returns the distance above the instance that calls the function. Thus, we used the ≥ relational operator applied to two real numbers, the value returned by `getDistanceAbove` and `1.0`. This way, we could add code that runs in a loop while the logical result of this comparison is `true`.

See also

▸ _Running conditional code_, in this chapter

Declaring and calling new functions

In this task, we will declare a new function for a class that will return the Boolean result of the evaluation of an expression. Then, we will use this new function to create an expression for a `while` loop.

Getting ready

We will be working on a project with an actor and a ground. Therefore, we will use an existing project that has a red bird and a grassy ground.

1. Open the project saved in the _Running a loop while a condition is true_ recipe in this chapter. Don't delete the existing statements because we will make changes to the existing code in the `run` procedure for the `MyScene` class.
2. Click on **Edit Code**, at the lower-right corner of the big scene preview. Alice will show a smaller preview of the scene and will display the **Code Editor** on a panel located at the right-hand side of the main window.
3. Click on the **class: MyScene** drop-down list and the list of classes that are part of the scene will appear.

How to do it...

Follow these steps to create a new function and use it in an expression for a `while` loop:

1. Select **MyRedbird | Declare Function**.
2. Enter `isAboveGround` in name, select `Boolean` in the **Return value type dropdown list**, and click **OK**. The code editor will add a new tab with the name of the new Boolean function, **isAboveGround**.

3. Make sure that `redbird (this)` is selected in the **instance** drop-down list located at the left-hand side of the main window, below the small scene preview. If you select another class, an **out-of-scope** label will appear and you won't be able to drag statements from the selected class. Make sure that `part : none` is selected in the drop-down list located at the right-hand side of the chosen instance.

4. Drag the **return _** statement, located at the top, and drop it on the **drop statement here** area located below the **do in order** label, inside the **isAboveGround** tab. Click on **true** and the following code will appear as a statement:

   ```
   return true
   ```

5. Click on the down arrow that appears with a gray background at the right-hand side of **true**. A drop-down menu will display different options to use to replace the current expression. Select the eleventh option that provides a cascade menu with six relational operators to apply to real numbers. Then, select **??? ≥ ??? | 1.0 | 1.0** in the cascade menus that appear. The following code will be displayed as the new statement:

   ```
   return (1.0 ≥ 1.0)
   ```

6. Activate the **Functions** tab.

7. Drag the **getDistanceAbove** function and drop it on the first **1.0** expression that appears before the ≥ operator. A black rectangle will surround the `1.0` value when you start dragging the **getDistanceAbove** function. Select `this` in the menu that appears. The following code will be displayed:

   ```
   return (this.getDistanceAbove(this) ≥ 1.0)
   ```

8. Drag the **getGround** function and drop it on the **this** keyword that appears before the ≥ operator. A black rectangle will surround `this` when you start dragging the **getGround** function. The following code will be displayed, as shown in the following screenshot:

   ```
   return (this.getDistanceAbove(this.getGround()) ≥ 1.0)
   ```

9. Now, click on **Edit code** and then on the **class: MyScene** drop-down list. The list of classes that are part of the scene will appear.

10. Select **MyScene | Edit run**.

11. Make sure that `redbird (this)` is selected in the **instance** drop-down list located at the left-hand side of the main window, below the small scene preview.

12. Drag the **isAboveGround** function and drop it on the expression defined for the while block: `(this.redbird.getDistanceAbove(this.grassyGround) ≥ 1.0)`. A black rectangle will surround this expression when you start dragging the **isAboveGround** function. The previously declared **isAboveGround** procedure will appear under **MyRedbird**. The following code will be displayed as the statement that defines the `while` block, as shown in the following screenshot:

```
while this.redbird.isAboveGround() is true
```

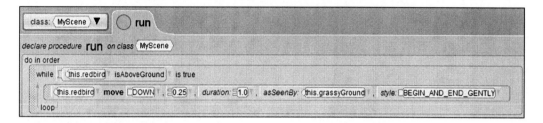

How it works...

We created a new function for the `MyRedbird` class that returns a Boolean value. The new function's name is `isAboveGround` and it is a parameterless function. The instance of the `MyRedbird` class that calls this function is accessed through the `this` keyword. Thus, the function can call the methods available from the `MyRedbird` class through `this`.

The function uses the `return` statement to return the Boolean result of an expression. The Boolean expression evaluates whether the real number returned by the `getDistanceAbove` function, with `this.getGround()` as a parameter, is greater than or equal to `1.0`. The `this.getGround` function passed as a parameter returns the ground instance defined in the scene in which the instance of the `MyRedbird` class is located. The result of `this.getGround` in this example is going to be `grassyGround`.

The `redbird` will move down until it reaches the green `grassyGround`. Alice calls the `move` procedure for the `redbird` while the condition defined in the while loop is `true`. The `while` statement evaluates whether the Boolean value returned by the `isAboveGround` function is `true`.

The statement included within the `while` block will run as many times as the expression evaluated in the `isAboveGround` function is `true`.

See also

▶ *Running a loop while a condition is true*, in this chapter

▶ *Declaring new procedures*, in *Chapter 3, Organizing Statements*

▶ *Using properties to call functions*, in *Chapter 6, Working with Properties*

5
Working with Variables

In this chapter, we will cover:

- ▶ Working with a local variable
- ▶ Changing values of variables
- ▶ Working with many local variables
- ▶ Working with constants
- ▶ Using arrays to control two instances
- ▶ Using variables to hold instances of generic classes
- ▶ Using variables to hold separate instances
- ▶ Working with parts of characters

Introduction

Alice 3 allows you to work with variables. When you have to define complex behaviors for the actors and the scenery, you can declare and change the values for variables with simple statements. This chapter provides many tasks that will allow us to use variables to control values for some parameters.

We will make many birds fly towards a fence. We will make these birds run different races. We will use variables to hold simple numbers but we will also use arrays to hold many instances of diverse kinds of birds. We will run conditional code according to the values of certain variables. In addition, we will use variables to work with parts of a hawk to make it move his wings while it moves. We will write the code to make the hawk fly.

Working with a local variable

In this recipe, we will declare a local variable with an initial value to define the number of units that a bird must advance. Then we will pass this variable as a parameter for the move procedure. The variable will allow us to use a descriptive name instead of a number as a parameter, and therefore it will be easier to understand the code.

Getting ready

Follow these steps to set a simple scene with four birds of different classes and a fence:

1. Select **File | New...** in the main menu to start a new project. A dialog box will display the six predefined templates with their thumbnail previews in the **Templates** tab.

2. Select GrassyProject.a3p as the desired template for the new project and click **OK**. Alice will display a grassy ground with a light blue sky.

3. Click on **Edit Scene**, at the lower-right corner of the scene preview. Alice will show a bigger preview of the scene and will display the **Model Gallery** at the bottom.

4. Add an instance of the Hawk class to the scene, and enter hawk for the name of this new instance. Follow the steps explained in the *Creating a new instance from a class in a gallery* recipe, in *Chapter 2, Working with Actors*.

5. Add instances of the four classes shown in the following table. Use the names shown in the Instance name column for each new instance:

Class	Instance name	Class created by Alice
Redbird	redbird	MyRedbird
Bluebird	bluebird	MyBluebird
BirdBaby	birdBaby	MyBirdBaby
Fence	fence	MyFence

6. Arrange the four birds and the fence as shown in the next image. The four birds from top to bottom are hawk, redbird, bluebird, and birdBaby. Pay special attention to the fence. Rotate the fence to make it appear in front of the four birds. The four birds must be behind the fence to make sure that the code works as expected.

How to do it...

Follow these steps to pass a local variable as a parameter to the move method for birdBady:

1. Click on **Edit code** and then on the **class: MyScene** drop-down list. The list of classes that are part of the scene will appear.

2. Select **MyScene | Edit run**.

3. Drag the **local...** statement, located at the top, and drop it on the **drop statement here** area located below the **do in order** label, inside the **run** tab. The **Declare Local** dialog box will appear.

4. Click on the **Value type** drop-down list and select **RealNumber**.

5. Enter stepBaby in **Name**.

6. Click on the **Initializer** drop-down list and select **0.25** as the initial value for the stepBaby variable. The following screenshot shows the **Declare Local** dialog box that declares the new stepBaby local variable:

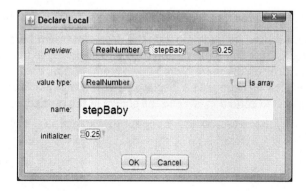

7. Click **OK** and the following code will be displayed as a new statement, as shown in the next screenshot:

```
RealNumber stepBaby ← 0.25
```

8. Drag the **while _** statement, located at the top, and drop it below the previously dropped statement. Click on **true** and a **drop statement here** placeholder will appear within the `while true is true` block.

9. Click on the down arrow that appears with a gray background at the right-hand side of **true**, before **is true**. A drop-down menu will display different options to use to replace the current expression. Select the eleventh option (**Relational (Real Number) { ==, !=, <, <=, >=, > }**) that provides a cascade menu with six relational operators to apply to real numbers. Then select **??? ≤ ??? | 1.0 | 0.25** in the cascade menus that appear. The following code will be displayed as the new statement that defines the `while` block:

```
while (1.0 ≤ 0.25) is true
```

10. Select `birdBaby` in the instance drop-down list located at the left-hand side of the main window, below the small scene preview. Make sure that `part: none` is selected in the drop-down list located at the right-hand side of the chosen instance.

11. Activate the **Functions** tab. Alice will display the functions for the `birdBaby`.

12. Drag the **getDistanceBehind** function and drop it on the **1.0** expression that appears before the ≤ operator. A black rectangle will surround the `1.0` value when you start dragging the **getDistanceBehind** function. Select `this.fence` in the menu that appears. The following code will be displayed as the statement that defines the definitive `while` block:

```
while (this.birdBaby.getDistanceBehind(this.fence) ≤ 0.25) is true
```

13. Activate the **Procedures** tab. Alice will display the procedures for the `birdBaby`.

14. Drag the **move** procedure and drop it on the **drop statement here** area located within the **while** block. Click on `FORWARD` and then on `stepBaby` in the cascade menu that appears. Click on the **more...** drop-down menu button, on `duration` and then on `0.5`. The following code will be displayed as the statement that will run while the previously specified condition is `true`, as shown in the next screenshot:

```
this.birdBaby.move(FORWARD, stepBaby, duration: 0.5)
```

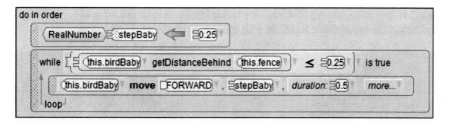

15. Select **File | Save as...** from Alice's main menu and give a new name to the project. Then you can make changes to the project according to your needs.

How it works...

The `birdBaby` will move forward until it reaches or goes through the `fence` located at the right-hand side of the scene. The `local...` statement allowed us to declare a local variable, named `stepBaby`, and to set the initial value for this variable to `0.25` in a single line of code. The line of code starts with the variable type (`RealNumber`), followed by the variable name (`stepBaby`), the **assignment operator** (←) and the variable's initial value (`0.25`).

```
RealNumber stepBaby ← 0.25
```

The line doesn't include the `local...` statement because the **Declare Local** dialog box generates the appropriate code according to the values we specify. We just drag the `local...` statement to the statements area to specify the parameters for the local variable declaration.

When we need a `RealNumber`, we can use `stepBaby`. We specified `stepBaby` as the value for the `amount` parameter when we called the `move` procedure for `birdBaby`. Because the value for `stepBaby` is always `0.25`, the move procedure receives `0.25` as the amount value while the condition defined for the `while` loop is `true`.

> The scope for this **local variable** is limited to the `run` procedure on the `MyScene` class. This means that we cannot see this variable from other procedures.

The following screenshot shows the last rendered frame where the `birdBaby` crosses the `fence` and stops its movement towards this `fence` in steps of `0.25` units:

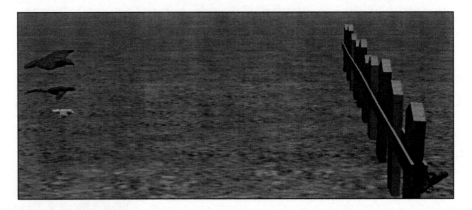

See also

▶ *Working with relational operators*, in *Chapter 4, Working with Functions and Conditions*

▶ *Controlling an actor with keystrokes*, in *Chapter 8, Working with Keyboard and Mouse Input*

Changing values of variables

In this task, we will use both the assignment and the sum operators to calculate and assign a new value to a local variable. We will increase the numeric value for an existing variable within a loop, and therefore a bird will increase its speed.

Getting ready

We will use the existing project that has four different birds and a fence. This project has a local variable declared to define the number of units that `birdBaby` has to advance in each step.

1. Open the project saved in the *Working with a local variable* recipe.

2. Click on **Edit Code**, at the lower-right corner of the big scene preview. Alice will show a smaller preview of the scene and will display the **Code Editor** on a panel located at the right-hand side of the main window.

3. Click on the **class: MyScene** drop-down list and the list of classes that are part of the scene will appear.

4. Select **MyScene | Edit run**.

How to do it...

Follow these steps to increase the value of the `stepBaby` variable each time that the `while` loop executes an iteration:

1. Drag the **stepBaby ← _** statement, located at the top of Alice's window, and drop it below the call to the `move` procedure within the `while` block.

2. Select **stepBaby** in the menu that appears.

3. Click on the down arrow that appears with a gray background at the right-hand side of the assignment operator ←. A drop-down menu will display different options to use to replace the current expression. Select **Math | stepBaby + ??? | Other Real Number...** in the cascade menus that appear, as shown in the next screenshot:

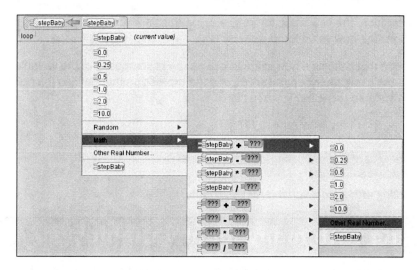

4. The **Enter custom real number** dialog box will appear. Enter `0.075` and click **OK**. The following code will be displayed as the second statement within the `while` block, as shown in the following screenshot:

```
stepBaby ← (stepBaby + 0.075)
```

5. Select **File | Save as...** from Alice's main menu and give a new name to the project. Then you can make changes to the project according to your needs.

How it works...

The `birdBaby` will move forward until it reaches or goes through the `fence` located at the right-hand side of the scene. The `birdBaby` accelerates the speed for each step it performs. Each new step is larger than the previous step because the value of the `stepBaby` variable increases in each iteration of the `while` loop.

The `stepBaby` ← _ statement allowed us to assign a new value for this variable. The new value is the result of applying the sum operator to the existing value of `stepBaby`. The initial value for `stepBaby` is `0.25`. In the second iteration, the new value for `stepBaby` is `0.25 + 0.075`, that is, `0.325`. Each iteration calls the `move` procedure, passes this variable as the value for the `amount` parameter, and then sums `0.075` to `stepBaby`. Thus, each iteration increases the number of units received in the `amount` parameter.

In the third iteration, the new value for `stepBaby` is `0.325 + 0.075`, that is, `0.4`. in the fourth iteration. The new value for `stepBaby` is `0.4 + 0.075`, that is, `0.475`.

The line of code that assigns a new value to `stepBaby` is composed of the variable name (`stepBaby`), the **assignment operator** (←) and the expression that defines the new value to assign to the variable (`stepBaby + 0.075`).

```
stepBaby ← (stepBaby + 0.075)
```

See also

▶ *Working with a local variable*, in this chapter

Working with many local variables

In this recipe, we will use two local variables to control the number of units that two different birds have to move forward in each iteration. We will use a descriptive name for each variable, and therefore the purpose of the code will be easier to understand.

Getting ready

We will use an existing project that has a local variable declared to define the number of units that `birdBaby` has to advance in each step. We will declare an additional local variable in the **run** procedure.

1. Open the project saved in the *Changing values of variables* recipe.

2. Click on **Edit Code**, at the lower-right corner of the big scene preview. Alice will show a smaller preview of the scene and will display the **Code Editor** on a panel located at the right-hand side of the main window.

3. Click on the **class: MyScene** drop-down list and the list of classes that are part of the scene will appear.

4. Select **MyScene | Edit run**.

How to do it...

Follow these steps to declare a new `stepBlue` variable and to increase its value each time that a new `while` loop executes an iteration:

1. Drag the **local...** statement, located at the top, and drop it below the first statement that declares the `stepBaby` local variable. The **Declare Local** dialog box will appear.

2. Click on the **Value type** drop-down list and select **RealNumber**.

3. Enter `stepBlue` in **Name**.

4. Click on the **Initializer** drop-down list and select **0.5** as the initial value for the `stepBlue` variable. Then click **OK** and the following code will be displayed as a new statement:

   ```
   RealNumber stepBlue ← 0.5
   ```

5. Drag the **do together** statement, located at the top, and drop it below the previously dropped statement, above the `while` block. Alice will display a green line indicating the position in which this new statement will be inserted. The `do together` statement will display a **drop statement here** placeholder.

6. Place the mouse pointer over the light shade at the left-hand side of the `while` block located below the `do together` placeholder. The mouse pointer will appear as a link select hand.

7. Drag the `while` block and drop it in the **drop statement here** area located within the `do together` block.

8. Drag the **while _** statement, located at the top of Alice's window, and drop it below the previously moved `while` block, within the `do together` block. Click on **true** and a **drop statement here** placeholder will appear within the `while true is true` block.

9. Click on the down arrow that appears with a gray background at the right-hand side of **true**, before **is true**. A drop-down menu will display different options to use to replace the current expression. Select the eleventh option (**Relational (Real Number) { ==, !=, <, <=, >=, > }**) that provides a cascade menu with six relational operators to apply to real numbers. Then select **??? ≤ ??? | 1.0 | 0.25** in the cascade menus that appear. The following code will be displayed as the new statement that defines the `while` block:

   ```
   while (1.0 ≤ 0.25) is true
   ```

10. Select `bluebird` in the instance drop-down list located at the left-hand side of the main window, below the small scene preview. Make sure that `part: none` is selected in the drop-down list located at the right-hand side of the chosen instance.

11. Activate the **Functions** tab. Alice will display the functions for the `bluebird`.

12. Drag the **getDistanceBehind** function and drop it on the **1.0** expression that appears before the ≤ operator. A black rectangle will surround the `1.0` value when you start dragging the **getDistanceBehind** function. Select `this.fence` in the menu that appears. The following code will be displayed as the statement that defines the definitive `while` block:

```
while (this.bluebird.getDistanceBehind(this.fence) ≤ 0.25) is true
```

13. Activate the **Procedures** tab. Alice will display the procedures for the `bluebird`.

14. Drag the **move** procedure and drop it on the **drop statement here** area located within the second **while** block. Click on `FORWARD` and then on `stepBlue` in the cascade menu that appears. Click on the **more...** drop-down menu button, on `duration` and then on `0.25`. The following code will be displayed as the statement that will run while the previously specified condition is `true`, as shown in the next screenshot:

```
this.bluebird.move(FORWARD, stepBlue, duration: 0.25)
```

15. Drag the **stepBlue ← _** statement, located at the top, and drop it below the previously dropped statement within the second `while` block.

16. Select **stepBlue** in the menu that appears.

17. Click on the down arrow that appears with a gray background at the right-hand side of the assignment operator ←. A drop-down menu will display different options to use to replace the current expression. Select **Math | stepBlue + ??? | Other Real Number...** in the cascade menus that appears.

18. The **Enter custom real number** dialog box will appear. Enter `0.085` and click **OK**. The following code will be displayed as the second statement within the new `while` block, as shown in the next screenshot:

```
stepBlue ← (stepBlue + 0.085)
```

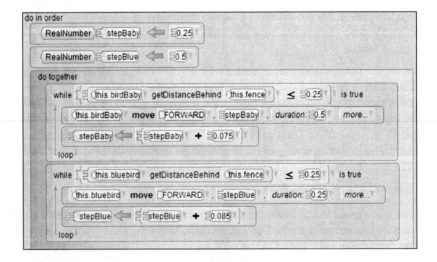

19. Select **File | Save as...** from Alice's main menu and give a new name to the project. Then you can make changes to the project according to your needs.

How it works...

The `run` procedure for the `MyScene` class has two independent local variables:

▶ `stepBaby`: Determines the number of units that the `birdBaby` has to move forward in each step

▶ `stepBlue`: Determines the number of units that the `bluebird` has to move forward in each step

Both `birdBaby` and `bluebird` move forward until they reach or go through the `fence` located at the right-hand side of the scene. Both birds move at the same time with different speeds.

The `local...` statement allowed us to declare a second local variable, named `stepBlue`, and to set the initial value for this variable to 0.5 in a single line of code. The line of code starts with the variable type (`RealNumer`), followed by the variable name (`stepBlue`), the assignment operator (←) and the variable's initial value (0.5).

```
RealNumber stepBlue ← 0.5
```

The `bluebird` accelerates the speed for each step it performs. Each new step is larger than the previous step because the value of the `stepBlue` variable increases in each iteration of the while loop.

The `stepBlue ← _` statement allowed us to assign a new value for this variable. The new value is the result of applying the sum operator to the existing value of `stepBlue`. In the second iteration, the new value for `stepBlue` is $0.5 + 0.085$, that is, 0.585. Each iteration calls the `move` procedure, passes this variable as the value for the `amount` parameter, and then sums 0.085 to `stepBlue`. Thus, each iteration increases the number of units received in the `amount` parameter.

The line of code that assigns a new value to `stepBlue` is composed of the variable name (`stepBlue`), the assignment operator (←) and the expression that defines the new value to assign to the variable (`stepBlue + 0.085`).

```
stepBlue ← (stepBlue + 0.085)
```

We added a `do together` statement that allowed us to create a block of code that runs two `while` loops at the same time. Each while loop controls the movement of one bird and both `while` loops start their execution together.

The `bluebird` flies faster than the `birdBaby`, and therefore `bluebird` wins the race. The following screenshot shows one of the rendered frames:

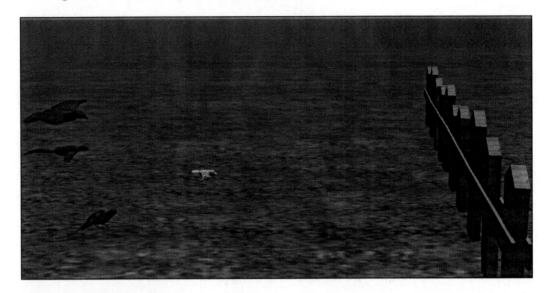

There's more...

When you have to specify a value of a specific type, Alice displays all the local variables declared for this type as options in the menu. For example, the second parameter for the move procedure is `amount` and its type is `RealNumber`. When you click on the down arrow that appears with a gray background for the current value of this parameter, Alice displays the two local variables of the `RealNumber` type, `stepBlue` and `stepBaby`, as the last two options. The next screenshot shows the menu with the two variables as options in the menu:

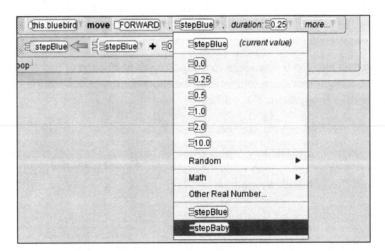

See also

▶ *Changing values of variables*, in this chapter

Working with constants

In this task, we will use four local variables as constants. These constants are variables that won't change their value and provide a friendly name. These constants will define values for the units to advance in each step and the acceleration for slow and fast birds. It will be easy to understand the purpose of each of the constants because of their descriptive names.

Getting ready

We will use an existing project that makes `birdBaby` and `bluebird` run a race.

1. Open the project saved in the *Working with many local variables* recipe.

2. Click on **Edit Code**, at the lower-right corner of the big scene preview. Alice will show a smaller preview of the scene and will display the **Code Editor** on a panel located at the right-hand side of the main window.

3. Click on the **class: MyScene** drop-down list and the list of classes that are part of the scene will appear.

4. Select **MyScene | Edit run**.

How to do it...

Follow these steps to declare four new variables and to use them as constants in the code:

1. Drag the **local...** statement, located at the top, and drop it above the first statement that declares the `stepBaby` local variable. The **Declare Local** dialog box will appear. Click on the **Value type** drop-down list, select **RealNumber** and enter STEP_SLOW in **Name**. Click on the **Initializer** drop-down list, select **0.25** as the initial value for the STEP_SLOW variable, and then click **OK**.

2. Drag new **local...** statements and follow the aforementioned step to declare the following three variables. Use the **Other Real Number...** option in the **Initializer** drop-down list to enter the initial values shown in the Initializer column for each new variable.

Value type	Name	Initializer
RealNumber	STEP_FAST	0.5
RealNumber	ACCELERATION_SLOW	0.075
RealNumber	ACCELERATION_FAST	0.085

The following code will be displayed as four new statements:

```
RealNumber STEP_SLOW ← 0.25
RealNumber STEP_FAST ← 0.5
RealNumber ACCELERATION_SLOW ← 0.075
RealNumber ACCELERATION_FAST ← 0.085
```

3. Go to the statement that declares the `stepBaby` variable. Click on its initial value, `0.25`, at the right-hand side of the assignment operator ←. A drop-down menu will display different options to replace the current expression. Select **STEP_SLOW** in the cascade menu that appears.

4. Go to the statement that declares the `stepBlue` variable. Click on its initial value, `0.25`, at the right-hand side of the assignment operator ←. A drop-down menu will display different options to replace the current expression. Select **STEP_FAST** in the cascade menu that appears.

5. Now go to the statement that increments the value of the `stepBaby` variable within the first `while` loop. Click on `0.075` at the right-hand side of the sum operator **+**. A drop-down menu will display different options to replace the current expression. Select **ACCELERATION_SLOW** in the cascade menu that appears. The following code will be displayed as the new assignment statement:

    ```
    stepBaby ← (stepBaby + ACCELERATION_SLOW)
    ```

6. Go to the statement that increments the value of the `stepBlue` variable within the second `while` loop. Click on `0.085` at the right-hand side of the sum operator **+**. A drop-down menu will display different options to replace the current expression. Select **ACCELERATION_FAST** in the cascade menu that appears. The following code will be displayed as the new assignment statement, as shown in the next screenshot:

    ```
    stepBlue ← (stepBlue + ACCELERATION_FAST)
    ```

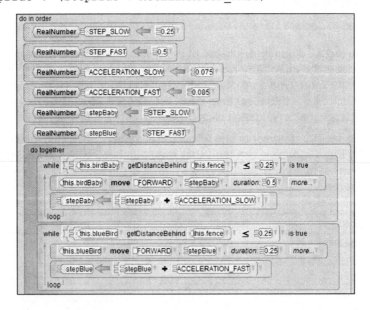

7. Select **File | Save as...** from Alice's main menu and give a new name to the project. Then you can make changes to the project according to your needs.

How it works...

We declared four variables and we set their initial values. However, because we don't change the values for these variables, we use them as **constants**. Alice doesn't provide a mechanism to declare constants but we call them constants because we don't assign new values to these variables. In fact, these constants appear with the assignment operator at the top, as shown in the following screenshot:

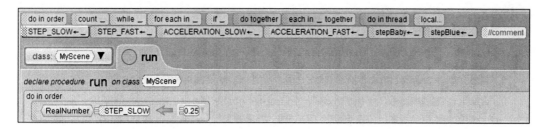

Many programming languages differentiate between constants and variables. We used uppercase letters to define the names for the four constants and we separated words with the low line character (_). This naming convention allows us to differentiate between variables that are supposed to have a constant value and variables that can change their values. Many programming languages such as C use this naming convention for constants.

The new code is easier to understand. When we read the code, we realize that `stepBaby` has a slow step value and `stepBlue` has a fast step value. In addition, if we want many birds to have a slow step value, we don't have to repeat the `0.25` value. We just have to assign `STEP_SLOW` to the new variable. Then if we want to test different slow step values, we can replace the `0.25` value assigned to `STEP_SLOW` with a new value. Constants are useful to define important values that we have to use in many parts of the code.

The same happens with the new acceleration constants, `ACCELERATION_SLOW` and `ACCELERATION_FAST`. Now when we read the code, we understand that each bird uses a different acceleration value to calculate the new step value. We realize that the code accelerates the step by reading a single line.

If we want the fast bird to fly faster, we can change the values for the first and only assignment for the constants with the `_FAST` suffix. This change in the code is easier to understand than a replacement of the `0.075` value at the right-hand side of the sum operator. Is `0.075` slow or fast? We have to read other lines and compare some numeric values to answer this question. However, it is clear that `ACCELERATION_FAST` is fast.

▶ *Working with many local variables*, in this chapter

Using arrays to control two instances

In this recipe, we will use an array to make the four birds cross the fence, one bird at a time. The array will act as a list of the birds that we must control within a loop. We will add code that runs for all the birds in the array.

Getting ready

We will use an existing project that makes `birdBaby` and `bluebird` run a race.

1. Open the project saved in the *Working with many local variables* recipe.
2. Click on **Edit Code**, at the lower-right corner of the big scene preview. Alice will show a smaller preview of the scene and will display the **Code Editor** on a panel located at the right-hand side of the main window.
3. Click on the **class: MyScene** drop-down list and the list of classes that are part of the scene will appear.
4. Select **MyScene | Edit run**.
5. Delete all the existing statements in the `run` procedure for the `MyScene` class.

How to do it...

Follow these steps to make the four birds fly from their initial position to the fence located at the right-hand side of the scene.

1. Drag the **local...** statement, located at the top, and drop it on the **drop statement here** area located below the **do in order** label, inside the **run** tab. The **Declare Local** dialog box will appear.
2. Click on the **type** drop-down list and a drop-down menu will appear. Select **Other Types | Model**.
3. Activate the **Is array** checkbox.
4. Enter `birds` in **Name**.
5. Click on the **Add...** drop-down menu button that appears at the right-hand side of **Initializer**. Click on `this.birdBaby` in the menu that appears.
6. Click on the **Add...** drop-down menu button that appears at the right-hand side of **Initializer** and below **[0] this.birdBaby**. Click on `this.bluebird` in the menu that appears.

7. Click on the new **Add...** drop-down menu button that appears and select `this.hawk`.

8. Click on the new **Add...** drop-down menu button that appears and select `this.redbird`. The dialog box will display the four elements that compose the `birds` array, as shown in the following screenshot:

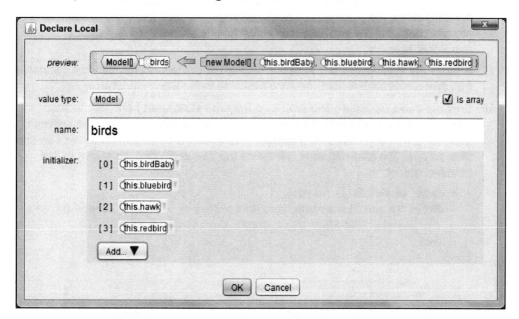

9. Click **OK** and the following code will be displayed as a new statement:

```
Model[] birds ← new Model[]{ this.birdBaby, this.bluebird, this.
hawk, this.redbird }
```

10. Drag the **local...** statement, located at the top, and drop it below the previously dropped variable declaration statement. The **Declare Local** dialog box will appear. Click on the **Value type** drop-down list, select **RealNumber** and enter `STEP_SLOW` in **Name**. Click on the **Initializer** drop-down list, select **0.25** as the initial value for the `STEP_SLOW` variable, and then click **OK**.

11. Drag the **for each in _** statement, located at the top, and drop it below the previously dropped statement. Click on **birds** to use this array as the data source for the loop.

12. Drag the **while _** statement, located at the top, and drop it in the **drop statement here** area located within the `for each Model m in birds` block. Click on **true** and a **drop statement here** placeholder will appear within the `while true is true` block.

13. Click on the down arrow that appears with a gray background at the right-hand side of **true**, before **is true**. A drop-down menu will display different options to use to replace the current expression. Select the eleventh option (**Relational (Real Number) { ==, !=, <, <=, >=, > }**) that provides a cascade menu with six relational operators to apply to real numbers. Then select **??? ≤ ??? | 1.0 | 0.25** in the cascade menus that appear.

14. Select `variable: m` in the instance drop-down list located at the left-hand side of the main window, below the small scene preview.

15. Activate the **Functions** tab. Alice will display the functions for the `birdBaby`.

16. Drag the **getDistanceBehind** function and drop it on the **1.0** expression that appears before the ≤ operator. A black rectangle will surround the `1.0` value when you start dragging the **getDistanceBehind** function. Select `this.fence` in the menu that appears.

17. Activate the **Procedures** tab. Alice will display the procedures for the local `m` variable that represents each `Model` instance available in the `birds` local array.

18. Drag the **move** procedure and drop it on the **drop statement here** area located within the **while** block. Click on `FORWARD` and then on `STEP_SLOW` in the cascade menu that appears. Click on the **more...** drop-down menu button, on `duration` and then on `0.5`. The following code will define the `for each` loop, as shown in the next screenshot:

```
for each (Model m in birds)
    while (m.getDistanceBehind(this.fence) ≤ 0.25) is true
        m.move(FORWARD, STEP_SLOW, duration: 0.5)
    loop
loop
```

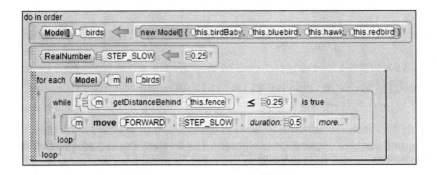

19. Select **File | Save as...** from Alice's main menu and give a new name to the project. Then you can make changes to the project according to your needs.

How it works...

The `local...` statement allowed us to declare an **array** of `Model`, named `birds`. The `Model` class is the generic superclass for all the 3D models. This means that any 3D model selected from the library inherits from a class that has `Model` as a superclass in some part of the hierarchy tree. We set the initial value for this variable to a new array of `Model` that has four instances, as shown in the following table:

Index	Value
0	this.birdBaby
1	this.bluebird
2	this.hawk
3	this.redbird

The line of code starts with the variable type (Model[]), where [] denotes an array, followed by the variable name (birds), the assignment operator (←), and the variable's initial value (new Model[] { this.birdBaby, this.bluebird, this.hawk, this.redbird }):

```
Model[] birds ← new Model[]{ this.birdBaby, this.bluebird, this.hawk,
this.redbird }
```

We used birds (plural) as the name for this array of Model because it provides access to many birds of our scene. This array has four elements, instances of diverse classes, but all of them are subclasses of Model. If we access birds[0], we will get a reference to birdBaby. If we access birds[2], we will get a reference to hawk.

The for each in _ statement allowed us to create a block of code that executes statements for each instance of the birds array. This array acts as a data source with four actors, and therefore the for each in _ statement runs the code specified in the block for each actor in the array.

The while loop within the for each in _ block runs while the m instance is behind the fence. This loop makes each instance in the array fly towards the fence The for each in _ block runs the code for each instance one at a time. Therefore each bird will fly alone towards the fence, one after the other. Each instance in the array is represented by the m variable within the for each in _ block. Alice runs the while loop for each of the Model instances specified after the in keyword, that is, the birds array.

Once the first call to the while loop finishes for birdBaby, the second call to this loop starts running for the second element of the array, bluebird. The following screenshot shows three of the rendered frames:

There's more...

We can change the value of a specific element of the array. For example, you can specify a new value for `birds[1]`. When you declare an array, Alice uses the array name to add two statements at the top:

▶ `arrayName ← _`: Allows creating and assigning a new array to the array variable

▶ `arrayName[_] ← _`: Allows assigning a new value to a specific element of the array

The following screenshot shows the two statements that Alice added for the `birds` array:

When you drop the `birds[_] ← _` statement, Alice displays a menu with the possible index values according to the previously assigned value for the `birds` array. Once you specify the index number, you can select the new value to assign to this element of the array, as shown in the following screenshot:

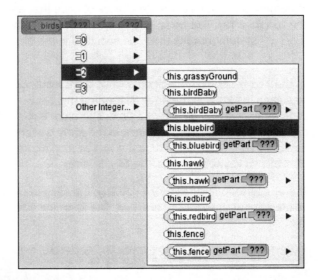

See also

▶ *Working with many local variables*, in this chapter

Using variables to hold instances of generic classes

In this task, we will use a variable that holds the generic `Model` class to make the four birds run a race. The four birds will fly towards the fence at the same time. We will create a block of code that will run for each `Model` found in an array, no matter the Model's subclass.

Getting ready

We will use an existing project that makes the four birds fly from their initial position to the fence located at the right-hand side of the scene.

1. Open the project saved in the *Using arrays to control two instances* recipe.
2. Click on **Edit Code**, at the lower-right corner of the big scene preview. Alice will show a smaller preview of the scene and will display the **Code Editor** on a panel located at the right-hand side of the main window.
3. Click on the **class: MyScene** drop-down list and the list of classes that are part of the scene will appear.
4. Select **MyScene | Edit run**.
5. Delete the `for each Model m in birds` block.

How to do it...

Follow these steps to make the four birds fly from their initial position to the fence located at the right-hand side of the scene, at the same time:

1. Drag the **each in _ together** statement, located at the top, and drop it below the last statement. Click on **birds** to use this array as the data source for the loop.
2. Drag the **while _** statement, located at the top, and drop it in the **drop statement here** area located within the `each Model m in birds together` block. Click on **true** and a **drop statement here** placeholder will appear within the `while true is true` block.
3. Click on the down arrow that appears with a gray background at the right-hand side of **true**, before **is true**. A drop-down menu will display different options to use to replace the current expression. Select the eleventh option (**Relational (Real Number) { ==, !=, <, <=, >=, > }**) that provides a cascade menu with six relational operators to apply to real numbers. Then select **??? ≤ ??? | 1.0 | 0.25** in the cascade menus that appear.
4. Select `variable: m` in the instance drop-down list located at the left-hand side of the main window, below the small scene preview.

5. Activate the **Functions** tab. Alice will display the functions for the birdBaby.

6. Drag the **getDistanceBehind** function and drop it on the **1.0** expression that appears before the ≤ operator. A black rectangle will surround the 1.0 value when you start dragging the **getDistanceBehind** function. Select this.fence in the menu that appears.

7. Activate the **Procedures** tab. Alice will display the procedures for the local m variable that represents each Model instance available in the birds local array.

8. Drag the **move** procedure and drop it on the **drop statement here** area located within the while block. Click on FORWARD and then on STEP_SLOW in the cascade menu that appears. Click on the **more...** drop-down menu button, on duration and then on 0.25. The following code will define the for each loop, as shown in the following screenshot:

```
each (Model m in birds) together
    while (m.getDistanceBehind(this.fence) ≤ 0.25) is true
        m.move(FORWARD, STEP_SLOW, duration: 0.25)
    loop
```

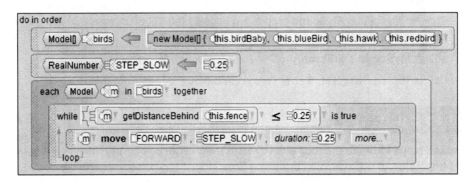

9. Select **File | Save as...** from Alice's main menu and give a new name to the project. Then you can make changes to the project according to your needs.

How it works...

The each in _ together statement allowed us to create a block of code that executes statements for each instance of the birds array. We had declared this array as a container for a generic class, Model. Therefore we could call the move method, defined in the Model class, for the m variable, defined by the each Model m in birds together block. In addition, we could call the getDistanceBehind function for m because this function is also defined in the generic Model class.

Alice runs the `while` loop for each of the `Model` instances specified after the `in` keyword, that is, the `birds` array. The `each Model m in birds together` block starts running the code for all the instances in the birds array together. This means that all the birds start flying at the same time and we didn't have to write code to control each bird. We could work with the `m` variable and the birds array provides all the subclasses of `Model` as a data source. Therefore all the birds will fly towards the `fence` concurrently. The next image shows three screenshots of the rendered frames:

See also

▶ *Using arrays to control two instances*, in this chapter

Using variables to hold separate instances

In this recipe, we will use an array to hold two instances. Then we will change the contents for this array to hold another two instances. Two birds will fly towards the fence at the same time and then two other birds will do the same. The same array will change the `Model` instances in its list.

Getting ready

We will use an existing project that makes the four birds fly towards the fence at the same time.

1. Open the project saved in the *Using variables to hold instances of generic classes* recipe.

2. Click on **Edit Code**, at the lower-right corner of the big scene preview. Alice will show a smaller preview of the scene and will display the **Code Editor** on a panel located at the right-hand side of the main window.

3. Click on the **class: MyScene** drop-down list and the list of classes that are part of the scene will appear.

4. Select **MyScene | Edit run**.

How to do it...

Follow these steps to make two groups of two birds fly towards the fence, one group after the other.

1. Go to the statement that declares the `birds` variable as an array of `Model`. Click on its initial value, `new Model[] { this.birdBaby, this.bluebird, this.hawk, this.redbird }`, at the right-hand side of the assignment operator ←. A drop-down menu will display different options to replace the current expression. Select **Other Array...** in the cascade menu and the **Enter Custom Array** dialog box will appear.

2. Place the mouse pointer over the index number 0, **[0]**, at the right-hand side of **Value**. The item will appear with a blue background and an **x** will appear at the right-hand side. Click on the **x** to remove this item from the array.

3. Repeat the aforementioned step three times, to remove all the items from the array.

4. Once you have removed all the elements from the array, a single **Add...** button should appear at the right-hand side of **Value:**, without index numbers or elements. Click **OK** and the following code will be displayed as the statement that declares the empty birds array:

   ```
   Model[] birds ← new Model[]{ }
   ```

5. Drag the **birds** ← _ statement, located at the top, and drop it below the previously modified statement. Select **Other Array...** in the cascade menu and the **Enter Custom Array** dialog box will appear.

6. Click on the **type** drop-down list and a drop-down menu will appear. Select **Other Types | Model**.

7. Click on the **Add...** drop-down menu button that appears at the right-hand side of **Initializer**. Click on `this.birdBaby` in the menu that appears.

8. Click on the **Add...** drop-down menu button that appears at the right-hand side of **Initializer** and below **[0] this.birdBaby**. Click on `this.hawk` in the menu that appears.

9. Click **OK** and the following code will be displayed as a new statement:

   ```
   birds ← new Model[]{ this.birdBaby, this.hawk }
   ```

10. Now drag the **birds** ← _ statement, located at the top, and drop it below the `each (Model m in birds) together` block. Select **Other Array...** in the cascade menu and the **Enter Custom Array** dialog box will appear.

11. Click on the **type** drop-down list and a drop-down menu will appear. Select **Other Types | Model**.

12. Click on the **Add...** drop-down menu button that appears at the right-hand side of **Initializer**. Click on `this.bluebird` in the menu that appears.

13. Click on the **Add...** drop-down menu button that appears at the right-hand side of **Initializer** and below **[0] this.bluebird**. Click on `this.redbird` in the menu that appears.

14. Click **OK** and the following code will be displayed as a new statement:

    ```
    birds ← new Model[]{ this.bluebird, this.redbird }
    ```

15. Drag the **each in _ together** statement, located at the top, and drop it below the last statement. Click on **birds** to use this array as the data source for the loop.

16. Drag the **while _** statement, located at the top, and drop it in the **drop statement here** area located within the second `each Model m in birds together` block. Click on **true** and a **drop statement here** placeholder will appear within the `while true is true` block.

17. Click on the down arrow that appears with a gray background at the right-hand side of **true**, before **is true**. A drop-down menu will display different options to use to replace the current expression. Select the eleventh option (**Relational (Real Number) { ==, !=, <, <=, >=, > }**) that provides a cascade menu with six relational operators to apply to real numbers. Then select **??? ≤ ??? | 1.0 | 0.25** in the cascade menus that appear.

18. Select the second `variable: m` item in the instance drop-down list located at the left-hand side of the main window, below the small scene preview.

19. Activate the **Functions** tab. Alice will display the functions for the `birdBaby`.

20. Drag the **getDistanceBehind** function and drop it on the **1.0** expression that appears before the ≤ operator. A black rectangle will surround the `1.0` value when you start dragging the **getDistanceBehind** function. Select `this.fence` in the menu that appears.

21. Activate the **Procedures** tab. Alice will display the procedures for the local `m` variable that represents each `Model` instance available in the `birds` local array.

22. Drag the **move** procedure and drop it on the **drop statement here** area located within the `while` block. Click on FORWARD and then on STEP_SLOW in the cascade menu that appears. Click on the **more...** drop-down menu button, on `duration` and then on `0.25`. The following code will define the `for each` loop, as shown in the next screenshot:

```
each (Model m in birds) together
    while (m.getDistanceBehind(this.fence) ≤ 0.25) is true
        m.move(FORWARD, STEP_SLOW, duration: 0.25)
    loop
```

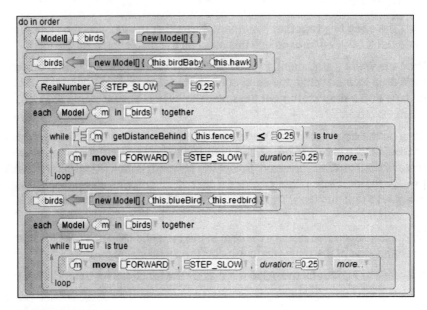

How it works...

We changed the statement that declared the `birds` array. The first statement in the run procedure declares the `birds` local variable as an empty array of `Model`. This means that, at this point, the birds array doesn't have elements. The next statement sets a new value for this variable to a new array of `Model` that has two instances: `this.birdBaby` and `this.hawk`.

Because the line of code assigns a new value to an existing variable, the line is composed of the variable name (`birds`), the assignment operator (←) and the variable's new value (new `Model[]{ this.birdBaby, this.hawk }`):

```
birds ← new Model[]{ this.birdBaby, this.hawk }
```

The first `each (Model m in birds) together` statement allowed us to create a block of code that executes statements for each instance of the `birds` array. Thus, `birdBaby` and `hawk` fly together towards the fence.

When the execution of the first `each (Model m in birds) together` block finishes, the next statement sets a new value for the `birds` local variable to a new array of `Model` that has two instances: `this.bluebird` and `this.redbird`. The line is composed of the variable name (`birds`), the assignment operator (←), and the variable's new value (`new Model[] { this.bluebird, this.redbird }`):

```
birds ← new Model[]{ this.bluebird, this.redbird }
```

The second `each (Model m in birds) together` statement allowed us to create a block of code that executes statements for each instance of the new `birds` array. This time, `bluebird` and `redbird` fly together towards the fence. The instances that compose the array changed and the block uses the new data source. The following image shows three screenshots of the rendered frames:

See also

▶ *Using variables to hold instances of generic classes*, in this chapter

Working with parts of characters

In this task, we will make the hawk move its wings while it flies towards the fence. We will declare a new procedure with the necessary parameters to make the hawk fly and move its wings. We will use local variables and conditional code to control the wings' rotation and the hawk's position.

Getting ready

We will use an existing project that has the hawk as one of its actors.

1. Open the project saved in the *Using variables to hold instances of generic classes* recipe.

2. Click on **Edit Code**, at the lower-right corner of the big scene preview. Alice will show a smaller preview of the scene and will display the **Code Editor** on a panel located at the right-hand side of the main window.

3. Click on the **class: MyScene** drop-down list and the list of classes that are part of the scene will appear.

4. Select **MyScene | Edit run**.

5. Delete all the existing statements in the run procedure for the MyScene class.

How to do it...

Follow these steps to declare and use a new fly procedure for the hawk class:

1. Click on **Edit code** and then on the **class: MyScene** drop-down list. The list of classes that are part of the scene will appear.

2. Click on the **class: MyScene** drop-down list and the list of classes that are part of the scene will appear.

3. Select **MyHawk | Declare procedure**. Enter fly in **Name** and click **OK**. The code editor will add a new tab with the name of the new procedure, **fly**.

4. Click on the **Add Parameter...** button and the **Declare Parameter** dialog box will appear.

5. Click on the **type** drop-down list and a drop-down menu will appear. Select **MoveDirection**.

6. Enter direction in name and click **OK**. The parameter will appear in the procedure declaration located at the top, below the **fly** tab.

7. Click on the **Add Parameter...** button and the **Declare Parameter** dialog box will appear.

8. Click on the **type** drop-down list and a drop-down menu will appear. Select **RealNumber**.

9. Enter amount in name and click **OK**. This second parameter will appear in the procedure declaration located at the top, below the **fly** tab.

10. Drag **local...** statements to declare the following three variables. Use the **Other Real Number...** option in the **Initializer** drop-down list to enter the initial values shown in the Initializer column for each new variable.

Value type	Name	Initializer
Other Types | RollDirection	`rollDirectionLeftWing`	`LEFT`
Other Types | RollDirection	`rollDirectionRightWing`	`RIGHT`
Integer	`counter`	`0`

The following code will be displayed as three new statements:

```
RollDirection rollDirectionLeftWing ← LEFT
RollDirection rollDirectionRightWing ← RIGHT
Integer counter ← 0
```

11. Drag the **count** statement, located at the top, and drop it below the last variable declaration statement, `Integer counter ← 0`. A list with some predefined values to count up to it will appear. Select **Other Integer...** and the **Enter custom integer** dialog box will appear. Enter 4 and click **OK**. The `count up to 4` statement will display a **drop statement here** placeholder.

12. Drag the **counter ← _** statement, located at the top, and drop it in the **drop statement here** area located within the `count up to 4` block.

13. Select **counter** in the menu that appears.

14. Click on the down arrow that appears with a gray background at the right-hand side of the assignment operator ←. A drop-down menu will display different options to use to replace the current expression. Select **Math | counter + ??? | 1** in the cascade menus that appear. The following code will be displayed as the first statement within the `count up to 4` block:

```
counter ← (counter + 1)
```

15. Drag the **do together** statement, located at the top, and drop it below the previously dropped statement, within the `count up to 4` block. The `do together` statement will display a **drop statement here** placeholder.

16. Select `hawk (this)` in the instance drop-down list located at the left-hand side of the main window, below the small scene preview.

17. Select `part: LeftWing` in the drop-down list located at the right-hand side of the chosen instance.

18. Activate the **Procedures** tab.

19. Drag the **roll** procedure and drop it in the **drop statement here** area within the do
    `together` block. A list with all the predefined direction values to pass to the first
    parameter and the two variables of the `RollDirection` type will appear. Click on
    `rollDirectionLeftWing` and then on `0.125` in the cascade menu that appears.
    Click on the **more...** drop-down menu button that appears at the right-hand side of
    the statement, on **duration** and then on **Other Real Number**. Enter `0.125` and click
    OK. The following line of code will appear:

    ```
    this.getPart(LeftWing).roll(rollDirectionLeftWing, 0.125,
    duration: 0.125)
    ```

20. Select `part: RightWing` in the drop-down list located at the right-hand side of the
    chosen instance.

21. Drag the **roll** procedure and drop it below the previously dropped statement within
    the do `together` block. A list with all the predefined direction values to pass to
    the first parameter and the two variables of the `RollDirection` type will appear.
    Click on `rollDirectionRightWing` and then on `0.125` in the cascade menu that
    appears. Click on the **more...** drop-down menu button that appears at the right-hand
    side of the statement, on **duration** and then on **Other Real Number**. Enter `0.125`
    and click **OK**. The following line of code will appear:

    ```
    this.getPart(RightWing).roll(rollDirectionRightWing, 0.125,
    duration: 0.125)
    ```

22. Now select `part: none` in the drop-down list located at the right-hand side of the
    chosen instance.

23. Drag the **move** procedure and drop it below the do `together` block, within
    the `count up to 4` block. Select `direction` and then `amount`. Click on the
    more... drop-down menu button that appears at the right-hand side of the statement,
    on **duration** and then on **Other Real Number**. Enter `0.125` and click **OK**.

24. Now click on the **amount** menu button that appears as a result of following the
    aforementioned step. Select **Math | amount / ??? | Other Real Number...** in the
    menu that appears. Enter 4 and click **OK**. The following line of code will appear:

    ```
    this.move(direction, (amount / 4.0), duration: 0.125)
    ```

25. Drag the **if _** statement, located at the top, and drop it below the previously
    dropped procedure call, within the `count up to 4` block. Click on **true** and two
    drop statement here placeholders will appear.

26. Now click on the down arrow that appears with a gray background at the right-hand
    side of **true**, before **is true then**. A drop-down menu will display different options to
    use to replace the current expression. Select the last option (**Relational (Integer)
    { ==, !=, <, <=, >=, > }**) that provides a cascade menu with six relational operators
    to apply to integer numbers. Then select **??? == ??? | counter | 0** in the cascade
    menus that appear.

27. Click on the down arrow that appears at the right-hand side of **counter**, before the **==** relational operator. Select **Math | divide, remainder | counter INTEGER_ REMAINDER ??? | 2**. The following code will be displayed as the new statement that defines the conditional `if` block:

```
if (counter.INTEGER_REMAINDER(2) == 0) is true then
```

28. Drag the **rollDirectionLeftWing** ← _ statement, located at the top, and drop it in the first **drop statement here** area located within the `if` block. Select **LEFT** in the menu that appears.

29. Drag the **rollDirectionRightWing** ← _ statement, located at the top, and drop it in below the previously dropped statement within the `if` block, before the `else` keyword. Select **RIGHT** in the menu that appears.

30. Drag the **rollDirectionLeftWing** ← _ statement, located at the top, and drop it in the **drop statement here** area located below the `else` keyword. Select **RIGHT** in the menu that appears.

31. Drag the **rollDirectionRightWing** ← _ statement, located at the top, and drop it below the previously dropped statement within the `else` block, after the **else** keyword. Select **LEFT** in the menu that appears. The following code will compose the `if` block within the `count up to 4` block, as shown in the next screenshot:

```
if (counter.INTEGER_REMAINDER(2) == 0) is true then
    rollDirectionLeftWing ← LEFT
    rollDirectionRightWing ← RIGHT
else
    rollDirectionLeftWing ← RIGHT
    rollDirectionRightWing ← LEFT
```

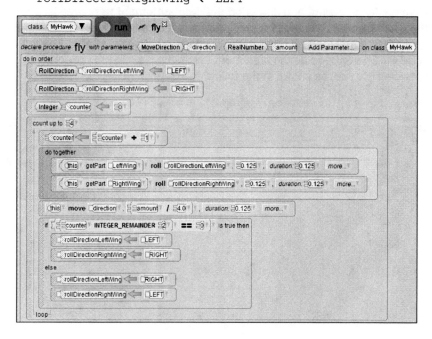

32. Select **MyScene | Edit run**.

33. Drag the **while _** statement, located at the top, and drop it below the previously dropped statement. Click on **true** and a **drop statement here** placeholder will appear within the `while true is true` block.

34. Click on the down arrow that appears with a gray background at the right-hand side of **true**, before **is true**. A drop-down menu will display different options to use to replace the current expression. Select the eleventh option (**Relational (Real Number) { ==, !=, <, <=, >=, > }**) that provides a cascade menu with six relational operators to apply to real numbers. Then select **??? ≤ ??? | 1.0 | 0.25** in the cascade menus that appear.

35. Select `hawk` in the instance drop-down list located at the left-hand side of the main window, below the small scene preview. Make sure that `part: none` is selected in the drop-down list located at the right-hand side of the chosen instance.

36. Activate the **Functions** tab. Alice will display the functions for the `hawk`.

37. Drag the **getDistanceBehind** function and drop it on the **1.0** expression that appears before the ≤ operator. A black rectangle will surround the `1.0` value when you start dragging the **getDistanceBehind** function. Select **this.fence.getPart ??? | CrossPost** in the menu that appears. The following code will be displayed as the statement that defines the definitive `while` block:

```
while (this.hawk.getDistanceBehind(this.fence.getPart(CrossPost))
≤ 0.25) is true
```

38. Activate the **Procedures** tab. Alice will display the procedures for the `hawk`.

39. Drag the **fly** procedure and drop it on the **drop statement here** area located within the **while** block. `fly` is the first procedure listed below the `MyHawk` label. Click on `FORWARD` and then on `0.25` in the cascade menus that appear. The following code will be displayed as the statement that will run while the previously specified condition is `true`, as shown in the following screenshot:

```
this.hawk.fly(direction: FORWARD, amount: 0.25)
```

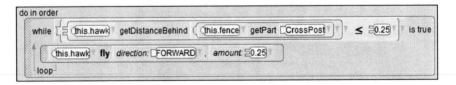

How it works...

We created a new procedure for the MyHawk class. The new procedure's name is fly and it receives two parameter, direction of the MoveDirection type, and amount of the RealNumber type. The instance of the MyHawk class that calls this procedure is accessed through the this keyword. Thus, the procedure can call the methods available from the MyHawk class through this.

The procedure runs a block of code four times and increments the value for the counter local variable in each iteration. When counter changes from an odd to an even value, the code in the if block changes the directions for the rolls of both the left wing and the right wing. The code determines whether the counter is odd or even by checking whether the integer remainder of the division of this counter by 2 is equal to 0 or not.

The rollDirectionLeftWing and rollDirectionRightWing variables change their value in each iteration to make the hawk move its wings up and down while it moves. Thus, the calls to the roll procedure for each wing uses these variables as the first parameter that indicates the desired direction. We called the roll procedure for LeftWing and RightWind, and therefore we controlled sub-parts of the hawk model. The next image shows four screenshots of the rendered frames with the hawk moving its wings while it moves:

The hawk flies until it reaches the CrossPost part of the fence. We used the getPart function to get a specific Model that composes the fence.

See also

▶ *Using variables to hold instances of generic classes*, in this chapter

6
Working with Properties

In this chapter, we will cover:

- ▸ Defining new properties to store real numbers
- ▸ Using properties to call procedures
- ▸ Changing the properties initial values
- ▸ Combining local variables and properties
- ▸ Calculating new values for properties
- ▸ Working with many instances of the same class
- ▸ Using properties to call functions
- ▸ Assigning values entered by the user to properties

Introduction

Alice 3 allows you to declare properties for the classes. When you have to associate values with specific instances of a class, you can declare, initialize, and change the values for properties with simple statements. This chapter provides many tasks that will allow us to use properties and to combine them with local variables and mathematic operations.

We will define new properties to allow many hawks to fly with their own speed values. We will use properties to call procedures, edit their initial values, and combine these properties with local variables and mathematic operations. In addition, we will request the user to enter values and we will assign these values to properties.

Defining new properties to store real numbers

In this recipe, we will declare a new property for the `MyHawk` class with an initial value. This property will define the number of units that an instance of the `MyHawk` class must advance in each step. We will be able to set different values associated with this property in each instance of the `MyHawk` class.

Getting ready

We will use an existing project that has four different birds and a fence. Follow these steps to leave the `hawk` as the only bird in the scene:

1. Open the project saved in the *Working with parts of characters* recipe, in *Chapter 5, Working with Variables*.

2. Delete the following three instances. Right-click on each instance name and select **Delete** in the context menu that appears.

   - `birdBaby`
   - `bluebird`
   - `redbird`

How to do it...

Follow these steps to declare a new property for the `MyHawk` class:

1. Click on **Edit code** and then on the **class: MyScene** drop-down list. The list of classes that are part of the scene will appear.

2. Select **MyHawk | Declare property**. The **Declare Property** dialog box will appear.

3. Click on the **Value type** drop-down list and select **RealNumber**.

4. Enter `Step` in **Name**.

5. Click on the **Initializer** drop-down list and select **0.25** as the initial value for the `Step` property. The following screenshot shows the **Declare Property** dialog box that declares the new `Step` property:

6. Click **OK** and Alice will add the `Step` property to the `MyHawk` class.

7. Select `hawk` in the instance drop-down list located at the left-hand side of the main window, below the small scene preview. Make sure that `part: none` is selected in the drop-down list located at the right-hand side of the chosen instance.

8. Activate the **Properties** tab. Alice will display the new `Step` property below **MyHawk**, as shown in the following screenshot:

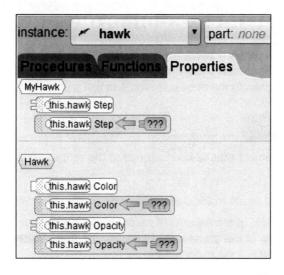

9. Select **File | Save as...** from Alice's main menu and give a new name to the project. Then you can make changes to the project according to your needs.

How it works...

We added the `Step` property to the `MyHawk` class. We set the initial value for this property of the `RealNumber` type to `0.25`. Thus, each new instance of the `MyHawk` class will have the value `0.25` for the `Step` property.

 The names for the properties for a class must start with an uppercase letter. Thus, we used `Step` as the name for the new property. However, there is an exception to the rule. When you add actors to a scene, the names for these properties start with a lowercase letter because they are instances that also appear as properties for the `MyScene` class.

When we declare a new property, Alice creates a read-write property. Alice doesn't allow us to create read-only properties.

See also

> ▶ *Inspecting the properties for each instance that composes a scene*, in *Chapter 1, Setting Scenes*

> ▶ *Defining a light's initial properties*, in *Chapter 1, Setting Scenes*

> ▶ *Working with parts of characters*, in *Chapter 5, Working with Variables*

Using properties to call procedures

In this task, we will use a property to control the number of units that a hawk has to fly. We will use an existing property that stores real numbers associated to each instance of the `MyHawk` class. This property will provide the necessary value to call a procedure.

Getting ready

We will use an existing project that has an instance of the `MyHawk` class and provides a `Step` property.

1. Open the project saved in the *Defining new properties to store real numbers* recipe.

2. Click on **Edit Code**, at the lower-right corner of the big scene preview. Alice will show a smaller preview of the scene and will display the **Code Editor** on a panel located at the right-hand side of the main window.

3. Click on the **class: MyScene** drop-down list and the list of classes that are part of the scene will appear.

4. Select **MyScene | Edit run**.

5. Delete all the existing statements in the `run` procedure for the `MyScene` class.

How to do it...

Follow these steps to declare and use a new `flyStep` procedure for the `MyHawk` class:

1. Click on **Edit code** and then on the **class: MyScene** drop-down list. The list of classes that are part of the scene will appear.

2. Select **MyHawk | Declare procedure**. Enter `flyStep` in **Name** and click **OK**. The code editor will add a new tab with the name of the new procedure, **flyStep**.

3. Click on the **Add Parameter...** button and the **Declare Parameter** dialog box will appear.

4. Click on the **type** drop-down list and a drop-down menu will appear. Select **Other Types | MoveDirection**.

5. Enter `direction` in name and click **OK**. The parameter will appear in the procedure declaration located at the top, below the **fly** tab.

6. Select `hawk (this)` in the instance drop-down list located at the left-hand side of the main window, below the small scene preview. Make sure that `part: none` is selected in the drop-down list located at the right-hand side of the chosen instance.

7. Activate the **Procedures** tab. Alice will display the procedures for the `hawk`.

8. Drag the **fly** procedure and drop it on the **drop statement here** area located below the **do in order** label, inside the **flyStep** tab. Click on `direction` and then on `this. Step` in the cascade menus that appear. The following code will be displayed as the new statement, as shown in the following screenshot:

   ```
   this.hawk.fly (direction: direction, amount: this.Step)
   ```

9. Select **MyScene | Edit run**.

10. Drag the **while _** statement, located at the top, and drop it below the previously dropped statement. Click on **true** and a **drop statement here** placeholder will appear within the `while true is true` block.

11. Click on the down arrow that appears with a gray background at the right-hand side of **true**, before **is true**. A drop-down menu will display different options to use to replace the current expression. Select the eleventh option (**Relational (Real Number) { ==, !=, <, <=, >=, > }**) that provides a cascade menu with six relational operators to apply to real numbers. Then select **??? ≤ ??? | 1.0 | 0.25** in the cascade menus that appear.

12. Select `hawk` in the instance drop-down list located at the left-hand side of the main window, below the small scene preview. Make sure that `part: none` is selected in the drop-down list located at the right-hand side of the chosen instance.

13. Activate the **Functions** tab. Alice will display the functions for the `hawk`.

14. Drag the **getDistanceBehind** function and drop it on the **1.0** expression that appears before the ≤ operator. A black rectangle will surround the `1.0` value when you start dragging the **getDistanceBehind** function. Select **this.fence.getPart ??? | CrossPost** in the menu that appears. The following code will be displayed as the statement that defines the definitive `while` block:

```
while (this.hawk.getDistanceBehind(this.fence.getPart(CrossPost))
≤ 0.25) is true
```

15. Activate the **Procedures** tab. Alice will display the procedures for the `hawk`.

16. Drag the **flyStep** procedure and drop it on the **drop statement here** area located within the **while** block. Click on FORWARD in the cascade menu. The following code will be displayed as the statement that will run while the previously specified condition is `true`, as shown in the next screenshot:

```
this.hawk.flyStep(direction: FORWARD)
```

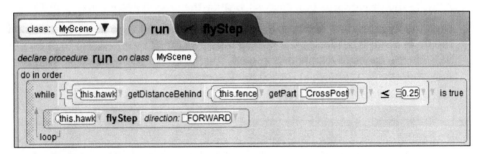

17. Select **File | Save as...** from Alice's main menu and give a new name to the project. Then you can make changes to the project according to your needs.

How it works...

We created a new procedure for the `MyHawk` class. The new procedure's name is `flyStep` and it receives one parameter, `direction` of the `MoveDirection` type. The instance of the `MyHawk` class that calls this procedure is accessed through the `this` keyword. Thus, the procedure can call the methods available from the `MyHawk` class through `this`. In addition, the procedure can access the instance's properties.

The procedure calls the `fly` method for the instance. The code passes the value received in the `direction` parameter to the `direction` parameter of the `fly` method. In addition, the code passes `this.Step` as the value for the amount parameter of the `fly` method. Thus, the value for `amount` will be the value of the `Step` property for the instance that is calling the `flyStep` method.

The `run` procedure calls the `flyStep` method within a `while` loop. The code passes `FORWARD` to the `direction` parameter. Because the code doesn't set a new value for the `Step` property of hawk, the calls to the `flyStep` procedure use the default value of this property, `0.25`.

The hawk flies until it reaches the `CrossPost` part of the `fence`. We used the `getPart` function to get a specific `Model` that composes the `fence`.

 Properties are also known as **fields**. If you need to specify a value related to an instance, you should consider adding a property to the class instead of using a local variable in your code. For example, if you are going to work with many instances that have different speed values, you can add a `Speed` property instead of declaring local variables with the speed values for each instance.

See also

▶ *Defining new properties to store real numbers*, in this chapter

Changing the properties initial values

In this recipe, we will change the initial value for the `Step` property. When we change the initial value for a property, this is going to be the default value for each new instance of the class that defines this property.

Getting ready

We will use an existing project that has an instance of the `MyHawk` class and provides a `flyStep` procedure that uses the value of the `Step` property.

1. Open the project saved in the *Using properties to call procedures* recipe.

2. Click on **Edit Code**, at the lower-right corner of the big scene preview. Alice will show a smaller preview of the scene and will display the **Code Editor** on a panel located at the right-hand side of the main window.

How to do it...

Follow these steps to edit the existing `Step` property of the `MyHawk` class:

1. Click on the **class: MyScene** drop-down list and the list of classes that are part of the scene will appear.

2. Select **MyHawk | Edit Step...** and the **Edit Field** dialog box will appear:

3. Click on the **Initializer** drop-down list and select **0.5** as the initial value for the `Step` property. The following screenshot shows the **Edit Field** dialog box with the information for the `Step` property:

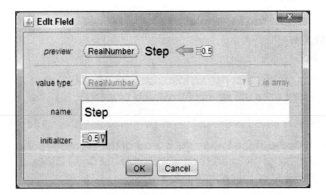

4. Select **File | Save as...** from Alice's main menu and give a new name to the project. Then you can make changes to the project according to your needs.

How it works...

We used the **Edit Field** dialog box to change the initial value for the Step property to 0.5. Thus, each new instance of the MyHawk class will have the value 0.5 for the Step property.

The run procedure calls the flyStep method within a while loop. The code passes FORWARD to the direction parameter. Because the code doesn't set a new value for the Step property of hawk, the calls to the flyStep procedure use the new default value of this property, 0.5. Thus, the hawk moves faster than the previous version.

There's more...

The **Edit Field** dialog box allows us to change the name and the initial value for an existing property. However, we cannot change the property's type.

 If you have to change the property's type, you have to delete the existing property. Then you have to create a new property with the same name and the new type.

See also

▸ *Using properties to call procedures*, in this chapter

Combining local variables and properties

In this task, we will request the user to enter the desired step value for a hawk. We will combine a local variable and a property to make the hawk fly according to the step value entered by the user.

Getting ready

We will use an existing project that uses the flyStep procedure to make the hawk fly towards the fence.

1. Open the project saved in the *Changing the properties initial values* recipe.
2. Click on **Edit Code**, at the lower-right corner of the big scene preview. Alice will show a smaller preview of the scene and will display the **Code Editor** on a panel located at the right-hand side of the main window.
3. Click on the **class: MyScene** drop-down list and the list of classes that are part of the scene will appear.
4. Select **MyScene | Edit run**.

How to do it...

Follow these steps to change the value of the Step property of the hawk instance with a value entered by the user:

1. Drag the **local...** statement, located at the top, and drop as the first statement, above the while block, inside the **run** tab. The **Declare Local** dialog box will appear.

2. Click on the **Value type** drop-down list and select **RealNumber**.

3. Enter stepHawk in **Name**.

4. Click on the **Initializer** drop-down list and select **1.0** as the initial value for the stepHawk variable.

5. Click **OK** and the following code will be displayed as a new statement:

   ```
   RealNumber stepHawk ← 1.0
   ```

6. Select scene (this) in the instance drop-down list located at the left-hand side of the main window, below the small scene preview.

7. Activate the **Functions** tab. Alice will display the functions for scene.

8. Drag the **getDoubleFromUser** function and drop it on the **1.0** expression that appears after the ← operator. A black rectangle will surround the 1.0 value when you start dragging the **getDoubleFromUser** function. Select **Other String...** and the **Enter Custom String** dialog box will appear. Enter Enter the desired step value for the hawk in the **value** textbox and click **OK**. The following code will appear as the statement that declares and initializes the stepHawk local variable:

   ```
   RealNumber stepHawk ← this.getDoubleFromUser("Enter the desired
   step value for the hawk")
   ```

9. Select hawk in the instance drop-down list located at the left-hand side of the main window, below the small scene preview. Make sure that part: none is selected in the drop-down list located at the right-hand side of the chosen instance.

10. Activate the **Properties** tab. Alice will display the properties for the hawk instance.

11. Drag the **Step** assignment statement and drop it below the stepHawk declaration statement. The **Step** assignment statement contains the **this.hawk** and **Step** labels followed by an arrow and three question marks **???**. Alice will display the stepHawk variable as an option in the menu. Select stepHawk, the desired RealNumber to assign to the hawk.Step property. The following code will appear before the while loop, as shown in the next screenshot:

    ```
    this.hawk.Step ← stepHawk
    ```

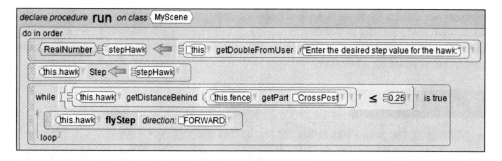

12. Select **File | Save as...** from Alice's main menu and give a new name to the project. Then you can make changes to the project according to your needs.

How it works...

When we run the project, Alice shows a dialog box requesting the user to enter a floating point number to use as the step value for the hawk, as shown in the following screenshot:

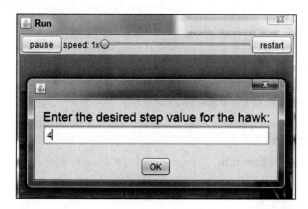

We declared the `stepHawk` variable and we assigned it the result of the `getDoubleFromUser` function. This function receives a string with the message to display in the dialog box as its unique parameter and returns the `RealNumber` value entered by the user. This way, the `stepHawk` variable holds the user's desired step value for the `hawk`. Then the code assigns the value of the `stepHawk` variable to `hawk.Step`, and therefore the `hawk` flies using the user's desired step value.

In this case, we used a local variable and then we assigned its value to a property. However, we could have assigned the result of the `getDoubleFromUser` function to `this.Step` without using an intermediate local variable. This recipe demonstrates the usage of a local variable to set a value for a property.

See also

▸ *Changing the properties initial values*, in this chapter

Calculating new values for properties

In this recipe we will use a mathematic operation to calculate a new value for a property. We will make the hawk fly according to a step value based on a number entered by the user.

Getting ready

We will use an existing project that requests the user to enter the desired step value for the hawk.

1. Open the project saved in the *Combining local variables and properties* recipe.
2. Click on **Edit Code**, at the lower-right corner of the big scene preview. Alice will show a smaller preview of the scene and will display the **Code Editor** on a panel located at the right-hand side of the main window.
3. Click on the **class: MyScene** drop-down list and the list of classes that are part of the scene will appear.
4. Select **MyScene | Edit run**.

How to do it...

Follow these steps to assign the result of a mathematic operation to the `Step` property of the `hawk` instance:

1. Go to the statement that assigns a value for the `this.hawk.Step` property. Click on its initial value, `stepHawk`, at the right-hand side of the assignment operator ←. A drop-down menu will display different options to replace the current expression.

2. Select **Math | stepHawk / ???** | **Other Real Number...** in the cascade menus that appear, as shown in the next screenshot:

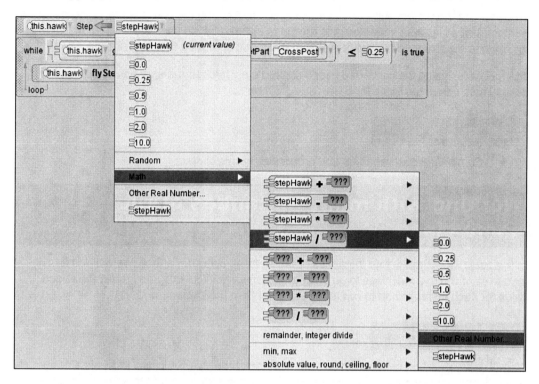

3. The **Enter custom real number** dialog box will appear. Enter `100` and click **OK**. The following code will be displayed as the assignment statement before the `while` loop, as shown in the following screenshot:

```
this.hawk.Step ← (stepHawk / 100.0)
```

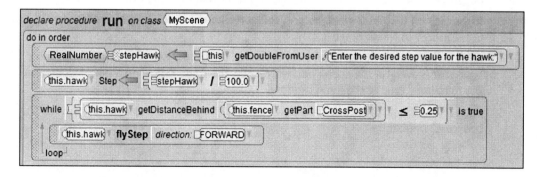

4. Select **File | Save as...** from Alice's main menu and give a new name to the project. Then you can make changes to the project according to your needs.

How it works...

When we run the project, Alice shows a dialog box requesting the user to enter a floating point number. The stepHawk variable holds the value entered by the user. We divided this variable by 100 and we assigned the result of this mathematic operation to hawk.Step.

The hawk flies using the converted user's desired step value. If the user enters 500 as the desired step value, the value for hawk.Step will be 5.

See also

▶ *Combining local variables and properties*, in this chapter

Working with many instances of the same class

In this task, we will make four instances of the MyHawk class run a race. We will add four instances of the MyHawk class to an array and then we will use this array to set the speed value for each instance and to run many statements at the same time.

Getting ready

We will use an existing project that has an instance of the MyHawk class, provides a Step property and defines a flyStep procedure. Follow these steps to add three new instances of the MyHawk class:

1. Open the project saved in the *Using properties to call procedures* recipe.
2. Click on **Edit Scene**, at the lower-right corner of the scene preview. Alice will show a bigger preview of the scene and will display the **Model Gallery** at the bottom.
3. Right-click on the hawk instance and select **Rename hawk...** in the context menu. Enter hawk0 in **Name** and click **OK**.
4. Click on **Edit Code**, at the lower-right corner of the big scene preview. Alice will show a smaller preview of the scene and will display the **Code Editor** on a panel located at the right-hand side of the main window.
5. Click on the **class: MyScene** drop-down list and the list of classes that are part of the scene will appear.

6. Select **MyHawk | Declare New Instance....** The **Declare Property** dialog box will appear. Enter `hawk1` in **Name**, as shown in the next screenshot, and click **OK**. Alice will create an instance of `MyHawk` named `hawk1`:

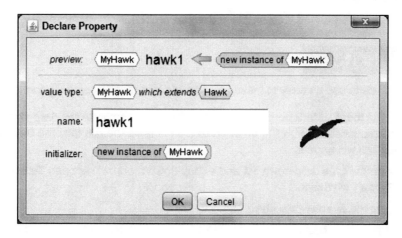

7. Repeat the aforementioned steps (5 and 6) to add two new instances of the `MyHawk` class. Use the following names for the new instances:

   ❑ hawk2

   ❑ hawk3

8. Place the four `hawk` instances in the edit scene screen as shown in the next screenshot. The four hawks from top to bottom are `hawk0`, `hawk1`, `hawk2`, and `hawk3`:

9. Click on the **class: MyScene** drop-down list and the list of classes that are part of the scene will appear.

10. Select **MyScene | Edit run**.

11. Delete all the existing statements in the run procedure for the `MyScene` class.

How to do it...

Follow these steps to use an array to make four hawks run a race by using random step values:

1. Drag the **local...** statement, located at the top, and drop it on the **drop statement here** area located below the **do in order** label, inside the **run** tab. The **Declare Local** dialog box will appear.

2. Click on the **type** drop-down list and a drop-down menu will appear. Select **My Types | MyHawk**.

3. Activate the **Is array** checkbox.

4. Enter `hawks` in **Name**.

5. Click on the **Add...** drop-down menu button that appears at the right-hand side of **Initializer**. Click on `this.hawk0` in the menu that appears.

6. Click on the **Add...** drop-down menu button that appears at the right-hand side of **Initializer** and below **[0] this.hawk0**. Click on `this.hawk1` in the menu that appears.

7. Click on the new **Add...** drop-down menu button that appears and select `this.hawk2`.

8. Click on the new **Add...** drop-down menu button that appears and select `this.hawk3`. The dialog box will display the four elements that compose the `hawks` array, as shown in the following screenshot:

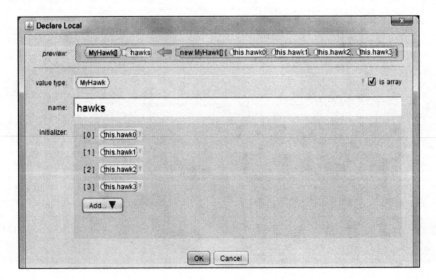

9. Click **OK** and the following code will be displayed as a new statement:

```
Model[] hawks ← new Model[]{ this.hawk0, this.hawk1, this.hawk2,
this.hawk3 }
```

10. Drag the **for each in _** statement, located at the top, and drop it below the previously dropped statement. Click on **hawks** to use this array as the data source for the loop.

11. Select `variable: m` in the instance drop-down list located at the left-hand side of the main window, below the small scene preview.

12. Activate the **Properties** tab. Alice will display the properties for the local `m` variable that represents each `Model` instance available in the `hawks` local array.

13. Drag the **Step** assignment statement, and drop it on the **drop statement here** area located within the `for each Model m in hawks` block. The **Step** assignment statement contains the **this.hawk** and **Step** labels followed by an arrow and three question marks **???**. Select `1.0` in the context menu.

14. Now click on the down arrow that appears with a gray background at the right-hand side of `1.0` on the previously defined statement, after the assignment operator ←. A drop-down menu will display different options used to replace the current expression.

15. Select **Random | nextRandomRealNumberInRange ???, ??? | 0.25 | 2.0**. The following code includes the expression that generates a real random number to pass it as a parameter:

```
m.Step ← nextRandomRealNumberInRange(0.25, 2.0)
```

16. Drag the **each in _ together** statement, located at the top, and drop it below the `for each Model m in hawks` block. Click on **hawks** to use this array as the data source for the loop.

17. Drag the **while _** statement, located at the top, and drop it in the **drop statement here** area located within the `each Model m in hawks together` block. Click on **true** and a **drop statement here** placeholder will appear within the `while true is true` block.

18. Click on the down arrow that appears with a gray background at the right-hand side of **true**, before **is true**. A drop-down menu will display different options to use to replace the current expression. Select the eleventh option (**Relational (Real Number) { ==, !=, <, <=, >=, > }**) that provides a cascade menu with six relational operators to apply to real numbers. Then select **??? ≤ ??? | 1.0 | 0.25** in the cascade menus that appear.

19. Select the second `variable: m` item in the instance drop-down list located at the left-hand side of the main window, below the small scene preview. Make sure that `part: none` is selected in the drop-down list located at the right-hand side of **variable: m**.

20. Activate the **Functions** tab. Alice will display the properties for the local `m` variable that represents each `Model` instance available in the `hawks` local array.

21. Drag the **getDistanceBehind** function and drop it on the **1.0** expression that appears before the ≤ operator. A black rectangle will surround the 1.0 value when you start dragging the **getDistanceBehind** function. Select **this.fence.getPart ???** **| CrossPost** in the menu that appears. The following code will be displayed as the statement that defines the definitive while block:

```
while (m.getDistanceBehind(this.fence.getPart(CrossPost)) ≤ 0.25)
is true
```

22. Activate the **Procedures** tab. Alice will display the procedures for the local m variable that represents each Model instance available in the hawks local array.

23. Drag the **flyStep** procedure and drop it on the **drop statement here** area located within the **while** block. Click on FORWARD in the cascade menu. The following code will be displayed as the statement that will run while the previously specified condition is true, as shown in the following screenshot:

```
m.flyStep(direction: FORWARD)
```

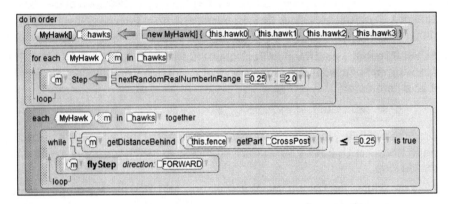

24. Select **File | Save as...** from Alice's main menu and give a new name to the project. Then you can make changes to the project according to your needs.

How it works...

The local... statement allowed us to declare an **array** of MyHawk, named hawks. We set the initial value for this variable to a new array of MyHawk that has four instances, as shown in the next table:

Index	Value
0	this.hawk0
1	this.hawk1
2	this.hawk2
3	this.hawk3

The `for each in _` statement allowed us to create a block of code that executes statements for each instance of the `hawks` array. The code assigns a random real number between `0.25` and `2.0` to the `Step` property of each `MyHawk` instance in the `hawks` array. This way, each hawk has a random `Step` value that will be used in the `flyStep` procedure.

The `each in _ together` statement allowed us to create a block of code that executes statements for each instance of the `hawks` array, at the same time. Alice runs the `while` loop for each of the `MyHawk` instances specified after the `in` keyword, that is, the `hawks` array. The `each MyHawk m in hawks together` block starts running the code for all the instances in the `hawks` array together. This means that all the hawks start flying at the same time. We could work with the `m` variable and the `hawks` array provides all the instances of `MyHawk` with their independent value of the `Step` property, as a data source. Therefore all the hawks will fly towards the `fence` concurrently, with diverse flying speeds. The next image shows three screenshots of the rendered frames:

There's more...

Because we worked with a property and an array of the `MyHawk` class, it is easy to add new hawks to the race. We just have to add a new instance of the `MyHawk` class and add this new instance to the `hawks` array. There is no need to make additional changes to the code, because both the `for each MyHawk m in hawks` block and the `each MyHawk m in hawks together` block will run code for all the instances in the `hawks` array.

If we had used local variables to define the step values for each hawk, it wouldn't be so easy to add a new instance of the `MyHawk` class to the race.

See also

> ▶ *Using properties to call procedures*, in this chapter

Using properties to call functions

In this recipe, we will define and use a new property to set the target that each hawk must reach. We will use this property as a parameter for a function that determines whether the hawk must go on flying or not.

Getting ready

We will use an existing project that has four instances of the `MyHawk` class.

1. Open the project saved in the *Working with many instances of the same class* recipe.

2. Click on **Edit Code**, at the lower-right corner of the big scene preview. Alice will show a smaller preview of the scene and will display the **Code Editor** on a panel located at the right-hand side of the main window.

3. Click on the **class: MyScene** drop-down list and the list of classes that are part of the scene will appear.

4. Select **MyScene | Edit run**.

How to do it...

Follow these steps to use a new property as a parameter for a function call:

1. Click on the **class: MyScene** drop-down list and the list of classes that are part of the scene will appear.

2. Select **MyHawk | Declare property**. The **Declare Property** dialog box will appear.

3. Click on the **Value type** drop-down list and select **Other Types | Model**.

4. Enter `Target` in **Name**.

5. Click on the **Initializer** drop-down list and select **this.grassyGround** as the initial value for the `Target` property.

6. Click **OK** and Alice will add the `Target` property to the `MyHawk` class.

7. Select the first `variable: m` item in the instance drop-down list located at the left-hand side of the main window, below the small scene preview. Make sure that `part: none` is selected in the drop-down list located at the right-hand side of **variable: m**.

8. Activate the **Properties** tab. Alice will display the properties for the local `m` variable that represents each `Model` instance available in the `hawks` local array.

9. Drag the **Target** assignment statement, and drop it below the `Step` assignment statement within the `for each Model m in hawks` block. Select **this.fence.getPart ??? | CrossPost** in the menu that appears. Alice will add the following code as a statement:

```
m.Target ← this.fence.getPart(CrossPost)
```

10. Select the second `variable: m` item in the instance drop-down list located at the left-hand side of the main window, below the small scene preview. Make sure that `part: none` is selected in the drop-down list located at the right-hand side of **variable: m**.

11. Activate the **Properties** tab. Alice will display the properties for the local `m` variable that represents each `Model` instance available in the `hawks` local array.

12. Drag the **Target** property and drop it on the **CrossPost** expression that appears in the statements that defines the `while (m.getDistanceBehind(this.fence. getPart(CrossPost)) ≤ 0.25) is true` block. A black rectangle will surround the `CrossPost` value when you start dragging the **Target** property. The **Step** property contains the **m** and **Target** labels with a yellow background. The following code will be displayed as the statement that defines the definitive `while` block, as shown in the next screenshot:

```
while (m.getDistanceBehind(m.Target) ≤ 0.25) is true
```

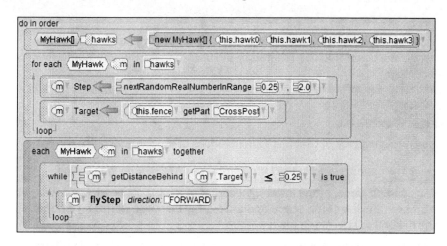

13. Select **File | Save as...** from Alice's main menu and give a new name to the project. Then you can make changes to the project according to your needs.

How it works...

We added the `Target` property of the `Model` type to the `MyHawk` class. Then we added a statement within the `for each MyHawk m in hawks` loop to set the value for `Target`. The new statement sets `this.fence.getPart(CrossPost)` to the `Target` property of each instance in the `hawks` array.

We used the `Target` property as a parameter for the `getDistanceBehind` function in the `each Hawk m in hawks together` loop. This way, each `MyHawk` instance will fly until it reaches the `Model` instance specified in the `Target` property. In this case, all the `MyHawk` instances will fly towards the `fence`. However, the existence of the `Target` property makes it easy to set different targets for the diverse `MyHawk` instances. In addition, the code is easier to understand.

See also

 ▶ *Working with many instances of the same class*, in this chapter

Assigning values entered by the user to properties

In this task, we will request the user to enter the desired step value for each of the four hawks. We will use the values entered by the user to make the four hawks fly with different speeds.

Getting ready

We will use an existing project that has four instances of the `MyHawk` class.

1. Open the project saved in the *Using properties to call functions* recipe.
2. Click on **Edit Code**, at the lower-right corner of the big scene preview. Alice will show a smaller preview of the scene and will display the **Code Editor** on a panel located at the right-hand side of the main window.
3. Click on the **class: MyScene** drop-down list and the list of classes that are part of the scene will appear.
4. Select **MyScene | Edit run**.

How to do it...

Follow these steps to set the `Step` property of many instances of the `MyHawk` class with values entered by the user:

1. Drag the **local...** statement, located at the top, and drop it as the first statement, above the `hawks` array declaration statement, inside the **run** tab. The **Declare Local** dialog box will appear.

2. Click on the **Value type** drop-down list and select **TextString**.

3. Enter `message` in **Name**.

4. Click on the **Initializer** drop-down list, select **Other String...** and the **Enter Custom String** dialog box will appear. Leave the **value** textbox without text and click **OK**. The following code will appear as the statement that declares and initializes the `message` local variable:

```
TextString message ← ""
```

5. Drag the **local...** statement, located at the top, and drop it below the `hawks` array declaration statement, inside the **run** tab. The **Declare Local** dialog box will appear.

6. Click on the **Value type** drop-down list and select **Integer**.

7. Enter `hawkCounter` in **Name**.

8. Click on the **Initializer** drop-down list and select 0. The following code will appear as the statement that declares and initializes the `hawkCounter` local variable:

```
Integer hawkCounter ← 0
```

9. Drag the **hawkCounter ← _** statement, located at the top of the window, and drop it as the first statement within the `for each MyHawk m in hawks` loop.

10. Select **hawkCounter** in the menu that appears.

11. Click on the down arrow that appears with a gray background at the right-hand side of the assignment operator ←. A drop-down menu will display different options to use to replace the current expression. Select **Math | hawkCounter + ??? | 1** in the cascade menus that appear. The following code will be displayed as the first statement within the `for each MyHawk m in hawks` block:

```
hawkCounter ← (hawkCounter + 1)
```

12. Drag the **message ← _** statement, located at the top, and drop it as the second statement within the `for each MyHawk m in hawks` loop.

13. Select **Other String...** and the **Enter Custom String** dialog box will appear. Enter `Enter step for hawk number:` in the **value** textbox and click **OK**.

14. Click on the down arrow that appears with a gray background at the right-hand side of the assignment operator ←. A drop-down menu will display different options to use to replace the current expression. Select **"Enter step for hawk number: " + ??? | hawkCounter** in the cascade menus that appear. The following code will be displayed as the second statement within the for each MyHawk m in hawks block:

```
message ← ("Enter step for hawk number:" + hawkCounter)
```

15. Select scene (this) in the instance drop-down list located at the left-hand side of the main window, below the small scene preview.

16. Activate the **Functions** tab. Alice will display the functions for scene.

17. Drag the **getDoubleFromUser** function and drop it on the **nextRandomRealNumberInRange(0.25, 2.0)** expression that appears after m.Step ←. A black rectangle will surround the nextRandomRealNumberInRange(0.25, 2.0) expression when you start dragging the **getDoubleFromUser** function. Select **Other String...** and the **Enter Custom String** dialog box will appear. Enter x in the **value** textbox and click **OK**.

18. Click on **"X"** in the recently modified statement. Select message in the menu and the following code will be displayed as the third statement within the for each MyHawk m in hawks block:

```
m.Step ← this.getDoubleFromUser(message)
```

19. Now click on getDoubleFromUser in the previously modified statement. A drop-down menu will display different options to replace the current expression.

20. Select **Math | this.getDoubleFromUser(message) / ??? | Other Real Number...** in the cascade menus that appear

21. The **Enter custom real number** dialog box will appear. Enter 100 and click **OK**. The following code will be displayed as the third statement within the for each MyHawk m in hawks block:

```
m.Step ← (this.getDoubleFromUser(message) / 100.0)
```

The following screenshot shows the code for the `run` procedure:

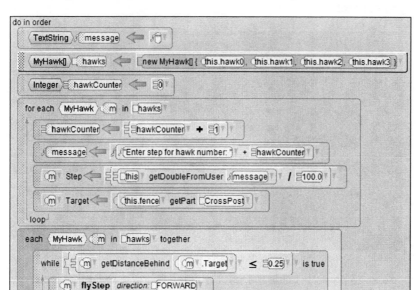

How it works...

We added a `message` local variable of the `TextString` type. This variable allowed us to create a customized message to request the user the step value for each hawk. We added a `hawkCounter` local variable of the `Integer` type.

Each iteration of the `for each MyHawk m in hawks` loop increases the value of `hawkCounter` by 1. Then the code assigns a new `TextString` to message with the concatenation of `"Enter step for hawk number: "` and the value of `hawkCounter` converted to a string. There is no need to include a statement to convert `hawkCounter` from `Integer` to a string, because Alice performs the type conversion automatically.

The dialog box that requests the user to enter a value indicates the hawk number, as shown in the following screenshot:

Each instance's Step property holds the value entered by the user for that instance. We divided the value by 100 and we assigned the result of this mathematic operation to m. Step within the for each MyHawk m in hawks loop.

The hawks fly using the converted user's desired step values. Thus, the user determines the speed for each hawk.

See also

- ▶ *Using properties to call functions*, in this chapter
- ▶ *Inspecting the properties for each instance that composes a scene*, in *Chapter 1, Setting Scenes*
- ▶ *Controlling an actor with keystrokes*, in *Chapter 8, Working with Keyboard and mouse input*
- ▶ *Controlling multiple actors with keystrokes*, in *Chapter 8, Working with Keyboard and Mouse Input*

7
Working with People

In this chapter, we will cover:

- ▸ Creating a random person
- ▸ Customizing a person's body
- ▸ Customizing a person's head
- ▸ Animating a person's body
- ▸ Animating a person's head
- ▸ Interaction between characters in the scene
- ▸ Speaking with other people
- ▸ Interacting with the environment

Introduction

Alice 3 includes the Sims 2 art assets and the Looking Glass Characters gallery. If you need to add people, you can create a customized person or take an existing one from the art assets. This chapter provides many tasks that will allow us to use people as actors in our scenes.

We will create a random person but we will also customize its body and its head. We will call simple procedures to perform complex animations with the person's body and its head. We will organize statements in different kinds of blocks to make people interact between them. We will create animations that show people talking to each other while performing realistic gestures and we will make people interact with the environment.

Creating a random person

In this recipe, we will use the Sims 2 art assets included in Alice 3 to add a random person to the scene. Sometimes, we cannot imagine the human character that we want to add to a scene. When this happens, we can use a function that makes Alice decide for you. Alice chooses a gender, a life stage, a head, a hair style, a skin tone, and an outfit and allows you to preview the new person before you add the new instance to the scene.

Getting ready

Follow these steps to set a simple scene without actors:

1. Select **File | New...** in the main menu to start a new project. A dialog box will display the six predefined templates with their thumbnail previews in the **Templates** tab.

2. Select `GrassyProject.a3p` as the desired template for the new project and click **OK**. Alice will display a grassy ground with a light blue sky.

How to do it...

Follow these steps to add a random person to the scene from The Sims 2 art assets:

1. Click on **Edit Scene**, at the lower-right corner of the scene preview. Alice will show a bigger preview of the scene and will display the **Model Gallery** at the bottom.

2. Click on the **Create Person...** button at the lower-left corner of Alice's main window. Alice will display a dialog box that gives you access to The Sims 2 art assets.

3. Click on the **Generate Random Selection** button at the top of the dialog box. Alice will display a preview of the 3D model that represents the randomly generated selection of the parameters that define a person at the left-hand side of the dialog box. The following screenshot shows the preview of the 3D model of a randomly generated child:

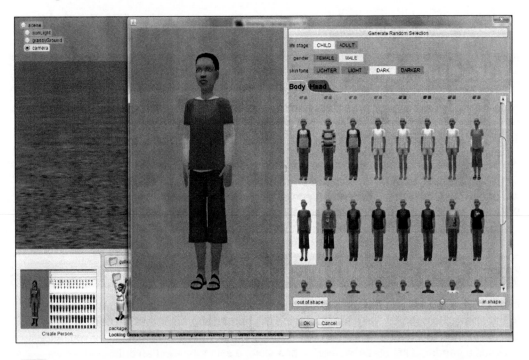

4. If you want to roll the dice again, you just have to click on **Generate Random Selection** and Alice will generate and preview another different random person.

5. Once you are happy with the randomly generated person, click **OK** and the **Declare Property** dialog box will appear.

6. Enter the desired name for the new instance and click **OK** to add it to the existing scene. The next screenshot shows a child added to the scene, as seen by the starting camera:

How it works...

Each time you click on the **Generate Random Selection** button, Alice selects random values for the following parameters to create a new instance of a person by using the Sims 2 art assets:

- ▶ Life state: child or adult
- ▶ Gender: female or male

- ▶ Skin tone: lighter, light, dark or darker
- ▶ Shape: a value that determines whether the person is out of shape (fat) or in shape (thin)

When we clicked on **OK**, the **Declare Property** dialog box provided information about what Alice was going to do:

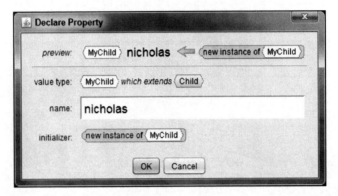

In this case, the resulting random life state was child, and therefore Alice defines a new class, MyChild, which extends Child. MyChild is a new value type for the project, a subclass of Child. The name for the new property that represents the new instance of MyChild is nicholas. This means that you can access this new person with the nicholas name and that this property is available for scene. Because the starting camera view is looking at the horizon, we see the child looking at the camera in the scene preview.

 If the life state was adult, Alice would define a new class, MyAdult, which extends Adult. The Sims 2 art assets included in Alice 3 uses different classes for children and adults.

There's more...

The Adult and Child classes expose six additional properties that allow you to control the person's look. The following table summarizes these six specific properties:

Property Name	Possible values
Gender	FEMALE or MALE
Outfit	Any instance of many subclasses of FemaleAdultFullBodyOutfit, FemaleChildFullBodyOutfit, MaleAdultFullBodyOutfit and MaleChildFullBodyOutfit
SkinTone	LIGHTER, LIGHT, DARK or DARKER

Property Name	Possible values
FitnessLevel	A real number between 0.0 and 1.0
EyeColor	LIGHT_BLUE, DARK_BLUE, GREEN, GRAY or DARK_BROWN
Hair	Any instance of many subclasses of FemaleAdultHair, FemaleChildHair, MaleAdultHair and MaleChildHair

 You can use statements to change the values for these properties.

See also

▶ _Working with many instances of the same class_, in _Chapter 6, Working with Properties_

▶ _Defining new properties_, in _Chapter 6, Working with Properties_

Customizing a person's body

In this task, we will browse the outfits provided by The Sims 2 art assets and we will dress a child's body. Alice provides many outfits for the person according to the selected gender and life stage. Alice allows you to preview the new person before you add the new instance to the scene.

Getting ready

Follow these steps to set a simple scene without actors:

1. Select **File | New...** in the main menu to start a new project. A dialog box will display the six predefined templates with their thumbnail previews in the **Templates** tab.

2. Select SandyProject.a3p as the desired template for the new project and click **OK**. Alice will display a sandy ground with a light blue sky.

How to do it...

Follow these steps to add a child wearing a t-shirt to the scene:

1. Click on **Edit Scene**, at the lower-right corner of the scene preview. Alice will show a bigger preview of the scene and will display the **Model Gallery** at the bottom.

2. Click on the **Create Person...** button at the lower-left corner of Alice's main window. Alice will display a dialog box that gives you access to the Sims 2 art assets.

3. Click on **CHILD** in **Life stage**.

4. Click on **MALE** in **Gender**.

5. Click on **LIGHT** in **Skin tone**. At this point, the dialog box will show a preview of the 3D model, as shown in the next screenshot:

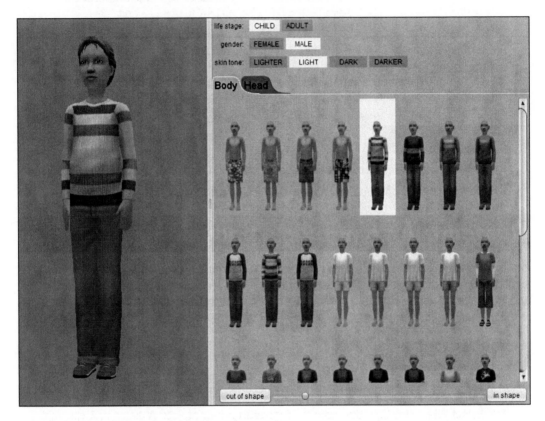

6. Make sure that the **Body** tab is activated. The dialog box will display the thumbnails of all the available outfits for a child. You can use the vertical scroll bar to scroll up and down.

7. Click on one of the thumbnails of the child wearing a t-shirt. The dialog box will update the preview of the 3D model, according to the selected outfit, as shown in the next screenshot. You can click on different outfits to see the difference in the bigger preview:

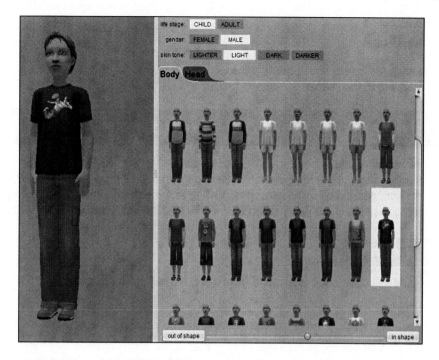

8. Use the slider located at the bottom of the dialog box to select the desired fitness level. If you move the slider to the left-hand side, the child will become fatter. If you move the slider to the right-hand side, the child will become thinner.

9. Once you are happy with the preview, click **OK** and the **Declare Property** dialog box will appear.

10. Enter **kevin** as the desired name for the new instance, and click **OK** to add it to the existing scene.

11. Select **File | Save as...** from Alice's main menu and give a new name to the project. Then you can make changes to the project according to your needs.

How it works...

We selected the life state, gender, skin tone and shape for a new child. We selected one of the available outfits to dress the child with a t-shirt, pants, and sneakers.

The **Body** tab displays thumbnails with all the available outfits for the selected gender and life state. This means that the available outfits are different for the following possible groups of values:

- ▶ Female adult
- ▶ Female child

> ▸ Male adult
>
> ▸ Male child

We used the live preview to check the appearance of the 3D model before we added the new `MyChild` instance to the scene.

Customizing a person's head

In this recipe, we will browse the hair and eye color configurations provided by the Sims 2 art assets and we will change the appearance of a child's head. Alice provides many hair styles and eye color configurations for the person according to the selected gender and life stage. Alice allows you to preview the new person before you add the new instance to the scene.

Getting ready

We want to add a second child to a scene. Therefore, we will use an existing project that has a child.

1. Open the project saved in the *Customizing a person's body* recipe in this chapter.
2. Click on **Edit Scene**, at the lower-right corner of the scene preview. Alice will show a bigger preview of the scene and will display the **Model Gallery** at the bottom.

How to do it...

Follow these steps to add a girl with red hair and gray eyes to the scene:

1. Click on the **Create Person...** button at the lower left corner of Alice's main window. Alice will display a dialog box that gives you access to The Sims 2 art assets.
2. Click on **CHILD** in **Life stage**.
3. Click on **FEMALE** in **Gender**.
4. Click on **LIGHTER** in **Skin tone**.
5. Activate the **Body** tab and select the desired outfit for the girl. Use the slider located at the bottom of the dialog box to select the desired fitness level.
6. Activate the **Head** tab. The dialog box will display the thumbnails of the available hairstyles for a girl. At this point, the dialog box will show a preview of the 3D model, as shown in the next screenshot:

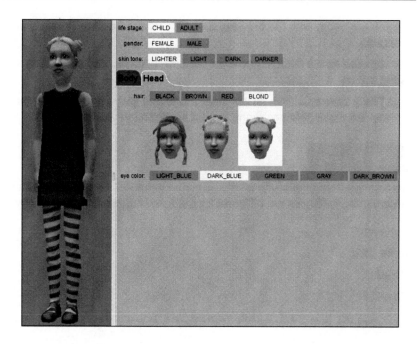

7. Click on **RED** in **Hair**.

8. Click on the thumbnail that displays the girl's hair with two braids.

9. Click on **GRAY** in **Eye color**. The dialog box will update the preview of the 3D model, according to the selected hairstyle and eyes color, as shown in the next screenshot. You can click on different hairstyles and colors to see the difference in the bigger preview:

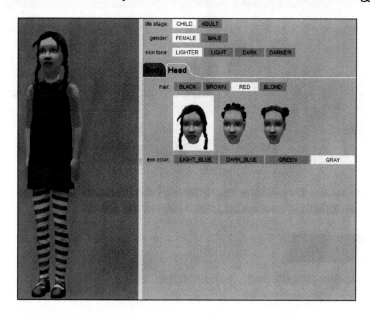

10. Once you are happy with the preview, click **OK** and the **Declare Property** dialog box will appear.

11. Enter **vanessa** as the desired name for the new instance, and click **OK** to add it to the existing scene.

12. Select **File | Save as...** from Alice's main menu and give a new name to the project. Then you can make changes to the project according to your needs.

How it works...

The **Head** tab displays thumbnails with all the available hairstyles for the selected gender and life state. The available hairstyles are different for the following possible groups of values:

- Female adult
- Female child
- Male adult
- Male child

The next screenshot shows the thumbnails of the twelve hairstyles for a man, that is, a male adult:

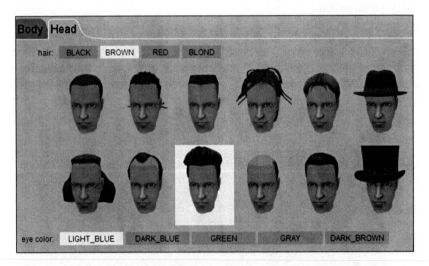

We used the live preview to check the appearance of the 3D model as we changed the hairstyle. Then we added the new MyChild instance to the scene.

See also

- *Customizing a person's body*, in this chapter

Animating a person's body

In this task, we will make a child dance by calling an existing procedure. The child will move his body because the procedure makes the child move the different models that compose a child. We will create an animation that includes complex movements of different parts of an instance.

Getting ready

We have to be working on a project with a person from the Sims 2 art assets. Therefore, we will use an existing project that has two children. kevin and vanessa are two instances of the MyChild class.

1. Open the project saved in the _Customizing a person's head_ recipe in this chapter.

2. Click on **Edit Code**, at the lower-right corner of the big scene preview. Alice will show a smaller preview of the scene and will display the **Code Editor** on a panel located at the right-hand side of the main window.

3. Click on the **class: MyScene** drop-down list and the list of classes that are part of the scene will appear.

4. Select **MyScene | Edit run**.

How to do it...

Follow these steps to make one of the children wave his arms:

1. Select **kevin** in the instance drop-down list located at the left-hand side of the main window, below the small scene preview.

2. Activate the **Procedures** tab. Alice will display the procedures for the previously selected child.

3. Drag the **dance** procedure and drop it in the **drop statement here** area located below the **do in order** label, inside the **run** tab. Select WAVE_ARMS as the value for the parameter. The following code will be displayed as a new statement, as shown in the next screenshot:

```
this.kevin.dance(WAVE_ARMS)
```

4. Select **File | Save as...** from Alice's main menu and give a new name to the project. Then you can make changes to the project according to your needs.

How it works...

We added a statement that calls the `dance` procedure for one of the `MyChild` instances, `kevin`. This procedure animates the child's body to make him dance. We selected `WAVE_ARMS` in the parameter that specifies the desired dancing style. The child waves his arms, as shown in the following four screenshots of the rendered frames:

The following dance styles are available for the `dance` procedure and you can use any of these values as the parameter:

- ▶ HEAD_BOP
- ▶ SWAY_SIDE_TO_SIDE
- ▶ WAVE_ARMS
- ▶ JUMP_AROUND
- ▶ ROCK_OUT
- ▶ SWING_ARMS

[Child dancing requires some background music. Check related recipes that explain how to play background music.]

There's more...

The `Adult` and `Child` classes provide dozens of procedures that allow you to animate a person's body with complex and realistic movements. For example, the `touchToes` procedure makes the person touch its toes with an excellent animation.

See also

- ▶ *Playing background music*, in *Chapter 1*, *Setting Scenes*
- ▶ *Checking the procedures and functions for each instance*, in *Chapter 1*, *Setting Scenes*
- ▶ *Customizing a person's head*, in this chapter

Animating a person's head

In this recipe, we will make a child shake his head while the other child dances by calling two existing procedures at the same time. We will create an animation that includes complex movements of different parts of two instances concurrently.

Getting ready

We have to be working on a project with two people from the Sims 2 art assets. Therefore, we will use an existing project that has two children. `kevin` and `vanessa` are two instances of the `MyChild` class.

1. Open the project saved in the *Animating a person's body* recipe in this chapter.
2. Click on **Edit Code**, at the lower-right corner of the big scene preview. Alice will show a smaller preview of the scene and will display the **Code Editor** on a panel located at the right-hand side of the main window.
3. Click on the **class: MyScene** drop-down list and the list of classes that are part of the scene will appear.
4. Select **MyScene | Edit run**.

How to do it...

Follow these steps to make one of the children shake her head while the other child dances:

1. Drag the **do together** statement, located at the top, and drop it above the first statement. Alice will display a green line indicating the position in which this new statement will be inserted. The `do together` statement will display a **drop statement here** placeholder.
2. Drag the **do in order** statement, located at the top, and drop it in the **drop statement here** area located within the `do together` block. The `do in order` statement will display a **drop statement here** placeholder.

3. Drag another **do in order** statement, located at the top, and drop it below the previously dropped statement. Make sure that this do in order statement becomes part of the statements for the do together block. This do in order statement will also display a **drop statement here** placeholder.

4. Place the mouse pointer over the light shade at the left-hand side of the statement below the do together placeholder. The mouse pointer will appear as a link select hand.

5. Drag the statement and drop it in the **drop statement here** area located within the first do in order block. The following code will be the statement for the first do in order block:

```
this.kevin.dance(WAVE_ARMS)
```

6. Select vanessa in the instance drop-down list located at the left-hand side of the main window, below the small scene preview.

7. Activate the **Procedures** tab. Alice will display the procedures for the previously selected child.

8. Drag the **delay** procedure and drop it in the **drop statement here** area located below the second do in order block. The delay procedure is the second one from the bottom procedure, above the playAudio procedure. Select 1.0 for the duration parameter.

9. Drag the **shakeHead** procedure and drop it below the previously dropped statement in the second do in order block. The following code will be displayed as the two statements for the second do in order block, as shown in the next screenshot:

```
this.vanessa.delay(1.0)
this.vanessa.shakeHead
```

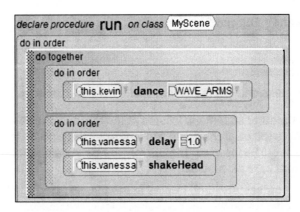

10. Select **File | Save as...** from Alice's main menu and give a new name to the project. Then you can make changes to the project according to your needs.

How it works...

We added a `do together` statement that allowed us to create a block of code that will run all the statements we add to the block at the same time. This means that all the statements added to this block will start their execution together.

We added two `do in order` statements within the `do together` block. Each of this `do in order` blocks will start their execution at the same time. We wanted to run an animation for `kevin` and to control `vanessa`'s head at the same time. Thus, the first `do in order` block has the statements that calls the `dance` procedure for `kevin` and the second `do in order` block includes two statements that control `vanessa`'s behavior.

First, the second `do in order` block calls the `delay` procedure to make `vanessa` wait for one second while `kevin` starts dancing. One second later, the next statement calls the `shakeHead` procedure to make `vanessa` shake her head. `vanessa` doesn't like `kevin`'s dance style, and therefore she starts shaking her head.

The scene shows two children performing actions at the same time, in parallel. This happens because each group of statements is executed in order in two independent blocks that run together. The next image shows four screenshots of the rendered frames:

 The names for the instances must start with lowercase letters. The names for classes must start with uppercase letters. Thus, you will notice that `vanessa` and `kevin` appear with lowercase in the explanations.

See also

▶ *Running statements for many actors*, in *Chapter 3, Organizing Statements*

▶ *Running conditional code*, in *Chapter 4, Working with Functions and Conditions*

▶ *Animating a person's body*, in this chapter

Interaction between characters in the scene

In this task, we will make two children interact. The interaction between two children requires running in parallel two blocks with calls to a different number of procedures. However, we also have to consider the time it takes for each procedure to complete its execution because we want each child to start an action at a certain time, when the other child is in execution or has already completed another action.

Getting ready

We have to be working on a project with two people from The Sims 2 art assets. Therefore, we will use an existing project that has two children. kevin and vanessa are two instances of the MyChild class.

1. Open the project saved in the *Animating a person's body* recipe in this chapter.

2. Click on **Edit Code**, at the lower-right corner of the big scene preview. Alice will show a smaller preview of the scene and will display the **Code Editor** on a panel located at the right-hand side of the main window.

3. Click on the **class: MyScene** drop-down list and the list of classes that are part of the scene will appear.

4. Select **MyScene | Edit run**.

5. Delete all the existing statements. Right-click on each statement or block of statements and select **Delete Statement** in the context menu that appears.

How to do it...

Follow these steps to make the two children perform coordinated actions at the same time:

1. Drag the **do together** statement, located at the top, in the **drop statement here** area located below the **do in order** label, inside the **run** tab. The do together statement will display a **drop statement here** placeholder.

2. Drag the **do in order** statement, located at the top, and drop it in the **drop statement here** area located within the do together block. The do in order statement will display a **drop statement here** placeholder.

3. Drag another **do in order** statement, located at the top, and drop it below the previously dropped statement. Make sure that this `do in order` statement becomes part of the statements for the `do together` block. This `do in order` statement will also display a **drop statement here** placeholder.

4. Select `kevin` in the instance drop-down list located at the left-hand side of the main window, below the small scene preview.

5. Activate the **Procedures** tab. Alice will display the procedures for `kevin`.

6. Drag the **turnToFace** procedure and drop it in the **drop statement here** area located within the first `do in order` block. Select **this.vanessa** as the value for the `target` parameter.

7. Drag the **yellForAttention** procedure and drop it below the previously dropped statement in the first `do in order block`.

8. Drag the **doTheTwist** procedure and drop it below the previously dropped statement in the first `do in order block`.

9. Drag the **jumpExcitedly** procedure and drop it below the previously dropped statement in the first `do in order block`. The following code will be displayed as the four statements for the first `do in order` block:

```
this.kevin.turnToFace(this.vanessa)
this.kevin.yellForAttention
this.kevin.doTheTwist
this.kevin.jumpExcitedly
```

10. Select `vanessa` in the instance drop-down list located at the left-hand side of the main window, below the small scene preview.

11. Activate the **Procedures** tab. Alice will display the procedures for `vanessa`.

12. Drag the **turnToFace** procedure and drop it in the **drop statement here** area located within the second `do in order` block. Select **this.kevin** as the value for the `target` parameter.

13. Drag the **actShocked** procedure and drop it below the previously dropped statement in the first `do in order block`.

14. Drag the **cheer** procedure and drop it below the previously dropped statement in the first `do in order` block. The following code will be displayed as the three statements for the second `do in order` block:

```
this.vanessa.turnToFace(this.kevin)
this.vanessa.actShocked
this.vanessa.cheer
```

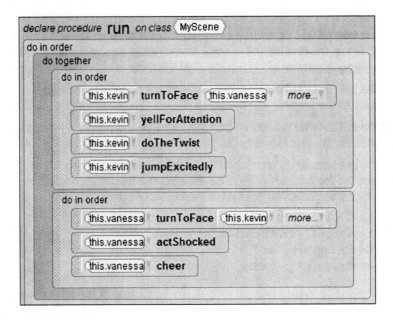

How it works...

We added two `do in order` statements within a `do together` block. Each of this `do in order` blocks will start their execution at the same time. The first `do in order` block has statements that call procedures for `kevin` and the second `do in order` block calls procedures for `vanessa`. This way, both code sequences run at the same time.

The scene shows two children performing actions at the same time, in parallel. Their actions were prepared to show a coordinated interaction between the two actors. For example, when `vanesa` cheers, she motivates `kevin` to jump excitedly. The next image shows four screenshots of the rendered frames:

See also

▸ *Animating a person's body*, in this chapter

Speaking with other people

In this recipe, we will combine speech bubbles with gestures. Two children will have a short conversation. We will make some of the speech bubbles appear while one of the children performs a specific gesture. This way, we will associate a specific gesture with a speech bubble and we will make the animation more realistic than a simple comic strip.

Getting ready

We have to be working on a project with two people from The Sims 2 art assets. Therefore, we will use an existing project that has two children. `kevin` and `vanessa` are two instances of the `MyChild` class.

1. Open the project saved in the *Animating a person's body* recipe in this chapter.

2. Click on **Edit Code**, at the lower-right corner of the big scene preview. Alice will show a smaller preview of the scene and will display the **Code Editor** on a panel located at the right-hand side of the main window.

3. Click on the **class: MyScene** drop-down list and the list of classes that are part of the scene will appear.

4. Select **MyScene | Edit run**.

5. Delete all the existing statements by right-clicking on each statement or block of statements and select **Delete Statement** in the context menu that appears.

How to do it...

Follow these steps to create an animation of a conversation between two children:

1. Drag the **do together** statement, located at the top, in the **drop statement here** area located below the **do in order** label, inside the **run** tab. The do together statement will display a **drop statement here** placeholder.

2. Drag the **do in order** statement, located at the top, and drop it in the **drop statement here** area located within the do together block. The do in order statement will display a **drop statement here** placeholder.

3. Drag another **do in order** statement, located at the top, and drop it below the previously dropped statement. Make sure that this do in order statement becomes part of the statements for the do together block. This do in order statement will also display a **drop statement here** placeholder.

4. Select **kevin** in the instance drop-down list located at the left-hand side of the main window, below the small scene preview.

5. Activate the **Procedures** tab. Alice will display the procedures for kevin.

6. Drag the **turnToFace** procedure and drop it in the **drop statement here** area located within the first do in order block. Select **this.vanessa** as the value for the target parameter. Click on the **more...** drop-down menu button that appears, on duration and then on **0.25** in the cascade menu that appears.

7. Drag the **say** procedure and drop it below the previously dropped statement in the first do in order block. The say procedure is located below addKeyListener and above think. Click **Other String...** and the **Enter Custom String** dialog box will appear. Enter **Hi, Vanessa**! in **Value** and click **OK**.

8. Drag the **do together** statement, located at the top, and drop it below the previously dropped statement in the first do in order block. Alice will display a green line indicating the position in which this new statement will be inserted. The do together statement will display a **drop statement here** placeholder.

9. Drag the **rubChin** procedure and drop it in the **drop statement here** area located within the previously dropped do together block.

10. Drag the **say** procedure and drop it below the previously dropped statement in the `do together` block. Click **Other String...** and the **Enter Custom String** dialog box will appear. Enter **Do you wanna dance?** in **Value** and click **OK**. Click on the **more...** drop-down menu button that appears, on `duration` and then on **2.0** in the cascade menu that appears. The following code will be displayed as the statements for the first `do in order` block:

```
this.kevin.turnToFace(this.vanessa, duration: 0.25)
this.kevin.say("Hi, Vanessa!")
do together
this.kevin.rubChin
this.kevin.say("Do you wanna dance?", duration 2.0)
```

11. Select **vanessa** in the instance drop-down list located at the left-hand side of the main window, below the small scene preview.

12. Activate the **Procedures** tab. Alice will display the procedures for **vanessa**.

13. Drag the **turnToFace** procedure and drop it in the **drop statement here** area located within the second `do in order` block. Select **this.kevin** as the value for the `target` parameter. Click on the **more...** drop-down menu button that appears, on `duration` and then on **1.0** in the cascade menu that appears.

14. Drag the **say** procedure and drop it below the previously dropped statement in the second `do in order` block. Click **Other String...** and the **Enter Custom String** dialog box will appear. Enter **Hi, Kevin!** in **Value** and click **OK**.

15. Drag the **delay** procedure and drop it below the previously dropped statement in the second `do in order` block. Select **1.0** for the duration parameter.

16. Drag the **do together** statement, located at the top, and drop it below the previously dropped statement in the second `do in order` block. Alice will display a green line indicating the position in which this new statement will be inserted. The `do together` statement will display a **drop statement here** placeholder.

17. Drag the **sigh** procedure and drop it in the **drop statement here** area located within the previously dropped `do together` block. Select **HAPPY** for the parameter.

18. Drag the **say** procedure and drop it below the previously dropped statement in the `do together` block. Click **Other String...** and the **Enter Custom String** dialog box will appear. Enter **Yeah!** in **Value** and click **OK**. Click on the **more...** drop-down menu button that appears, on **duration** and then on **2.0** in the cascade menu that appears. The following code will be displayed as the statements for the second `do in order` block, as shown in the next screenshot:

```
this.vanessa.turnToFace(this.kevin, duration: 1.0)
this.vanessa.say("Hi, Kevin!")
this.vanessa.delay(1.0)
do together
```

```
this.vanessa.sigh(HAPPY)
this.vanessa.say("Yeah!", duration 2.0)
```

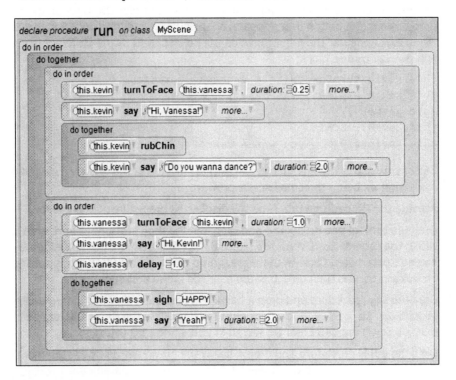

How it works...

We added two do in order statements within a do together block. Each of this do in order blocks will start their execution at the same time. The first do in order block has statements that call procedures for kevin and the second do in order block calls procedures for vanessa. This way, both code sequences run at the same time.

We added a do together block within the first do in order block that is part of the main do together block. We did this to run the rubChin procedure at the same time that kevin asks "Do you wanna dance?". This way, kevin performs a gesture while the speech bubble appears.

We added a do together block within the second do in order block that is part of the main do together block. We did this to run the sigh(HAPPY) procedure at the same time that vanessa says "Yeah!" and accepts kevin's invitation to dance. There is a one second delay before this do together block to make vanessa listen to kevin's question. This way, vanessa performs a happy gesture while her speech bubble appears. The next image shows three screenshots of the rendered frames:

See also

▶ *Animating a person's body*, in this chapter

Interacting with the environment

In this task, we will add a child from the Looking Glass Characters to make him interact with a palm tree and a skateboard. The child will walk to the skateboard. While he walks, he will move his legs and feet. Then the child will look at one of the palm tree's leaves.

Getting ready

We will be working on a project with a character from the Looking Glass Characters gallery. Therefore, we will create a new project and set a simple scene:

1. Select **File | New...** in the main menu to start a new project. A dialog box will display the six predefined templates with their thumbnail previews in the **Templates** tab.

2. Select `SandyProject.a3p` as the desired template for the new project and click **OK**. Alice will display a sandy ground with a light blue sky.

3. Click on **Edit Scene**, at the lower-right corner of the scene preview. Alice will show a bigger preview of the scene and will display the **Model Gallery** at the bottom.

4. Add an instance of the `Trevor` class to the scene, and enter `trevor` for the name of this new instance. You can locate the `Trevor` class in the `kids` package within the `Looking Glass Characters` gallery. First, Alice will create the `MyTrevor` class to extend `Trevor`. Then Alice will create an instance of `MyTrevor` named `trevor`. Follow the steps explained in the *Creating a new instance from a class in a gallery* recipe, in *Chapter 2, Working with Actors*.

5. Add an instance of the `TrevorsSkateBoard` class, and enter `trevorsSkateBoard` for the name of this new instance.

6. Add an instance of the `Palmtree` class, and enter `palmtree` for the name of this new instance.

7. Place the skate board and the palm tree at the right-hand side of `trevor`.

How to do it...

Follow these steps to make the child walk to the skateboard and then look at one of the palm tree's leaves:

1. Click on **Edit Code**, at the lower-right corner of the big scene preview. Alice will show a smaller preview of the scene and will display the **Code Editor** on a panel located at the right-hand side of the main window.

2. Click on the **class: MyScene** drop-down list and the list of classes that are part of the scene will appear.

3. Select **MyScene | Edit run**.

4. Select `trevor` in the instance drop-down list located at the left-hand side of the main window, below the small scene preview.

5. Activate the **Procedures** tab. Alice will display the procedures for the previously selected child.

6. Drag the **walkTo** procedure and drop it in the **drop statement here** area located below the **do in order** label, inside the **run** tab. Select **this.trevorsSkateboard** as the target. Click on the **more...** drop-down menu button that appears, on `spatialRelation` and then on `IN_FRONT_OF` in the cascade menu that appears.

7. Drag the **sitOn** procedure and drop it below the previously dropped statement. Select **this.trevorsSkateboard** as the target.

8. Drag the **lookAt** procedure and drop it below the previously dropped statement. A list with all the possible instances to pass to the `target` parameter will appear. Select **this. palmtree.getPart ???** and then **Leave04**. The following code will be displayed, as shown in the next screenshot:

```
this.trevor.walkTo(this.trevorsSkateboard, spatialRelation: IN_
FRONT_OF)
this.trevor.sitOn(this.trevorsSkateboard)
this.trevor.lookAt(this.palmtree.getPart(Leave04))
```

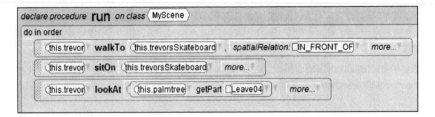

How it works...

The `Trevor` class is part of the `Looking Glass Characters` gallery. This gallery provides classes with specific procedures that make it simple to perform complex animations and to interact with other actors. For example, the `walkTo` procedure allows you to make `trevor` walk to a target. When `trevor` walks, he moves his feet, and therefore he performs a real-life walking animation. The `moveTo` procedure moves the actor but it doesn't perform additional animations while the actor changes its position. The `walkTo` procedure makes it simple to make the actor walk while it moves to a target. Unfortunately, this procedure isn't available for the Sims 2 art assets included in Alice 3.

`trevor` walks to his skateboard (`this.trevorsSkateboard`), sits on it (`this.trevorsSkateboard`) and then looks at one of the palm tree's leaves (`this.palmtree.getPart(Leave04)`). `trevor` shows realistic movements for each action, as shown in the following four screenshots of the rendered frames.

There's more...

The different classes included in the `Looking Glass Characters` gallery provide many procedures that perform complex animations. For example, the `Trevor` class provides the `touch` procedure that makes the actor touch a target with one of its hands or one of his feet.

See also

- ▶ *Browsing galleries*, in *Chapter 2, Working with Actors*
- ▶ *Moving an actor with relative positions*, in *Chapter 2, Working with Actors*

8
Working with Keyboard and Mouse Input

In this chapter, we will cover:

- ▶ Defining a mouse button listener
- ▶ Reacting to mouse events
- ▶ Controlling an actor with the mouse
- ▶ Defining a key listener
- ▶ Reacting to keyboard events
- ▶ Controlling an actor with keystrokes
- ▶ Controlling the camera with the keyboard
- ▶ Controlling multiple actors with keystrokes

Introduction

Alice 3 allows you to read inputs from both the keyboard and the mouse. When you want the user to interact with a scene or you have to develop a game, it is very important to react to keyboard and mouse events. This chapter provides many tasks that will allow us to control actors and the camera view with the keyboard and the mouse.

We will define mouse and keyboard listeners and we will learn to program code in response to certain events. We will combine properties and conditional code to make sure that the user performs one action at a time with the keystrokes. We will allow the user to drag and drop actors to new locations in the scene. In addition, we will control the camera with the keyboard to provide dozens of exciting points of view for our scenes.

Defining a mouse button listener

In this recipe, we will make two robots dance when the user clicks on the scene. We will define a mouse button listener and we will add the necessary code to make two robots dance when the user clicks on the scene.

Getting ready

We have to be working on a project with two characters from the Looking Glass Characters gallery. Therefore, we will create a new project and set a simple scene:

1. Select **File | New...** in the main menu to start a new project. A dialog box will display the six predefined templates with their thumbnail previews in the **Templates** tab.

2. Select `SnowyProject.a3p` as the desired template for the new project and click **OK**. Alice will display a snowy ground with a light blue sky.

3. Click on **Edit Scene**, at the lower-right corner of the scene preview. Alice will show a bigger preview of the scene and will display the **Model Gallery** at the bottom.

4. Add an instance of the `Biff` class to the scene, and enter `biff` for the name of this new instance. First, Alice will create the `MyBiff` class to extend `Biff`. Then Alice will create an instance of `MyBiff` named `biff`. Follow the steps explained in the *Creating a new instance from a class in a gallery* recipe, in *Chapter 2, Working with Actors*.

5. Add an instance of the `Gina` class and enter `gina` for the name of this new instance. `gina` is the default name proposed by Alice.

6. Place `gina` at the right-hand side of biff, as shown in the following screenshot:

How to do it...

Follow these steps to run the code that makes `biff` and `gina` dance when the user clicks on the scene:

1. Click on **Edit Code**, at the lower-right corner of the big scene preview. Alice will show a smaller preview of the scene and will display the **Code Editor** on a panel located at the right-hand side of the main window.

2. Click on the **class: MyScene** drop-down list and the list of classes that are part of the scene will appear.

3. Select **MyScene | Declare property**. The **Declare Property** dialog box will appear.

4. Click on the **Value type** drop-down list and select **Boolean**.

5. Enter `Dancing` in **Name**.

6. Click on the **Initializer** drop-down list and select `false` as the initial value for the `Dancing` property. Click **OK** and Alice will add the `Dancing` property to the `MyScene` class.

7. Click on the **class: MyScene** drop-down list and the list of classes that are part of the scene will appear.

8. Select **MyScene | Declare procedure**. Enter `dance` in **Name** and click **OK**. The code editor will add a new tab with the name of the new procedure, **dance**.

9. Select `biff` in the instance drop-down list located at the left-hand side of the main window, below the small scene preview. Make sure that `part: none` is selected in the drop-down list located at the right-hand side of the chosen instance.

10. Activate the **Procedures** tab. Alice will display the procedures for `biff`.

11. Drag the **Flex** procedure and drop it on the **drop statement here** area located below the **do in order** label, inside the **dance** tab.

12. Select `gina` in the instance drop-down list located at the left-hand side of the main window, below the small scene preview. Make sure that `part: none` is selected in the drop-down list located at the right-hand side of the chosen instance.

13. Drag the **FlirtWith** procedure and drop it below the previously dropped statement. Select `this.biff` as the value for the `who` parameter.

14. Drag the **do together** statement, located at the top, and drop below the previously dropped statement. The `do together` statement will display a **drop statement here** placeholder.

15. Select `biff` in the instance drop-down list located at the left-hand side of the main window.

16. Drag the **MoonWalk** procedure and drop it on the **drop statement here** area located within the `do together` block.

17. Select `gina` in the instance drop-down list located at the left-hand side of the main window.

18. Drag the **Dance** procedure and drop it below the previously dropped statement, within the `do together` block. Select `1.0` as the value for the `length` parameter. The following code will be displayed for the `dance` procedure, as shown in the following screenshot:

Some models from the Looking Glass Characters gallery provide procedures that don't follow the naming convention for procedures. For example, the `MoonWalk` procedure starts with an uppercase letter.

19. Click on the **class: MyScene** drop-down list and the list of classes that are part of the scene will appear.

20. Select **MyScene | Edit run**.

21. Select `scene (this)` in the instance drop-down list located at the left-hand side of the main window, behind the small scene preview.

22. Click on the **Procedures** tab on the panel located behind the aforementioned drop-down list. Alice will display all the available procedures for `scene`.

23. Drag the **addMouseButtonListener** procedure and drop it on the **drop statement here** area located below the **do in order** label, inside the **run** tab. The `addMouseButtonListener` procedure will add a `mouseButtonClicked` procedure declaration with a **drop statement here** placeholder, as shown in the following screenshot:

24. Drag the **if _** statement, located at the top, and drop it on the **drop statement here** placeholder within the `mouseButtonClicked` procedure. Click on **this.Dancing** and two **drop statement here** placeholders will appear.

25. Now click on the last down arrow that appears with a gray background at the right-hand side of the previously defined expression for the `if` block, before **is true then**. A drop-down menu will display different options to use to replace the current expression.

26. Select the fifth option that adds a `NOT` operator to the existing expression. The following code will be displayed as the new statement that defines the conditional `if` block:

```
if NOT(this.Dancing) is true then
```

27. Activate the **Properties** tab. Alice will display the properties for `scene`.

28. Drag the **Dancing** assignment statement and drop it on the first **drop statement here** area located within the `if` block. The **Dancing** assignment statement contains the **this.scene** and **Dancing** labels followed by an arrow and three question marks **???**. Select `true`, the desired `Boolean` to assign to the `scene.Dancing` property.

29. Activate the **Procedures** tab. Alice will display the procedures for `scene`.

30. Drag the **dance** procedure and drop it below the previously dropped statement, within the `if` block and above the `else` keyword.

31. Activate the **Properties** tab. Alice will display the properties for `scene`.

32. Drag the **Dancing** assignment statement and drop it below the previously dropped statement, within the `if` block and above the `else` keyword. Select `false`, the desired `Boolean` to assign to the `scene.Dancing` property. The following statements will appear after the `if` declaration, before the `else` keyword:

```
this.Dancing ← true
this.dance
this.Dancing ← false
```

The next screenshot shows the code for the run procedure:

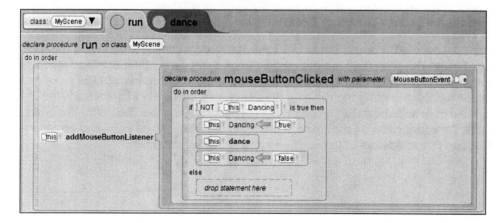

33. Select **File | Save as...** from Alice's main menu and give a new name to the project. Then you can make changes to the project according to your needs.

How it works...

When we run the project, `biff` and `gina` appear in the scene. If we click on the scene, the code written for the `mouseButtonClicked` procedure runs. `biff` and `gina` perform many movements and then they start dancing with their own styles. The following images shows one of the rendered frames when `biff` and `gina` are dancing as a result of a click on the scene:

The `run` procedure calls the `addMouseButtonListener` procedure for `scene`. The `addMouseButtonListener` procedure declares a `mouseButtonClicked` procedure that will run its code when the user clicks on the scene. Each time the user clicks on the scene, the code in this `mouseButtonClicked` procedure runs. Thus, it is necessary to check whether the code for this procedure is already running before starting the whole dance again. If the user clicks on the scene while `biff` and `gina` are dancing, we don't want to run the code again to make them start a new dance. We want them to finish their dance. If the user clicks on the scene after `biff` and `gina` finished their dance, the code in the `mouseButtonClicked` procedure must run again.

Because the code in the `mouseButtonClicked` procedure cannot access local variables declared in the `run` procedure, we declared a `Dancing` property of the `Boolean` type for `scene`. When a click fires the execution of the code in the `mouseButtonClicked` procedure, an `if` block checks whether the value for the `Dancing` property is `false`. If the value is `false`, the code sets the `Dancing` property to `true`, indicating that the dance has begun. This way, if the user clicks on the scene at this time, `Dancing` will be `true` and no code will be executed by this new call to the `mouseButtonClicked` procedure.

The first call to the `mouseButtonClicked` procedure calls the `dance` procedure that makes both `biff` and `gina` move their bodies. Then when the dance procedure has finished its execution, the code sets the `Dancing` property to `false`. This way, if the user clicks on the scene at this time, `Dancing` will be `false` and the `mouseButtonClicked` procedure will run the code to make both `biff` and `gina` move their bodies.

 We used the `Dancing` property as a **flag**. This `Boolean` flag allowed us to make sure that only one `mouseButtonClicked` procedure is going to be fired at a time.

Reacting to mouse events

In this task, we will allow the user to move the actors and the camera with the mouse. We will call a procedure that adds a default model manipulation to all our actors in the scene.

Getting ready

We will use an existing project that has two characters from the Looking Glass Characters gallery.

1. Open the project saved in the *Defining a mouse button listener* recipe.
2. Click on **Edit Code**, at the lower-right corner of the big scene preview. Alice will show a smaller preview of the scene and will display the **Code Editor** on a panel located at the right-hand side of the main window.
3. Click on the **class: MyScene** drop-down list and the list of classes that are part of the scene will appear.
4. Select **MyScene | Edit run**.

How to do it...

Follow these steps to allow the user to manipulate the actors and the camera with the mouse:

1. Select `scene (this)` in the instance drop-down list located at the left-hand side of the main window, below the small scene preview.
2. Activate the **Procedures** tab. Alice will display the procedures for `scene`.

3. Drag the **addDefaultModelManipulation** procedure and drop it as the first statement, above the call to the `addMouseButtonListener` procedure, inside the **run** tab. The following code will be displayed as a new statement, as shown in the following screenshot:

```
This.addDefaultModelManipulation
```

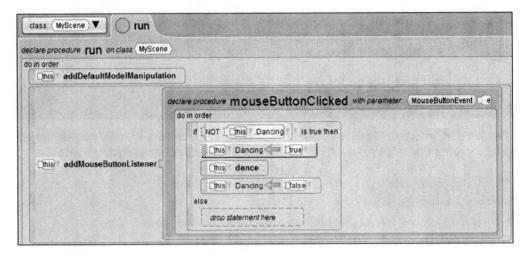

4. Select **File | Save as...** from Alice's main menu and give a new name to the project. Then you can make changes to the project according to your needs.

How it works...

When we run the project, the `addDefaultModelManipulation` procedure for `scene` assigns events that get fired when the user performs the following actions with the mouse:

▶ Drag an instance: Move the instance to a new location

▶ Double click on an instance: Point the camera to the instance

We can follow these steps to change `biff`'s location when the project is running:

1. Place the mouse pointer over `biff`.

2. Press the mouse button and drag biff to the desired position in the rendered frame.

3. Place the actor in the desired position and release the mouse button. The following image shows biff in a new location. It is possible to move biff while he and gina are dancing.

If we double-click on gina, the camera will point at her, as shown in the next screenshot:

There's more...

The Scene class provides the removeDefaultModelManipulation procedure. This procedure allows you to remove the events that get fired when the user performs the actions supported by the addDefaultModelManipulation procedure.

MyScene is a subclass of Scene, and therefore, MyScene inherits the removeDefaultModelManipulation procedure from Scene. Because scene is an instance of MyScene, we can call the removeDefaultModelManipulation procedure when we want to remove the possibility to move instances and change the location of the camera with the mouse.

See also

▶ *Defining a mouse button listener*, in this chapter

Controlling an actor with the mouse

In this recipe, we will make the robots dance when the user clicks on them. The user has to place the mouse pointer over the 3D model that represents the robot and click to make it dance. We will add code that Alice will execute when each robot gets clicked.

Getting ready

We will use an existing project that has two characters from the Looking Glass Characters gallery.

1. Open the project saved in the *Reacting to mouse events* recipe.
2. Click on **Edit Code**, at the lower-right corner of the big scene preview. Alice will show a smaller preview of the scene and will display the **Code Editor** on a panel located at the right-hand side of the main window.
3. Click on the **class: MyScene** drop-down list and the list of classes that are part of the scene will appear.
4. Select **MyScene | Edit run**.
5. Delete all the existing statements in the run procedure for the MyScene class.

How to do it...

Follow these steps to allow the user to make each actor dance with a click on its rendered model:

1. Select biff in the instance drop-down list located at the left-hand side of the main window, below the small scene preview.
2. Click on the **class: MyScene** drop-down list and the list of classes that are part of the scene will appear.
3. Select **MyBiff | Declare property**. The **Declare Property** dialog box will appear.
4. Click on the **Value type** drop-down list and select **Boolean**.
5. Enter DancingAlone in **Name**.
6. Click on the **Initializer** drop-down list and select false as the initial value for the DancingAlone property. Click **OK** and Alice will add the DancingAlone property to the MyBiff class.
7. Click on the **class: MyScene** drop-down list and the list of classes that are part of the scene will appear.
8. Select **MyBiff | Declare procedure**. Enter danceAlone in **Name** and click **OK**. The code editor will add a new tab with the name of the new procedure, **danceAlone**.

9. Drag the **if _** statement, located at the top, and drop it on the **drop statement here** placeholder within the `danceAlone` tab. Click on **this.DancingAlone** and two **drop statement here** placeholders will appear.

10. Now click on the last down arrow that appears with a gray background at the right-hand side of the previously defined expression for the `if` block, before **is true then**. A drop-down menu will display different options to use to replace the current expression.

11. Select the fifth option that adds a `NOT` operator to the existing expression. The following code will be displayed as the new statement that defines the conditional `if` block:

    ```
    if NOT(this.DancingAlone) is true then
    ```

12. Activate the **Properties** tab. Alice will display the properties for `biff`.

13. Drag the **DancingAlone** assignment statement and drop it on the first **drop statement here** area located within the `if` block. The **DancingAlone** assignment statement contains the **this.hawk** and **Step** labels followed by an arrow and three question marks **???**. Select `true` as the desired `Boolean` to assign to the `DancingAlone` property.

14. Activate the **Procedures** tab. Alice will display the procedures for `biff`.

15. Drag the **MoonWalk** procedure and drop it below the previously dropped statement, within the `if` block and above the `else` keyword.

16. Activate the **Properties** tab. Alice will display the properties for `biff`.

17. Drag the **DancingAlone** assignment statement and drop it below the previously dropped statement, within the `if` block and above the `else` keyword. Select `false`, the desired `Boolean` to assign to the `DancingAlone` property.

    The next screenshot shows the code for the `danceAlone` procedure:

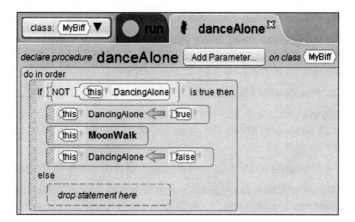

18. Select `gina` in the instance drop-down list located at the left-hand side of the main window, below the small scene preview.

19. Click on the **class: MyScene** drop-down list and the list of classes that are part of the scene will appear.

20. Select **MyGina | Declare property**. The **Declare Property** dialog box will appear.

21. Click on the **Value type** drop-down list and select **Boolean**.

22. Enter `DancingAlone` in **Name**.

23. Click on the **Initializer** drop-down list and select `false` as the initial value for the `DancingAlone` property. Click **OK** and Alice will add the `DancingAlone` property to the `MyGina` class.

24. Click on the **class: MyScene** drop-down list and the list of classes that are part of the scene will appear.

25. Select **MyGina | Declare procedure**. Enter `danceAlone` in **Name** and click **OK**. The code editor will add a new tab with the name of the new procedure, **danceAlone**.

26. Drag the **if _** statement, located at the top, and drop it on the **drop statement here** placeholder within the `danceAlone` tab. Click on **this.DancingAlone** and two **drop statement here** placeholders will appear.

27. Now click on the last down arrow that appears with a gray background at the right-hand side of the previously defined expression for the `if` block, before **is true then**. A drop-down menu will display different options to use to replace the current expression.

28. Select the fifth option that adds a `NOT` operator to the existing expression. The following code will be displayed as the new statement that defines the conditional `if` block:

```
if NOT(this.DancingAlone) is true then
```

29. Activate the **Properties** tab. Alice will display the properties for `gina`.

30. Drag the **DancingAlone** assignment statement and drop it on the first **drop statement here** area located within the `if` block. Select `true`, the desired `Boolean` to assign to the `DancingAlone` property.

31. Activate the **Procedures** tab. Alice will display the procedures for `gina`.

32. Drag the **Dance** procedure and drop it below the previously dropped statement, within the `if` block and above the `else` keyword. Select `1.0` as the value for the `length` parameter.

33. Activate the **Properties** tab. Alice will display the properties for `gina`.

34. Drag the **DancingAlone** assignment statement and drop it below the previously dropped statement, within the `if` block and above the `else` keyword. Select `false`, the desired `Boolean` to assign to the `DancingAlone` property.

The next screenshot shows the code for the `danceAlone` procedure:

35. Click on the **class: MyScene** drop-down list and the list of classes that are part of the scene will appear.

36. Select **MyScene | Edit run**.

37. Select `biff` in the instance drop-down list located at the left-hand side of the main window, behind the small scene preview.

38. Click on the **Procedures** tab on the panel located behind the aforementioned drop-down list. Alice will display all the available procedures for `biff`.

39. Drag the **addMouseButtonListener** procedure and drop it on the **drop statement here** area located below the **do in order** label, inside the **run** tab. The `addMouseButtonListener` procedure will add a `mouseButtonClicked` procedure declaration with a **drop statement here** placeholder.

40. Drag the **danceAlone** procedure and drop it on the **drop statement here** placeholder within the `mouseButtonClicked` procedure.

41. Now select `gina` in the instance drop-down list located at the left-hand side of the main window, behind the small scene preview.

42. Activate the **Procedures** tab. Alice will display the procedures for `gina`.

43. Drag the **addMouseButtonListener** procedure and drop it below the existing `addMouseButtonListener` call, inside the **run** tab. The `addMouseButtonListener` procedure will add a `mouseButtonClicked` procedure declaration with a **drop statement here** placeholder.

44. Drag the **danceAlone** procedure and drop it on the **drop statement here** placeholder within the `mouseButtonClicked` procedure. The following screenshot shows the code for the `run` procedure:

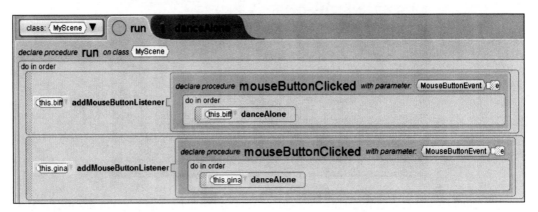

45. Select **File | Save as...** from Alice's main menu and give a new name to the project. Then you can make changes to the project according to your needs.

How it works...

When we run the project, `biff` and `gina` appear in the scene. If we click on `biff`, the code written for his `mouseButtonClicked` procedure runs and he starts his moonwalk dance. If we click on `gina`, the code written for her `mouseButtonClicked` procedure runs and she starts her dance. If we click on `biff` and then on `gina`, they will dance at the same time because both `mouseButtonClicked` procedures will run concurrently.

We declared the `DancingAlone` property to use it as a `Boolean` flag for the instances of both the `MyBiff` and the `MyGina` classes. The `run` procedure calls the `addMouseButtonListener` procedure for `biff` and then for `gina`. Each call to the `addMouseButtonListener` procedure declares a `mouseButtonClicked` procedure that will run its code when the user clicks on the instance that is calling the `addMouseButtonListener` procedure. Each time the user clicks on the actor, the code in its `mouseButtonClicked` procedure runs. Thus, it is necessary to check whether the code for this procedure is already running before starting the actor's dance again. If the user clicks on `biff` while he is dancing, we don't want to run the code again to make him start a new dance. We want him to finish his dance. If the user clicks after `biff` finished his dance, the code in `biff`'s `mouseButtonClicked` procedure must run again. The same happens with `gina`.

Because the code called by the `mouseButtonClicked` procedure cannot access local variables declared in the `run` procedure, we declared a `DancingAlone` property of the `Boolean` type for both the `MyBiff` and `MyGina` classes. When a click fires the execution of the code in the `mouseButtonClicked` procedure, the `danceAlone` procedure uses an `if` block to check whether the value for the `DancingAlone` property is `false`. If the value is `false`, the code in `danceAlone` sets the `DancingAlone` property to `true` for the instance, indicating that the dance has begun. This way, if the user clicks on the same actor at this time, `DancingAlone` will be `true` and no code will be executed by this new call to the `danceAlone` procedure.

Before the `danceAlone` procedure has finished its execution, the code sets the `DancingAlone` property to `false`. This way, if the user clicks on the actor at this time, `DancingAlone` will be `false` and the `danceAlone` procedure will run the code to make the actor move its body.

See also

▶ *Reacting to mouse events*, in this chapter

Defining a key listener

In this recipe, we will make the robots dance when the user presses certain keys. The user has to press a specific key to make each robot dance. We will add code that Alice will execute when certain keys get pressed.

Getting ready

We will use an existing project that has two characters from the Looking Glass Characters gallery, `biff` and `gina`. This project has a `danceAlone` procedure defined for the `MyBiff` and the `MyGina` classes.

1. Open the project saved in the *Controlling an actor with the mouse* recipe.

2. Click on **Edit Code**, at the lower-right corner of the big scene preview. Alice will show a smaller preview of the scene and will display the **Code Editor** on a panel located at the right-hand side of the main window.

3. Click on the **class: MyScene** drop-down list and the list of classes that are part of the scene will appear.

4. Select **MyScene | Edit run**.

How to do it...

Follow these steps to allow the user to make each actor dance by pressing certain keys:

1. Select `biff` in the instance drop-down list located at the left-hand side of the main window, below the small scene preview.

2. Activate the **Procedures** tab. Alice will display the procedures for `biff`.

3. Drag the **addKeyListener** procedure and drop it as the last statement, below the last `addMouseButtonListener` call, inside the **run** tab. The `addKeyListener` procedure will add a `keyPressed` procedure declaration with a **drop statement here** placeholder, as shown in the next screenshot:

4. Drag the **if _** statement, located at the top, and drop it on the **drop statement here** placeholder within the `keyPressed` procedure. Click on **true** and two **drop statement here** placeholders will appear.

5. Now click on the last down arrow that appears with a gray background at the right-hand side of the previously defined expression for the `if` block, before **is true then**. A drop-down menu will display different options to use to replace the current expression.

6. Select **e.IsKey ???** | **letters (A-M)** | **B** in the cascade menus that appear. The following code will be displayed as the new statement that defines the conditional `if` block:

   ```
   if (e.IsKey(B)) is true then
   ```

7. Drag the **danceAlone** procedure and drop it on the first **drop statement here** area located within the `if` block.

8. Now select `gina` in the instance drop-down list located at the left-hand side of the main window, below the small scene preview.

9. Activate the **Procedures** tab. Alice will display the procedures for `gina`.

10. Drag the **addKeyListener** procedure and drop it as the last statement, below the previously added `addKeyListener` call, inside the **run** tab. The `addKeyListener` procedure will add a `keyPressed` procedure declaration with a **drop statement here** placeholder.

11. Drag the **if _** statement, located at the top, and drop it on the **drop statement here** placeholder within the `keyPressed` procedure for `gina`. Click on **true** and two **drop statement here** placeholders will appear.

12. Now click on the last down arrow that appears with a gray background at the right-hand side of the previously defined expression for the `if` block, before **is true then**. A drop-down menu will display different options to use to replace the current expression.

13. Select **e.IsKey ??? | letters (A-M) | G** in the cascade menus that appear. The following code will be displayed as the new statement that defines the conditional `if` block:

    ```
    if (e.IsKey(G)) is true then
    ```

14. Drag the **danceAlone** procedure and drop it on the first **drop statement here** area located within the `if` block. The following screenshot shows the two `addKeyListener` calls added to the `run` procedure:

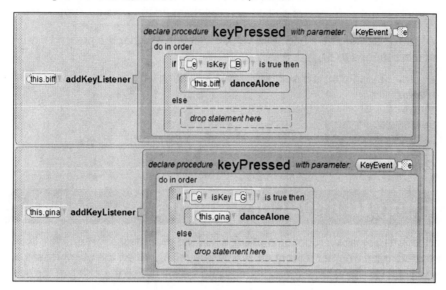

15. Select **File | Save as...** from Alice's main menu and give a new name to the project. Then you can make changes to the project according to your needs.

How it works...

When we run the project, `biff` and `gina` appear in the scene. If we press **B**, `biff` starts his moonwalk dance. If we press **G**, `gina` dances.

When we press any key, Alice executes the two `keyPressed` procedures because we added these procedures as key listeners for `biff` and `gina`. These procedures receive the `e` parameter of the `KeyEvent` type. This parameter contains the key that was pressed by the user. The `e.isKey` function receives a key value as a parameter and returns a `Boolean` value indicating whether the user pressed this key.

The `keyPressed` procedure for `biff` uses an `if` block to determine whether the pressed key was *B*. If `e.isKey(B)` returns `true`, the procedure calls the `danceAlone` procedure for `biff`.

The `keyPressed` procedure for `gina` uses an `if` block to determine whether the pressed key was *G*. If `e.isKey(G)` returns `true`, the procedure calls the `danceAlone` procedure for `gina`.

There's more...

The `KeyEvent` class provides two additional functions that are useful when we need to evaluate the key pressed by the user in a `keyPressed` procedure. The following two functions don't receive parameters and we can call them for the e parameter:

> ► `e.isDigit`: Returns a `Boolean` value indicating whether the pressed key is a number (from 0 to 9)

> ► `e.isLetter`: Returns a `Boolean` value indicating whether the pressed key is a letter

See also

> ► *Controlling an actor with the mouse*, in this chapter

Reacting to keyboard events

In this recipe, we will make a robot stop rolling when the user presses a key. We will use a property to determine whether a robot must continue rolling. When the user presses a specific key, Alice will change the value for this property and we will notice the effect in the scene.

Getting ready

We will use an existing project that has an instance of `gina` as one of two characters from the Looking Glass Characters gallery.

1. Open the project saved in the *Defining a key listener* recipe.
2. Click on **Edit Code**, at the lower-right corner of the big scene preview. Alice will show a smaller preview of the scene and will display the **Code Editor** on a panel located at the right-hand side of the main window.
3. Click on the **class: MyScene** drop-down list and the list of classes that are part of the scene will appear.
4. Select **MyScene | Edit run**.
5. Delete all the existing statements in the `run` procedure for the `MyScene` class.

How to do it...

Follow these steps to allow the user to press a key to stop `gina`'s dance:

1. Select `gina` in the instance drop-down list located at the left-hand side of the main window, below the small scene preview.

2. Click on the **class: MyScene** drop-down list and the list of classes that are part of the scene will appear.

3. Select **MyGina | Declare property**. The **Declare Property** dialog box will appear.

4. Click on the **Value type** drop-down list and select **Boolean**.

5. Enter `StopRolling` in **Name**.

6. Click on the **Initializer** drop-down list and select `false` as the initial value for the `StopRolling` property. Click **OK** and Alice will add the `StopRolling` property to the `MyGina` class.

7. Activate the **Procedures** tab. Alice will display the procedures for `gina`.

8. Drag the **turn** procedure and drop it on the **drop statement here** area located below the **do in order** label, inside the **run** tab. Select `LEFT` for the first parameter and then click on `0.5`. Click on the **more...** drop-down menu button that appears, on `duration` and then on `1.0` in the cascade menu that appears. The following code will appear as a new statement:

   ```
   this.gina.turn(LEFT, 0.5, duration: 1.0)
   ```

9. Drag the **addKeyListener** procedure and drop it as the last statement, below the previously dropped `turn` call, inside the **run** tab. The `addKeyListener` procedure will add a `keyPressed` procedure declaration with a **drop statement here** placeholder.

10. Drag the **if _** statement, located at the top, and drop it on the **drop statement here** placeholder within the `keyPressed` procedure. Click on **true** and two **drop statement here** placeholders will appear.

11. Now click on the last down arrow that appears with a gray background at the right-hand side of the previously defined expression for the `if` block, before **is true then**. A drop-down menu will display different options to use to replace the current expression.

12. Select **e.IsKey ??? | letters (N-Z) | S** in the cascade menus that appear. The following code will be displayed as the new statement that defines the conditional `if` block:

    ```
    if (e.IsKey(S)) is true then
    ```

13. Activate the **Properties** tab. Alice will display the properties for `gina`.

14. Drag the **StopRolling** assignment statement and drop it on the first **drop statement here** area located within the if block. Select true, the desired Boolean to assign to the StopRolling property.

15. Drag the **while _** statement, located at the top, and drop it as the last statement, below the addKeyListener call, inside the **run** tab. Click on **true** and a **drop statement here** placeholder will appear within the while true is true block.

16. Drag the **StopRolling** property and drop it on the first **true** expression that appears in the statement that defines the while true is true block. A black rectangle will surround the true value when you start dragging the **StopRolling** property. The **StopRolling** property contains the **this.gina** and **StopRolling** labels with a yellow background.

17. Click on the down arrow that appears with a gray background at the right-hand side of **this.gina.StopRolling**, before **is true**. A drop-down menu will display different options to use to replace the current expression. Select the fifth option that adds a NOT operator to the existing expression. The following code will be displayed as the statement that defines the definitive while block:

    ```
    While NOT(this.gina.StopRolling) is true
    ```

18. Activate the **Procedures** tab. Alice will display the procedures for gina.

19. Drag the **RollForward** procedure and drop it on the **drop statement here** area located within the **while** block. Select 0.25 as the value for the distance parameter. The following screenshot shows the code for the run procedure:

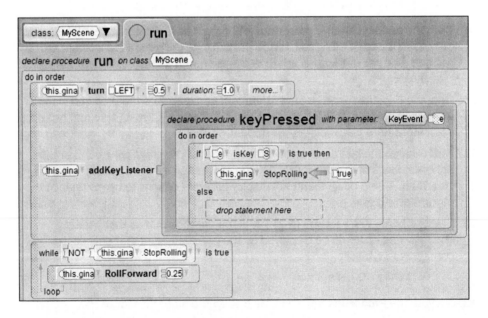

20. Select **File | Save as...** from Alice's main menu and give a new name to the project. Then you can make changes to the project according to your needs.

How it works...

When we run the project, `gina` turns to the left and starts rolling towards the horizon. `gina` keeps rolling while the value of her `StopRolling` property is `true`.

When we press any key, Alice executes the `keyPressed` procedure because we added this procedure as a key listener for `gina`. This procedure uses an `if` block to determine whether the pressed key was *S*. If `e.isKey(S)` returns `true`, the procedure changes the value of the `gina.StopRolling` property to `true`. Thus, the expression defined in the `while` loop in the `run` procedure evaluates to `false`, this loop stops running and `gina` keeps quiet on the scene. The following image shows the rendered frame when `gina` stops rolling after we pressed the *S* key:

We could stop the execution of a `while` loop by changing the value of a property in the `keyPressed` procedure fired by a key listener.

See also

▶ *Defining a key listener*, in this chapter

Controlling an actor with keystrokes

In this task, we will use the arrow keys to control a robot's movement. We will add code associated with each of the four arrow keys. We will use a property to avoid the robot to perform two movements at the same time.

Getting ready

We will use an existing project that has an instance of `gina` as one of two characters from the Looking Glass Characters gallery.

1. Open the project saved in the *Reacting to keyboard events* recipe.

2. Click on **Edit Code**, at the lower-right corner of the big scene preview. Alice will show a smaller preview of the scene and will display the **Code Editor** on a panel located at the right-hand side of the main window.

3. Click on the **class: MyScene** drop-down list and the list of classes that are part of the scene will appear.

4. Select **MyScene | Edit run**.

5. Delete all the existing statements in the `run` procedure for the `MyScene` class.

How to do it...

Follow these steps to allow the user to control `biff`'s movements with the arrow keys:

1. Click on the **class: MyScene** drop-down list and the list of classes that are part of the scene will appear.

2. Select **MyBiff | Declare property**. The **Declare Property** dialog box will appear.

3. Click on the **Value type** drop-down list and select **RealNumber**.

4. Enter `Step` in **Name**.

5. Click on the **Initializer** drop-down list and select **0.25** as the initial value for the `Step` property. Click **OK** and Alice will add the `Step` property to the `MyBiff` class.

6. Click on the **class: MyBiff** drop-down list. Then select **MyBiff | Declare property**. The **Declare Property** dialog box will appear.

7. Click on the **Value type** drop-down list and select **Boolean**.

8. Enter `Moving` in **Name**.

9. Click on the **Initializer** drop-down list and select **false** as the initial value for the `Moving` property. Click **OK** and Alice will add the `Moving` property to the `MyBiff` class.

10. Click on the **class: MyBiff** drop-down list. Then select **MyBiff | Declare procedure**. Enter `moveStep` in **Name** and click **OK**. The code editor will add a new tab with the name of the new procedure, **moveStep**.

11. Click on the **Add Parameter...** button and the **Declare Parameter** dialog box will appear.

12. Click on the **type** drop-down list and a drop-down menu will appear. Select **Other Types | MoveDirection**.

13. Enter `direction` in name and click **OK**. The parameter will appear in the procedure declaration located at the top, below the **moveStep** tab.

14. Select `biff (this)` in the instance drop-down list located at the left-hand side of the main window, below the small scene preview. Make sure that `part: none` is selected in the drop-down list located at the right-hand side of the chosen instance.

15. Drag the **if _** statement, located at the top, and drop it on the **drop statement here** placeholder within the `moveStep` tab. Click on **this.Moving** and two **drop statement here** placeholders will appear.

16. Click on the last down arrow that appears with a gray background at the right-hand side of the previously defined expression for the `if` block, before **is true then**. A drop-down menu will display different options to use to replace the current expression.

17. Select the fifth option that adds a `NOT` operator to the existing expression. The following code will be displayed as the new statement that defines the conditional `if` block:

```
if NOT(this.Moving) is true then
```

18. Activate the **Properties** tab. Alice will display the properties for `biff`.

19. Drag the **Moving** assignment statement and drop it on the first **drop statement here** area located within the `if` block. Select `true`, the desired `Boolean` to assign to the `Moving` property.

20. Activate the **Procedures** tab. Alice will display the procedures for `biff`.

21. Drag the **move** procedure and drop it below the previously dropped statement, within the `if` block and above the `else` keyword. Click on `direction` and then on `this.Step` in the cascade menus that appear. Click on the **more...** drop-down menu button, on `duration` and then on `0.25`. Click on the additional **more...** drop-down menu that appears, on `asSeenBy` and then on `this`.

22. Activate the **Properties** tab. Alice will display the properties for `biff`.

23. Drag the **Moving** assignment statement and drop it below the previously dropped statement, within the `if` block and above the `else` keyword. Select `false`, the desired `Boolean` to assign to the `Moving` property.

The next screenshot shows the code for the `moveStep` procedure:

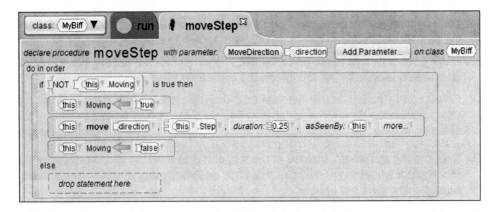

24. Click on the **class: MyBiff** drop-down list and the list of classes that are part of the scene will appear. Then select **MyScene | Edit run**.

25. Activate the **Procedures** tab. Alice will display the procedures for `biff`.

26. Drag the **addKeyListener** procedure and drop it in the **drop statement here** area located below the **do in order** label, inside the **run** tab. The `addKeyListener` procedure will add a `keyPressed` procedure declaration with a **drop statement here** placeholder.

27. Drag the **if _** statement, located at the top, and drop it on the **drop statement here** placeholder within the `keyPressed` procedure. Click on **true** and two **drop statement here** placeholders will appear.

28. Click on the last down arrow that appears with a gray background at the right-hand side of the previously defined expression for the `if` block, before **is true then**. A drop-down menu will display different options to use to replace the current expression.

29. Select **e.IsKey ??? | arrows | LEFT** in the cascade menus that appear.

30. Drag the **moveStep** procedure and drop it on the first **drop statement here** area located within the `if` block. Select `LEFT` as the value for the direction parameter. The following code will be displayed as the block that defines the conditional `if` block:

```
if (e.IsKey(LEFT)) is true then
        this.biff.moveStep(direction: LEFT)
```

31. Drag the **if _** statement, located at the top, and drop it below the previously dropped `if` block, within the `keyPressed` procedure. Click on **true** and two **drop statement here** placeholders will appear.

32. Click on the last down arrow that appears with a gray background at the right-hand side of the previously defined expression for the `if` block, before **is true then**. A drop-down menu will display different options to use to replace the current expression.

33. Select **e.IsKey ???** | **arrows** | **RIGHT** in the cascade menus that appear.

34. Drag the **moveStep** procedure and drop it on the first **drop statement here** area located within the `if` block. Select `RIGHT` as the value for the direction parameter. The following code will be displayed as the block that defines the second conditional `if` block:

```
if (e.IsKey(RIGHT)) is true then
    this.biff.moveStep(direction: RIGHT)
```

35. Drag the **if _** statement, located at the top, and drop it below the previously dropped `if` block, within the `keyPressed` procedure. Click on **true** and two **drop statement here** placeholders will appear.

36. Click on the last down arrow that appears with a gray background at the right-hand side of the previously defined expression for the `if` block, before **is true then**. A drop-down menu will display different options to use to replace the current expression.

37. Select **e.IsKey ???** | **arrows** | **UP** in the cascade menus that appear.

38. Drag the **moveStep** procedure and drop it on the first **drop statement here** area located within the `if` block. Select `FORWARD` as the value for the direction parameter. The following code will be displayed as the block that defines the third conditional `if` block:

```
if (e.IsKey(UP)) is true then
    this.biff.moveStep(direction: FORWARD)
```

39. Drag the **if _** statement, located at the top, and drop it below the previously dropped `if` block, within the `keyPressed` procedure. Click on **true** and two **drop statement here** placeholders will appear.

40. Click on the last down arrow that appears with a gray background at the right-hand side of the previously defined expression for the `if` block, before **is true then**. A drop-down menu will display different options to use to replace the current expression.

41. Select **e.IsKey ???** | **arrows** | **DOWN** in the cascade menus that appear.

42. Drag the **moveStep** procedure and drop it on the first **drop statement here** area located within the `if` block. Select `BACKWARD` as the value for the direction parameter. The following code will be displayed as the block that defines the fourth conditional `if` block:

```
if (e.IsKey(DOWN)) is true then
    this.biff.moveStep(direction: BACKWARD)
```

The next screenshot shows the code for the `run` procedure:

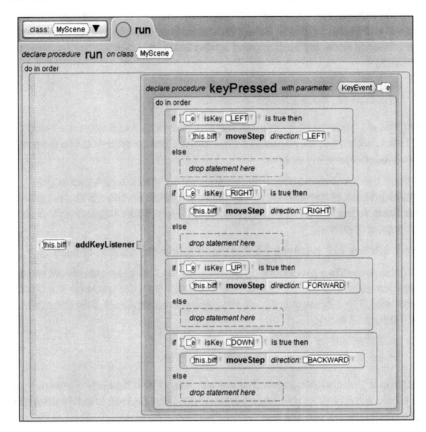

43. Select **File | Save as...** from Alice's main menu and give a new name to the project. Then you can make changes to the project according to your needs.

How it works...

When we run the project, we can use the arrow keys to make `biff` move. When we press any key, Alice executes the `keyPressed` procedure because we added this procedure as a key listener for `biff`. This procedure uses many `if` blocks to perform actions according to the arrow key that the user pressed. For example, if we press the DOWN key, the `keyPressed` procedure calls the `moveStep` procedure for `biff` with BACKWARD as the value for the `direction` parameter. The `moveStep` procedure uses the `Moving` property as a Boolean flag to avoid many movements to run at the same time.

The `keyPressed` procedure reacts to four arrow keys and performs movements as seen by `biff`:

▶ LEFT: Moves `biff` to his left-hand side

▶ RIGHT: Moves `biff` to his right-hand side

▶ UP: Moves `biff` forward

▶ DOWN: Moves `biff` backward

> The key listener keeps listening to the keys pressed by the user while the project is running.

The following screenshot shows the rendered frame after biff moved to his left-hand side and forward many times:

There's more...

You can create a more efficient key listener by taking advantage of the `else` keyword in each `if` block. In this task, we defined four `if` blocks that Alice will execute for each key pressed by the user. If we change the location of the second, third, and fourth `if` blocks to start after each previous else keyword, the code will be more efficient. For example, when the user presses the right arrow, Alice will evaluate only two `if` blocks, the first one and the second one. Then Alice will leave the `keyPressed` procedure because the remaining two `if` blocks appear after the second `else` keyword.

See also

▶ *Reacting to keyboard events*, in this chapter

Controlling the camera with the keyboard

In this recipe, we will use two keys to zoom in and zoom out of the scene. We will move the camera towards and away from one of the actors according to the key pressed by the user. The rendered view will show the effects of the camera's movement.

Getting ready

We will use an existing project that has one key listener defined for `biff`, one of the two characters we have been using from the Looking Glass Characters gallery.

1. Open the project saved in the *Controlling an actor with keystrokes* recipe.

2. Click on **Edit Code**, at the lower-right corner of the big scene preview. Alice will show a smaller preview of the scene and will display the **Code Editor** on a panel located at the right-hand side of the main window.

3. Click on the **class: MyScene** drop-down list and the list of classes that are part of the scene will appear.

4. Select **MyScene | Edit run**.

How to do it...

Follow these steps to allow the user to move the camera with two keys:

1. Select `camera` in the instance drop-down list located at the left-hand side of the main window, below the small scene preview.

2. Activate the **Procedures** tab. Alice will display the procedures for `camera`.

3. Drag the **addKeyListener** procedure and drop it below the existing `addKeyListener` call, inside the **run** tab. The `addKeyListener` procedure will add a `keyPressed` procedure declaration with a **drop statement here** placeholder.

4. Drag the **if _** statement, located at the top, and drop it on the **drop statement here** placeholder within the `keyPressed` procedure for the `camera` key listener. Click on **true** and two **drop statement here** placeholders will appear.

5. Click on the last down arrow that appears with a gray background at the right-hand side of the previously defined expression for the `if` block, before **is true then**. A drop-down menu will display different options to use to replace the current expression.

6. Select **e.IsKey ??? | letters (N-Z) | T** in the cascade menus that appear.

7. Drag the **moveToward** procedure and drop it on the first **drop statement here** area located within the `if` block. Select `0.25` for the first parameter and then click on `this.biff`. Click on the **more...** drop-down menu button that appears, on `duration` and then on `0.25` in the cascade menus.

8. Drag another **if _** statement, located at the top, and drop it below the `else` keyword, within the previously dropped `if` block. Click on **true** and two **drop statement here** placeholders will appear.

9. Click on the last down arrow that appears with a gray background at the right-hand side of the previously defined expression for the `if` block, before **is true then**. A drop-down menu will display different options to use to replace the current expression.

10. Select **e.IsKey ??? | letters (A-M) | G** in the cascade menus that appear.

11. Drag the **moveAwayFrom** procedure and drop it on the first **drop statement here** area located within the recently added `if` block. Select `0.25` for the first parameter and then click on `this.biff`. Click on the **more...** drop-down menu button that appears, on `duration` and then on `0.25` in the cascade menus.

The following screenshot shows the code for the new key listener:

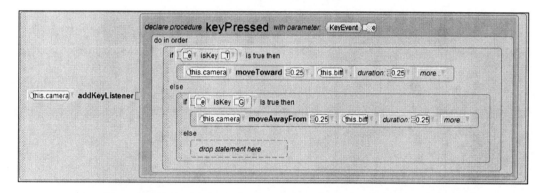

12. Select **File | Save as...** from Alice's main menu and give a new name to the project. Then you can make changes to the project according to your needs.

How it works...

When we run the project, we can press the following two keys to move the camera towards and away from `biff`:

- ▶ **T**: Moves the camera towards `biff`, and therefore, zooms in. The following image shows the result of pressing this key many times:

- ▶ **G**: Moves the camera away from biff, and therefore, zooms out. The following image shows the result of pressing this key many times:

When we press any key, Alice executes the two `keyPressed` procedures because we added two key listeners, one for `biff` and the other for `camera`. The `keyPressed` procedure for the `camera`'s key listener uses two chained `if` blocks to perform actions according to the key that the user pressed. We didn't use a `Boolean` flag because we want the camera to go on moving if the user keeps one of the defined keys pressed for many seconds.

See also

- ▶ *Controlling an actor with keystrokes*, in this chapter
- ▶ *Controlling the output*, in *Chapter 10, Customizing the Output*
- ▶ *Following characters*, in *Chapter 10, Customizing the Output*

Controlling multiple actors with keystrokes

In this task, we will use two sets of keys to control two different robot's movements. We will declare and call specific procedures to handle the necessary movements for the robots. We will evaluate many expressions to determine the key pressed by the user and run the necessary code according to this key.

Getting ready

We will use an existing project that allows the user to move `biff` by using the arrow keys. This project also includes `gina` in the scene, another character from the Looking Glass Characters gallery.

1. Open the project saved in the *Controlling the camera with the keyboard* recipe.

2. Click on **Edit Code**, at the lower-right corner of the big scene preview. Alice will show a smaller preview of the scene and will display the **Code Editor** on a panel located at the right-hand side of the main window.

3. Click on the **class: MyScene** drop-down list and the list of classes that are part of the scene will appear.

4. Select **MyScene | Edit run**.

How to do it...

Follow these steps to allow the user to control `biff` and `gina` with two sets of keys:

1. Click on the **class: MyScene** drop-down list and the list of classes that are part of the scene will appear.

2. Select **MyBiff | Declare procedure**. Enter `rotate` in **Name** and click **OK**. The code editor will add a new tab with the name of the new procedure, **rotate**.

3. Select `biff (this)` in the instance drop-down list located at the left-hand side of the main window, below the small scene preview. Make sure that `part: none` is selected in the drop-down list located at the right-hand side of the chosen instance.

4. Activate the **Properties** tab. Alice will display the properties for `biff`.

5. Drag the **Moving** assignment statement and drop it on the first **drop statement here** area. Select `true`, the desired `Boolean` to assign to the `Moving` property.

6. Activate the **Procedures** tab. Alice will display the procedures for `biff`.

7. Drag the **turn** procedure and drop it below the previously dropped statement. Select `RIGHT` for the first parameter and then click on `0.25`. Click on the **more...** drop-down menu button that appears, on `duration` and then on `0.25`. Click on the additional **more...** drop-down menu that appears, on `asSeenBy` and then on `this`.

8. Activate the **Properties** tab. Alice will display the properties for `biff`.

9. Drag the **Moving** assignment statement and drop it below the previously dropped statement. Select `false`, the desired `Boolean` to assign to the `Moving` property.

   The next screenshot shows the code for the `rotate` procedure:

10. Click on the **class: MyBiff** drop-down list and the list of classes that are part of the scene will appear.

11. Select **MyGina | Declare property**. The **Declare Property** dialog box will appear.

12. Click on the **Value type** drop-down list and select **Boolean**.

13. Enter `Moving` in **Name**.

14. Click on the **Initializer** drop-down list and select **false** as the initial value for the `Moving` property. Click **OK** and Alice will add the `Moving` property to the `MyGina` class.

15. Click on the **class: MyGina** drop-down list. Select **MyGina | Declare procedure**. Enter `rotate` in **Name** and click **OK**. The code editor will add a new tab with the name of the new procedure, **rotate**.

16. Repeat the aforementioned steps (3 to 9) to declare the same `rotate` procedure for the `MyGina` class. Use `gina` instead of `biff`.

17. Follow the steps explain the *Controlling an actor with keystrokes* recipe, in this chapter, to declare a `moveStep` procedure for the `MyGina` class. Use `gina` instead of `biff`.

18. Click on the **class: MyGina** drop-down list and the list of classes that are part of the scene will appear.

19. Select **MyScene | Edit run**.

20. Select `biff` in the instance drop-down list located at the left-hand side of the main window, below the small scene preview.

21. Activate the **Procedures** tab. Alice will display the procedures for `biff`.

22. Drag the **if _** statement, located at the top, and drop it below the last if block within the `keyPressed` procedure for `biff`'s key listener. Click on **true** and two **drop statement here** placeholders will appear.

23. Click on the last down arrow that appears with a gray background at the right-hand side of the previously defined expression for the if block, before **is true then**. A drop-down menu will display different options to use to replace the current expression.

24. Select **e.IsKey ???** | **letters (A-M)** | **M** in the cascade menus that appear.

25. Drag the **rotate** procedure and drop it on the first **drop statement here** area located within the if block.

26. Drag and drop the if blocks that evaluate the different arrow keys pressed in the keyPressed procedure for biff's key listener and organize them as shown in the next screenshot. Each if block appears after the else keyword of the previous if block, as shown in the next screenshot:

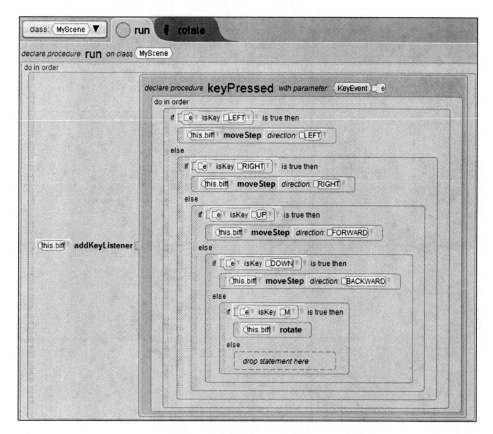

27. Select gina in the instance drop-down list located at the left-hand side of the main window, below the small scene preview.

28. Activate the **Procedures** tab. Alice will display the procedures for gina.

29. Drag the **addKeyListener** procedure and drop it below the last `addKeyListener` call in the list, inside the **run** tab. The `addKeyListener` procedure will add a `keyPressed` procedure declaration with a **drop statement here** placeholder.

30. Add the same `if` blocks used in the previously edited `keyPressed` procedure to this new `keyPressed` procedure. However, change the value passed as a parameter to the `isKey` function according to the following table:

`biff`'s value for the `isKey` parameter	`gina`'s value for the `isKey` parameter
LEFT	A
RIGHT	D
UP	W
DOWN	S
M	R

The next screenshot shows the code for the new key listener:

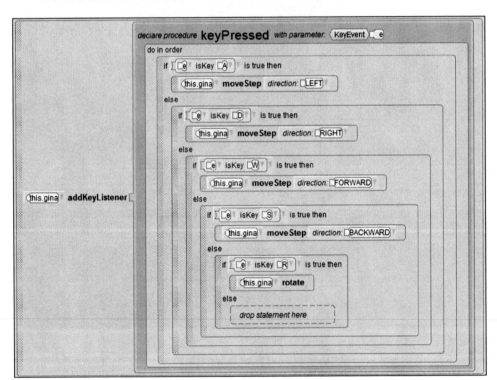

How it works...

When we run the project, we can use the arrow keys to move `biff`. If we press the _M_ key, `biff` rotates `90` degrees. The new `rotate` procedure calls the `turn` procedure with `0.25` as the value for the `amount` parameter. This value means that the model must turn `360` degrees x `0.25` = `90` degrees. This new procedure sets the `Moving` property to `true` before calling the `turn` procedure and then sets this property to `false`.

The procedure doesn't use an `if` block to check whether `Moving` is false in order to turn the model, and therefore, the user can keep the key pressed and the model rotates continuously. However, because the rotate procedure sets the `Moving` property to `true` before calling the `turn` procedure, the user cannot use the arrow keys to move the model while it is rotating.

The `keyPressed` procedure for `gina`'s key listener reacts to five keys and performs movements as seen by `gina`:

- **A**: Moves `gina` to her left-hand side
- **D**: Moves `gina` to her right-hand side
- **W**: Moves `gina` forward
- **S**: Moves `gina` backward
- **R**: Turns `gina` 90 degrees to her right-hand side

The multiple key listeners allow the user to control two actors in the scene. The following images shows one of the rendered frames when `biff` and `gina` have been rotated as a result of many pressed keys:

See also

- _Controlling an actor with keystrokes_, in this chapter
- _Controlling the camera with the keyboard_, in this chapter

9
Creating Interactive Stories

In this chapter, we will cover:

- ▸ Dressing a person
- ▸ Building a house
- ▸ Talking at the cafeteria
- ▸ Managing an amusement park
- ▸ Organizing the layout of a bedroom
- ▸ Creating an epic story
- ▸ Enabling a person to throw a basketball through a hoop
- ▸ Working with animals on a farm

Introduction

Alice 3 provides an extensive gallery of 3D models that allows you to create dazzling interactive stories. This chapter provides many tasks that will provide examples of how to combine all the things learned in previous chapters with some good ideas and the capabilities of the 3D models included in the galleries.

We will change a girl's outfit, build a house, make people talk at a cafeteria and allow the user to customize the layout of an amusement park. We will make a medieval knight kneel before a princess, animate the coach to throw a basketball through a hoop, and show living animals at a farm. In addition, we will allow the user to customize the layout of a bedroom.

Dressing a person

In this recipe, we will change a girl's outfit when the user clicks on the desired costume. We will add five girls with different outfits. Then we will define mouse button listeners for four girls and we will add the necessary code to change the value of a property for one of the girls to copy the outfit of the clicked girl.

Getting ready

Follow these steps to create a new project and display the **Model Gallery**:

1. Select **File | New...** in the main menu to start a new project. A dialog box will display the six predefined templates with their thumbnail previews in the **Templates** tab.

2. Select `GrassyProject.a3p` as the desired template for the new project and click **OK**. Alice will display a grassy ground with a light blue sky.

3. Click on **Edit Scene**, at the lower-right corner of the scene preview. Alice will show a bigger preview of the scene and will display the **Model Gallery** at the bottom.

How to do it...

Follow these steps to add five girls with different outfits and define mouse button listeners for four girls:

1. Add five girls with the same head and body but with different outfits. Follow the steps explained in the *Customizing a person's head* and *Customizing a person's body* recipes, in *Chapter 7, Working with People*.

2. Use `sarah` as the first girl's name and locate her at the center of the scene. Use `outfit0`, `outfit1`, `outfit2`, and `outfit3` as the names for the other four girls. Locate `outfit0` and `outfit1` at the left-hand side of `sarah`. Locate `outfit2` and `outfit3` at the right-hand side of `sarah`, as shown in the next screenshot:

3. Click on the **class: MyScene** drop-down list and the list of classes that are part of the scene will appear. Select **MyChild | Declare procedure**, enter `dressAs` in **Name** and click **OK**. The code editor will add a new tab with the name of the new procedure, **dressAs**.

4. Click on the **Add Parameter...** button and the **Declare Parameter** dialog box will appear.

5. Click on the **Value type** drop-down list and a drop-down menu will appear. Select **MyTypes | MyChild**.

6. Enter `child` in name and click **OK**. The parameter will appear in the procedure declaration located at the top, below the **dressAs** tab.

7. Make sure that `sarah (this)` is selected in the **instance** drop-down list located at the left-hand side of the main window, below the small scene preview.

8. Activate the **Properties** tab. Alice will display the properties for the `MyChild` class. `sarah` is an instance of `MyChild`.

9. Drag the **Outfit** assignment statement and drop it in the **drop statement here** area in the `dressAs` tab. The **Outfit** assignment statement contains the **this** and **Outfit** labels followed by an arrow and three question marks **???**.

10. Select female **child | FemaleChildFullBodyOutfitBlazerPleats | PVTSCHOOLBLUE**.

11. Now select `parameter: child` in the **instance** drop-down list located at the left-hand side of the main window, below the small scene preview.

12. Activate the **Properties** tab. Alice will display the properties for the `MyChild` instance received as a parameter.

13. Drag the **Outfit** property and drop it on `PVTSCHOOLBLUE`, at the right-hand side of the assignment operator ← of the recently added statement. A black rectangle will surround the `PVTSCHOOLBLUE` value when you start dragging the **Outfit** property. The **Outfit** property contains the **child** and **Outfit** labels with a yellow background. The following code will appear as the first statement for the `dressAs` procedure:

```
this.Outfit ← child.Outfit
```

14. Select `sarah (this)` in the **instance** drop-down list located at the left-hand side of the main window, below the small scene preview.

15. Activate the **Procedures** tab. Alice will display the procedures for the `MyChild` class.

16. Drag the **joglnPlace** procedure and drop it below the previously dropped statement. The following code will be displayed as the second statement for the `dressAs` procedure, as shown in the next screenshot:

```
this.jogInPlace
```

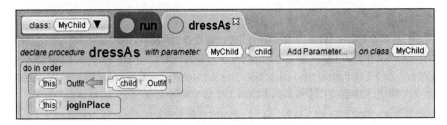

17. Click on the **class: MyChild** drop-down list and the list of classes that are part of the scene will appear.

18. Select **MyScene | Edit run**.

19. Select `outfit0` in the instance drop-down list located at the left-hand side of the main window, behind the small scene preview.

20. Click on the **Procedures** tab on the panel located behind the aforementioned drop-down list. Alice will display all the available procedures for `outfit0`.

21. Drag the **addMouseButtonListener** procedure and drop it on the **drop statement here** area located below the **do in order** label, inside the **run** tab. The `addMouseButtonListener` procedure will add a `mouseButtonClicked` procedure declaration with a **drop statement here** placeholder.

22. Select `sarah` in the instance drop-down list located at the left-hand side of the main window, behind the small scene preview.

23. Activate the **Procedures** tab. Alice will display the procedures for `sarah`.

24. Drag the **dressAs** procedure and drop it on the **drop statement here** placeholder within the `mouseButtonClicked` procedure for the `outfit0`'s mouse button listener. Click on `outfit0` and the following code will appear:

```
this.sarah.dressAs(child: this.outfit0)
```

25. Repeat the aforementioned steps (19 to 24) to declare the same mouse button listener for `outfit1`, `outfit2` and `outfit3`. Replace `outfit0` by the corresponding instance name. The following screenshot shows the final code with the four mouse button listeners in the `run` procedure:

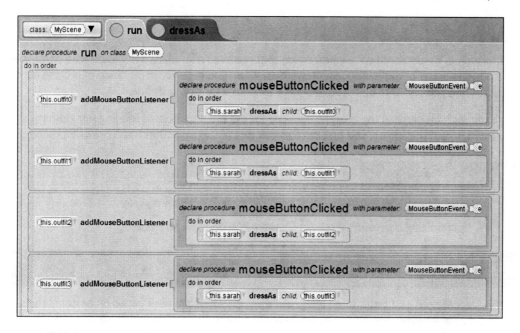

How it works...

When we run the project, `sarah` appears in the middle of the scene. If we click on one of the four girls with different outfits, the code written for her `mouseButtonClicked` procedure runs and `sarah` changes her clothes.

If we click on `outfit1`, the code written for her `mouseButtonClicked` procedure runs, and therefore Alice calls the `dressAs` procedure for `sarah` with `outfit1` as the value for the `child` parameter. `sarah` dresses as `outfit1` and then jogs in her place with her new costume. The following screenshot shows one of the rendered frames when `sarah` is jogging in her place after dressing as `outfit1`:

There's more...

In this recipe, we declared a new procedure that received a `MyChild` instance as a parameter and accessed one of the instance's properties. When you receive an instance of a class as a parameter, you can also call procedures or functions for this instance.

For example, you can call the `clap` procedure for the instance that is lending her clothing to `sarah`. In order to do so, you just have to call `child.clap` within the `dressAs` procedure.

See also

▶ *Customizing a person's head*, in *Chapter 7, Working with People*

▶ *Customizing a person's body*, in *Chapter 7, Working with People*

Building a house

In this task, we will add parts to an incomplete house when the user clicks on certain labels. We will create a new procedure to make a model appear by increasing the value of its opacity from 0 to 100%. Then we will call this procedure with a specific model as a parameter when the user clicks on the 3D text that represents the model.

Getting ready

Follow these steps to create a new project and display the **Model Gallery**:

1. Select **File | New...** in the main menu to start a new project. A dialog box will display the six predefined templates with their thumbnail previews in the **Templates** tab.

2. Select `GrassyProject.a3p` as the desired template for the new project and click **OK**. Alice will display a grassy ground with a light blue sky.

3. Click on **Edit Scene**, at the lower-right corner of the scene preview. Alice will show a bigger preview of the scene and will display the **Model Gallery** at the bottom.

How to do it...

Follow these steps to allow the user to build a house by clicking on labels:

1. Add an instance of the `BrickHouse` class to the scene, and enter `house` for the name of this new instance. Follow the steps explained in the *Creating a new instance from a class in a gallery* recipe, in *Chapter 2, Working with Actors*. Rotate the house to make both the door and the chimney visible, as shown in the next screenshot:

2. Click on the **Create 3D Text...** button located at the lower-right corner. The **Create 3D Text** dialog box will appear.

3. Enter **door** in **text** and the same value will appear in **instance**, as shown in the next screenshot:

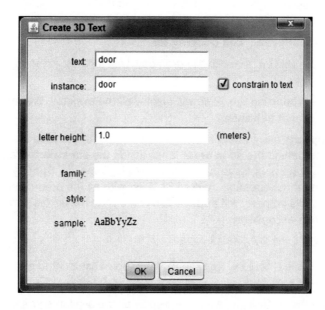

4. Click **OK**. Alice will add a 3D label with the door text. First, Alice will create the MyText class to extend Text. Then Alice will create an instance of MyText named door.

5. Place **door** at the right-hand side of the `house`.

6. Click on the **Create 3D Text...** button located at the lower-right corner. The **Create 3D Text** dialog box will appear.

7. Enter **roof** in **Text** and the same value will appear in **Instance**. Click **OK** and Alice will add a 3D label with the **roof** text.

8. Place **roof** above **door** at the right-hand side of the **house**. The font sizes are the same for both labels. However, when you change the position of one of the labels, Alice will render it with a smaller size in the 2D window as shown in the next screenshot:

9. Click on the **class: MyScene** drop-down list and the list of classes that are part of the scene will appear.

10. Select **MyBrickHouse | Edit constructor**.

11. Select `part: Walls_Door` in the drop-down list located at the right-hand side of `house (this)`.

12. Activate the **Properties** tab. Alice will display all the available properties for the `Wall_Doors` part of `house`.

13. Drag the **Opacity** assignment statement and drop it in the **drop statement here** area located behind the **do in order** label, inside the **constructor** tab. The **Opacity** assignment statement contains the **this's Walls_Door** and **Opacity** labels followed by an arrow and three question marks **???**. A list with all the predefined opacity values to assign to this property will appear. Click on `0.0` to make this part invisible. The following code will appear:

```
this.getPart(Walls_Door).Opacity ← 0.0
```

14. Now select `part: Walls_Roof` in the drop-down list located at the right-hand side of `house (this)`.

15. Activate the **Properties** tab. Alice will display all the available properties for the `Wall_Roof` part of `house`.

16. Drag the **Opacity** assignment statement and drop it below the previously dropped assignment statement. The **Opacity** assignment statement contains the **this's Walls_Roof** and **Opacity** labels followed by an arrow and three question marks **???**. A list with all the predefined opacity values to assign to this property will appear. Click on **0.0** to make this part invisible. The following code will appears as the second statement for the constructor, as shown in the next screenshot:

```
this.getPart(Walls_Roof).Opacity ← 0.0
```

17. Click on the **class: MyBrickHouse** drop-down list and the list of classes that are part of the scene will appear. Select **MyBrickHouse | Declare procedure**, enter `showPart` in **Name** and click **OK**. The code editor will add a new tab with the name of the new procedure, **showPart**.

18. Click on the **Add Parameter...** button and the **Declare Parameter** dialog box will appear.

19. Click on the **Value type** drop-down list and a drop-down menu will appear. Select **OtherTypes | Model**.

20. Enter `part` in name and click **OK**. The parameter will appear in the procedure declaration located at the top, below the **showPart** tab.

21. Drag the **local...** statement, located at the top, and drop it on the **drop statement here** area located below the **do in order** label, inside the **showPart** tab. The **Declare Local** dialog box will appear.

22. Click on the **Value type** drop-down list and select **RealNumber**.

23. Enter **opacity** in **Name**.

24. Click on the **Initializer** drop-down list and select **0.0** as the initial value for the `opacity` variable. The following code will appear:

```
RealNumber opacity ← 0.0
```

25. Drag the **count** statement, located at the top, and drop it below the `opacity` variable declaration statement. A list with some predefined values to count up to it will appear. Select **Other Integer...** and the **Enter custom integer** dialog box will appear. Enter **10** and click **OK**. The `count up to 10` statement will display a **drop statement here** placeholder.

26. Drag the **opacity ← _** statement, located at the top, and drop it in the **drop statement here** area located within the `count up to 10` block.

27. Select **opacity** in the menu that appears.

28. Click on the down arrow that appears with a gray background at the right-hand side of the assignment operator **←**. A drop-down menu will display different options to use to replace the current expression. Select **Math | opacity + ??? | Other Real Number...** in the cascade menus that appear. The **Enter custom real number** dialog box will appear. Enter **0.1** and click **OK**. The following code will be displayed as the first statement within the `count up to 10` block:

```
opacity ← (opacity + 0.1)
```

29. Now select `parameter: part` in the **instance** drop-down list located at the left-hand side of the main window, below the small scene preview.

30. Activate the **Properties** tab. Alice will display the properties for the `Model` instance received as a parameter.

31. Drag the **Opacity** assignment statement and drop it below the previously dropped statement, within the `count up to 10` block. The **Opacity** assignment statement contains the **part** and **Opacity** labels followed by an arrow and three question marks **???**. Select **opacity** and the following code will be displayed as the second statement within the `count up to 10 block`, as shown in the next screenshot:

```
part.Opacity ← opacity
```

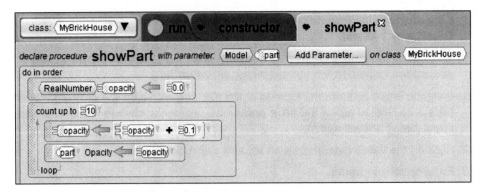

32. Click on the **class: MyBrickHouse** drop-down list and the list of classes that are part of the scene will appear.

33. Select **MyScene | Edit run**.

34. Select `door` in the instance drop-down list located at the left-hand side of the main window, behind the small scene preview.

35. Activate the **Procedures** tab. Alice will display the procedures for `door`.

36. Drag the **addMouseButtonListener** procedure and drop it on the **drop statement here** area located below the **do in order** label, inside the **run** tab. The `addMouseButtonListener` procedure will add a `mouseButtonClicked` procedure declaration with a **drop statement here** placeholder.

37. Select `house` in the instance drop-down list located at the left-hand side of the main window, behind the small scene preview.

38. Activate the **Procedures** tab. Alice will display the procedures for `house`.

39. Drag the **showPart** procedure and drop it on the **drop statement here** placeholder within the `mouseButtonClicked` procedure for `door`'s mouse button listener. Select **this.house.getPart ??? | Walls_Door** in the menu and the following code will appear:

```
this.house.showPart(this.house.getPart(Walls_Door))
```

40. Now select **roof** in the instance drop-down list located at the left-hand side of the main window, behind the small scene preview.

41. Activate the **Procedures** tab. Alice will display the procedures for **roof**.

42. Drag the **addMouseButtonListener** procedure and drop it on the **drop statement here** area located below the **do in order** label, inside the **run** tab. The `addMouseButtonListener` procedure will add a `mouseButtonClicked` procedure declaration with a **drop statement here** placeholder.

43. Select `house` in the instance drop-down list located at the left-hand side of the main window, behind the small scene preview.

44. Activate the **Procedures** tab. Alice will display the procedures for `house`.

45. Drag the **showPart** procedure and drop it on the **drop statement here** placeholder within the `mouseButtonClicked` procedure for `roof`'s mouse button listener. Select **this.house.getPart ??? | Walls_Roof** in the menu. The following code will appear, as shown in the next screenshot:

```
this.house.showPart(this.house.getPart(Walls_Roof))
```

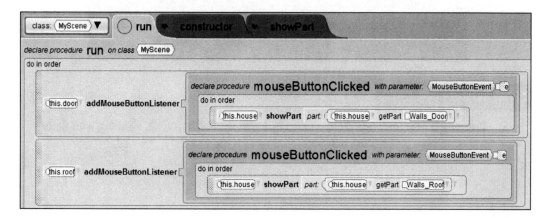

How it works...

When we run the project, the house appears without the door and the roof. We added two statements in the constructor for the `MyBrickHouse` class that makes the `Walls_Door` and `Walls_Roof` parts invisible by setting the value of their `Opacity` property to `0`.

If we click on one of the two 3D labels with text, the code written for their `mouseButtonClicked` procedure runs and a new part of the `house` appears.

If we click on `door`, the code written for its `mouseButtonClicked` procedure runs, and therefore Alice calls the `showPart` procedure for `house` with the `Model` returned by `getPart(Walls_Door)` as the value for the `part` parameter. The `showPart` procedure performs an animation that increases the value of the `Opacity` property for the `Model` received as a parameter. The following screenshot shows one of the rendered frames when the roof is becoming visible:

See also

  ▶ *Creating a new instance from a class in a gallery, in Chapter 2, Working with Actors*

Talking at the cafeteria

In this recipe, we will make three people have a short conversation at a cafeteria. We will add three characters and we will make them look at the target of his/her words before displaying the speech bubbles. We will also add the necessary code to animate these characters.

Getting ready

Follow these steps to create a new project and display the **Model Gallery**:

1. Select **File | New...** in the main menu to start a new project. A dialog box will display the six predefined templates with their thumbnail previews in the **Templates** tab.

2. Select `GrassyProject.a3p` as the desired template for the new project and click **OK**. Alice will display a grassy ground with a light blue sky.

3. Click on **Edit Scene**, at the lower-right corner of the scene preview. Alice will show a bigger preview of the scene and will display the **Model Gallery** at the bottom.

How to do it...

Follow these steps to allow the user to build a house by clicking on labels:

1. Add an instance of the `Cafeteria` class to the scene, and enter `cafeteria` for the name of this new instance.

2. Add instances of the nine classes shown in the following table. Use the names shown in the `Instance name` column for each new instance:

Class	Instance name	Class created by Alice
BigTable	bigTable0	MyBigTable
BigTable	bigTable1	MyBigTable
Chair	chair0	MyChair
Chair	chair1	MyChair
Chair	chair2	MyChair
Chair	chair3	MyChair
LunchLady	lunchLady	MyLunchLady
TheRoyalButler	theRoyalButler	MyTheRoyalButler
MrsMiller	mrsMiller	MyMrsMiller

3. Place and rotate the instances as shown in the next screenshot:

4. Click on the **class: MyScene** drop-down list and the list of classes that are part of the scene will appear.

5. Select **MyScene | Edit run**.

6. Select `mrsMiller` in the instance drop-down list located at the left-hand side of the main window, behind the small scene preview.

7. Activate the **Procedures** tab. Alice will display the procedures for `mrsMiller`.

8. Drag the **lookAt** procedure and drop it on the **drop statement here** area located below the **do in order** label, inside the **run** tab. Select **this.theRoyalButler**. The following code will appear:

    ```
    this.mrsMiller.lookAt(this.theRoyalButler)
    ```

9. Drag the **say** procedure and drop it below the previously dropped statement. Click **Other String...** and the **Enter Custom String** dialog box will appear. Enter `Hey, Jim! Have you checked the repaired chairs?` in **Value** and click **OK**. Click on the **more...** drop-down menu button that appears, on `duration` and then on **Other Real Number....** The **Enter custom real number** dialog box will appear. Enter **3.0**, click **OK**. and the following code will appear:

    ```
    this.mrsMiller.say("Hey, Jim! Have you checked the repaired
    chairs?", duration: 3.0)
    ```

10. Select `theRoyalButler` in the instance drop-down list located at the left-hand side of the main window, behind the small scene preview.

11. Drag the **lookAt** procedure and drop it on the **drop statement here** area located below the **do in order** label, inside the **run** tab. Select **this.mrsMiller**. The following code will appear:

    ```
    this.theRoyalButler.lookAt(this.mrsMiller)
    ```

12. Drag the **say** procedure and drop it below the previously dropped statement. Click **Other String...** and the **Enter Custom String** dialog box will appear. Enter The repaired chairs are OK. in **Value** and click **OK**. Click on the **more...** drop-down menu button that appears, on duration and then on 2.0 in the cascade menu. The following code will appear:

    ```
    this.theRoyalButler.say("The repaired chairs are OK.", duration: 2.0)
    ```

13. Select lunchLady in the instance drop-down list located at the left-hand side of the main window, behind the small scene preview.

14. Drag the **walkTo** procedure and drop it in the **drop statement here** area located below the **do in order** label, inside the **run** tab. Select **this.mrsMiller** as the target. Click on the **more...** drop-down menu button that appears, on spatialRelation and then on IN_FRONT_OF in the cascade menu. Click on the new **more...** drop-down menu that appears, on offset and then on 1.0. The following code will appear:

    ```
    this.lunchLady.walkTo(this.mrsMiller, spatialRelation: IN_FRONT_OF, offset: 1.0)
    ```

15. Drag the **lookAt** procedure and drop it on the **drop statement here** area located below the **do in order** label, inside the **run** tab. Select **this.mrsMiller**. The following code will appear:

    ```
    this.lunchLady.lookAt(this.mrsMiller)
    ```

16. Drag the **say** procedure and drop it below the previously dropped statement. Click **Other String...** and the **Enter Custom String** dialog box will appear. Enter Are the chairs ready? in **Value** and click **OK**. Click on the **more...** drop-down menu button that appears, on duration and then on 2.0 in the cascade menu. The following code will appear:

    ```
    this.lunchLady.say("Are the chairs ready?", duration: 2.0)
    ```

17. Select mrsMiller in the instance drop-down list located at the left-hand side of the main window, behind the small scene preview.

18. Drag the **lookAt** procedure and drop it on the **drop statement here** area located below the **do in order** label, inside the **run** tab. Select **this.lunchLady**. The following code will appear:

    ```
    this.mrsMiller.lookAt(this.lunchLady)
    ```

19. Drag the **say** procedure and drop it below the previously dropped statement. Click **Other String...** and the **Enter Custom String** dialog box will appear. Enter `Yes!` in **Value** and click **OK**. Click on the **more...** drop-down menu button that appears, on `duration` and then on **1.0** in the cascade menu. The following code will appear, as shown in the next screenshot:

```
this.mrsMiller.say("Yes!", duration: 1.0)
```

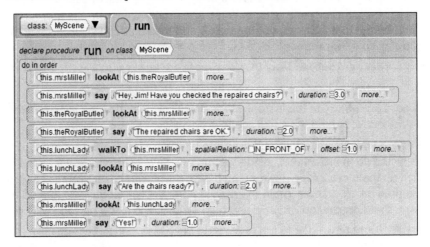

How it works...

We added three characters to the cafeteria: `mrsMiller`, `theRoyalButler` and `lunchLady`. We placed the `cafeteria` on top of the `grassyGround`, and therefore the three characters can talk inside a `cafeteria`.

Each character looks at the target of his/her words before talking. Thus, we can see the characters moving their heads and then displaying their speech bubbles. The following screenshot shows one of the rendered frames when `mrsMiller` is looking at `lunchLady` and says `Yes!`

Managing an amusement park

In this task, we will allow the user to organize the layout of an amusement park. We will set a scene of an amusement park with ten 3D models. Then we will add the necessary code to assign events that get fired when the user performs actions with the mouse. These events will make it possible for the user to drag and drop models and to rotate them.

Getting ready

Follow these steps to create a new project and display the **Model Gallery**:

1. Select **File | New...** in the main menu to start a new project. A dialog box will display the six predefined templates with their thumbnail previews in the **Templates** tab.

2. Select `GrassyProject.a3p` as the desired template for the new project and click **OK**. Alice will display a grassy ground with a light blue sky.

3. Click on **Edit Scene**, at the lower right corner of the scene preview. Alice will show a bigger preview of the scene and will display the **Model Gallery** at the bottom.

How to do it...

Follow these steps to set a scene with an amusement park:

1. Add instances of the ten classes shown in the following table. Use the names shown in the `Instance name` column for each new instance:

Class	Instance name	Class created by Alice
Carousel	Carousel	MyCarousel
FerrisWheel	ferrisWheel	MyFerrisWheel
Coaster	coaster	MyChair
Octopus	octopus	MyOctopus
Teacups	teacups	MyTeacups
Popcorncart	popcorncart	MyPopcorncart
RaceHorseGame	raceHorseGame	MyRaceHorseGame
HotDogCart	hotDogCart	MyHotDogCart
HauntedHouse	hauntedHouse	MyHauntedHouse
RingToss	ringToss	MyRingToss

2. Place, resize, and rotate the instances as shown in the next screenshot:

3. Click on the **class: MyScene** drop-down list and the list of classes that are part of the scene will appear.

4. Select **MyScene | Edit run**.

5. Select `scene (this)` in the instance drop-down list located at the left-hand side of the main window, below the small scene preview.

6. Activate the **Procedures** tab. Alice will display the procedures for `scene`.

7. Drag the **addDefaultModelManipulation** procedure and drop it as the first statement, above the call to the `addMouseButtonListener` procedure, inside the **run** tab. The following code will be displayed as a new statement, as shown in the next screenshot:

```
This.addDefaultModelManipulation
```

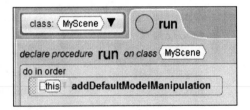

How it works...

When we run the project, the `addDefaultModelManipulation` procedure for `scene` assigns events that get fired when the user performs actions with the mouse.

We can use the mouse to drag an instance to a new location. In addition, we can press the *Ctrl* key while we move the mouse to rotate an instance. We can organize the layout of the amusement park and then we can double click on an instance to point the camera to this instance.

The following screenshot shows one of the rendered frames with a new layout for the amusement park:

Organizing the layout of a bedroom

In this task, we will allow the user to organize the layout of a bedroom. We will set a scene of a bedroom with six 3D models placed in different parts of the bedroom. Then we will add the necessary code to assign events that get fired when the user performs actions with the mouse. These events will make it possible for the user to drag and drop models and to rotate them.

Getting ready

Follow these steps to create a new project and display the **Model Gallery**:

1. Select **File | New...** in the main menu to start a new project. A dialog box will display the six predefined templates with their thumbnail previews in the **Templates** tab.

2. Select `GrassyProject.a3p` as the desired template for the new project and click **OK**. Alice will display a grassy ground with a light blue sky.

3. Click on **Edit Scene**, at the lower-right corner of the scene preview. Alice will show a bigger preview of the scene and will display the **Model Gallery** at the bottom.

How to do it...

Follow these steps to set a scene with a bedroom:

1. Add an instance of the Room class located in **Gallery | Looking Glass Scenery | bedroom**. Enter **room** for the name of this new instance.

2. Add instances of the six classes shown in the following table. Use the names shown in the Instance name column for each new instance:

Class	Instance name	Class created by Alice
OldBed	oldBed	MyOldBed
CatClock	catClock	MyCatClock
Endtable2	endtable2	MyEndtable2
Lamp	lamp	MyLamp
CuckooClock	cuckooClock	MyCuckooClock
PictureFrame	pictureFrame	MyPictureFrame

3. Place, rotate, and resize the instances as shown in the next screenshot:

4. Click on the **class: MyScene** drop-down list and the list of classes that are part of the scene will appear.

5. Select **MyScene | Edit run**.

6. Select `scene (this)` in the instance drop-down list located at the left-hand side of the main window, below the small scene preview.

7. Activate the **Procedures** tab. Alice will display the procedures for `scene`.

8. Drag the **addDefaultModelManipulation** procedure and drop it as the first statement, inside the **run** tab. The following code will be displayed as a new statement, as shown in the next screenshot:

```
this.addDefaultModelManipulation
```

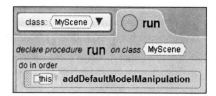

How it works...

We added six elements to a `room` to transform it into a bedroom. We added an old bed, a cat clock, an end table, a lamp, a cuckoo clock and a picture frame. These elements appear in different initial positions within the 3D area covered by the `room`. We placed the `room` on top of the `grassyGround`, and therefore the user can move and rotate the six elements inside the `room`.

When we run the project, the `addDefaultModelManipulation` procedure for `scene` assigns events that get fired when the user performs actions with the mouse. For example, we can use the mouse to drag the `lamp` to a new location. In addition, we can press the Ctrl key while we move the mouse to rotate the `lamp`. We can organize the layout of the six elements inside the `room`.

The following screenshot shows one of the rendered frames with a new layout for the bedroom:

Creating an epic story

In this recipe, we will make a knight kneel before a princess in a medieval scene. We will call procedures that perform realistic and complex animations for medieval characters. The knight will walk towards the princess and then he will kneel before her.

Getting ready

Follow these steps to create a new project and display the **Model Gallery**:

1. Select **File | New…** in the main menu to start a new project. A dialog box will display the six predefined templates with their thumbnail previews in the **Templates** tab.

2. Select `GrassyProject.a3p` as the desired template for the new project and click **OK**. Alice will display a grassy ground with a light blue sky.

3. Click on **Edit Scene**, at the lower-right corner of the scene preview. Alice will show a bigger preview of the scene and will display the **Model Gallery** at the bottom.

How to do it…

Follow these steps to set a medieval scene with a princess and a knight as the main characters:

1. Add instances of the eight classes shown in the following table. Use the names shown in the `Instance name` column for each new instance:

Class	Instance name	Class created by Alice
Princess	princess	MyPrincess
WaterFall	waterFall	MyWaterFall
Castle	Castle	MyCastle
Knight	Knight	MyKnight
Tent	Tent	MyTent
Crispy	crispy	MyCrispy
Tower	tower	MyTower
Horse	horse	MyHorse

2. Place, rotate, and resize the instances as shown in the next screenshot. You will need excessive resizing for some of the instances to accomplish this. Remember that you can switch between the `Starting Camera View` and the `Layout View`.

3. Click on the **class: MyScene** drop-down list and the list of classes that are part of the scene will appear.

4. Select **MyScene | Edit run**.

5. Select `knight` in the instance drop-down list located at the left-hand side of the main window, below the small scene preview.

6. Activate the **Procedures** tab. Alice will display the procedures for `knight`.

7. Drag the **Yes** procedure and drop it on the **drop statement here** area located below the **do in order** label, inside the **run** tab. The following code will appear:

```
this.knight.Yes
```

8. Drag the **KneelBefore** procedure and drop it below the previously dropped statement. Select `this.princess` as the value for the `who` parameter. The following code will be displayed as the second statement for the `run` procedure, as shown in the next screenshot:

```
this.knight.kneelBefore(this.princess)
```

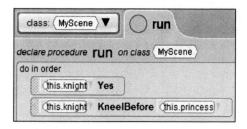

How it works...

The `Knight` class is part of the `Generic Alice Models | medieval` gallery. This class provides specific procedures that make it simple to perform complex animations and to interact with other actors. `knight` is an instance of `MyKnight`, and `MyKnight` inherits from `Knight`. For example, the `KneelBefore` procedure allows you to make `knight` walk to a target and kneel before it. When `knight` walks, he moves his feet, and therefore he performs a real-life walking animation and ends up kneeling before the `princess`. The `Yes` procedure makes it simple to make the actor perform a gesture because he found the `princess` before walking towards her.

The `knight` shows realistic movements for each action, as shown in the following four screenshots of the rendered frames:

 Some models from the `Generic Alice Models | medieval` gallery provide procedures that don't follow the naming convention for procedures. For example, the `KneelBefore` procedure starts with an uppercase letter.

Enabling a person to throw a basketball through a hoop

In this task, we will make a coach throw a basketball through a hoop. We will work with subparts of a complex model to set the target for the basketball. In addition, we will add code that makes a basketball bounce many times.

Getting ready

Follow these steps to create a new project with a gym in the scene.

1. Select **File | New...** in the main menu to start a new project. A dialog box will display the six predefined templates with their thumbnail previews in the **Templates** tab.

2. Select `GrassyProject.a3p` as the desired template for the new project and click **OK**. Alice will display a grassy ground with a light blue sky.

3. Click on **Edit Scene**, at the lower-right corner of the scene preview. Alice will show a bigger preview of the scene and will display the **Model Gallery** at the bottom.

4. Add an instance of the `Gym` class located in **Gallery | Looking Glass Scenery | gym**. Enter **gym** for the name of this new instance.

How to do it...

Follow these steps to animate a coach and a basketball:

1. Add an instance of the `Coach` class located in **Gallery | Looking Glass Characters | adults**. Enter `coach` for the name of this new instance.

2. Add instances of the three classes shown in the following table. Use the names shown in the `Instance name` column for each new instance:

Class	Instance name	Class created by Alice
Basketball	basketball	MyBasketball
Lana	lana	MyLana
Leon	leon	MyLeon

3. Place, resize, and rotate the instances as shown in the next screenshot. The `basketball` must be at the right-hand side of the `coach`:

4. Click on the **class: MyScene** drop-down list and the list of classes that are part of the scene will appear.

5. Select **MyScene | Edit run**.

6. Drag the **do together** statement, located at the top, and drop it on the **drop statement here** area located below the **do in order** label, inside the **run** tab. Alice will display a green line indicating the position in which this new statement will be inserted. The `do together` statement will display a **drop statement here** placeholder.

7. Select `coach` in the instance drop-down list located at the left-hand side of the main window, below the small scene preview.

8. Activate the **Procedures** tab. Alice will display the procedures for `coach`.

9. Drag the **Cheer** procedure and drop it in the **drop statement here** area located within the `do together` block.

10. Select `basketball` in the instance drop-down list located at the left-hand side of the main window, below the small scene preview.

11. Drag the **moveTo** procedure and drop it as the second statement within the `do together` block. Select **this.gym.getPart ??? | Gym_PoleHoop01_BBoard01_Rim01_Net01**. The following code will define the `do together` block:

```
do together
    this.coach.Cheer
    this.basketball.moveTo(this.gym.getPart(Gym_PoleHoop01_
    BBoard01_Rim01_Net01))
```

12. Drag the **move** procedure and drop it below the `do together` block. Select DOWN and then `1.0`. The following code will be displayed:

```
this.basketball.move(DOWN, 1.0)
```

13. Drag the **local...** statement, located at the top, and drop it below the previously dropped statement. The **Declare Local** dialog box will appear.

14. Click on the **Value type** drop-down list and select **RealNumber**.

15. Enter `bounceDistance` in **Name**.

16. Click on the **Initializer** drop-down list and select **1.0** as the initial value for the `bounceDistance` variable. Click **OK** and the following code will be displayed as a new statement:

```
RealNumber bounceDistance ← 1.0
```

17. Drag the **count** statement, located at the top, and drop it below the variable declaration statement. A list with some predefined values to count up to it will appear. Select **Other Integer...** and the **Enter custom integer** dialog box will appear. Enter **5** and click **OK**. The `count up to 5` statement will display a **drop statement here** placeholder.

18. Drag the **bounceDistance ← _** statement, located at the top, and drop it in the **drop statement here** area located within the `count up to 5` block. Select **bounceDistance** in the menu that appears.

19. Click on the down arrow that appears with a gray background at the right-hand side of the assignment operator ←. A drop-down menu will display different options to use to replace the current expression. Select **Math | bounceDistance / ??? | 2.0** in the cascade menus that appear. The following code will be displayed as the first statement within the `count up to 5` block:

```
bounceDistance ← (bounceDistance / 2.0)
```

20. Drag the **move** procedure and drop it below the previously dropped statement, within the `count up to 5` block. Select **UP** and then `bounceDistance`. Click on the **more...** drop-down menu button, on `duration` and then on `0.5` in the cascade menu that appears. The following code will be displayed as a new statement:

```
this.basketball.move(UP, bounceDistance, duration: 0.5)
```

21. Drag the **move** procedure and drop it below the previously dropped statement, within the `count up to 5` block. Select `DOWN` and then `bounceDistance`. Click on the **more...** drop-down menu button, on `duration` and then on `0.5` in the cascade menu that appears. The following code will be displayed as a new statement, as shown in the next screenshot:

```
this.basketball.move(DOWN, bounceDistance, duration: 0.5)
```

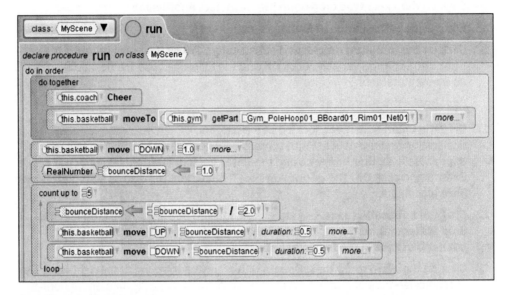

How it works...

We added a `do together` statement that allowed us to create a block of code that runs all the statements we added to the block at the same time. This means that all the statements added to this block will start their execution together, and therefore when the `coach` starts cheering, the `basketball` begins moving. The coach moves his two hands and throws the `basketball`.

The basketball reaches the basketball net's bottom and then goes down to the floor. Then the code makes the basketball bounce by moving it up and down five times, half the distance each time. The `bounceDistance` local variable allows us to divide the previous distance by 2 in each count loop iteration. The next screenshot shows four screenshots of the rendered frames:

There's more...

In this recipe, we added the code to make the `basketball` bounce in the `run` procedure. However, we might define a new `bounce` procedure for the `MyBasketball` class, with the `Model` instance that represents the floor as a parameter.

Then we can call the bounce procedure in the `run` procedure as many times as necessary.

See also

- ▶ *Declaring new procedures*, in *Chapter 3, Organizing Statements*
- ▶ *Using properties to call functions*, in *Chapter 6, Working with Properties*

Working with animals on a farm

In this recipe, we will set a scene with animals in the farm and we will make the animals move. We will create a complex animation that makes many animals perform diverse random movements concurrently. Each time that we run the project, we will have a different animation on the screen.

Getting ready

Follow these steps to create a new project and display the **Model Gallery**:

1. Select **File | New...** in the main menu to start a new project. A dialog box will display the six predefined templates with their thumbnail previews in the **Templates** tab.

2. Select GrassyProject.a3p as the desired template for the new project and click **OK**. Alice will display a grassy ground with a light blue sky.

3. Click on **Edit Scene**, at the lower-right corner of the scene preview. Alice will show a bigger preview of the scene and will display the **Model Gallery** at the bottom.

How to do it...

Follow these steps to animate animals in the farm:

1. Add instances of the twelve classes shown in the following table. Use the names shown in the Instance name column for each new instance:

Class	Instance name	Class created by Alice
FarmHouse	farmHouse	MyFarmHouse
Barn	barn	MyBarn
Cornfield	Cornfield	MyCornfield
Scarecrow	scarecrow	MyScarecrow
Pitchfork	pitchfork	MyPitchfork
WeatherVane	weatherVane	MyWeatherVane
Cow	cow	MyCow
Horse	horse	MyHorse
Chicken	chicken	MyChicken
Rabbit	rabbit	MyRabbit
Fence	fence	MyFence
Man	man	MyMan

2. Place, resize, and rotate the instances as shown in the next screenhsot:

3. Click on the **class: MyScene** drop-down list and the list of classes that are part of the scene will appear.

4. Select **MyScene | Edit run**.

5. Drag the **count** statement, located at the top, and drop it on the **drop statement here** area located below the **do in order** label, inside the **run** tab. A list with some predefined values to count up to it will appear. Select **Other Integer...** and the **Enter custom integer** dialog box will appear. Enter 20 and click **OK**. The count up to 20 statement will display a **drop statement here** placeholder.

6. Drag the **do together** statement, located at the top, and drop it on the **drop statement here** area located within the count up to 20 block. The do together statement will display a **drop statement here** placeholder.

7. Select cow in the instance drop-down list located at the left-hand side of the main window, below the small scene preview. Make sure that part: none is selected in the drop-down list located at the right-hand side of the chosen instance.

8. Drag the **move** procedure and drop it within the do together block. Select FORWARD and then 1.0.

9. Now click on the down arrow that appears with a gray background at the right-hand side of `1.0` on the previously defined statement, after **move**. A drop-down menu will display different options to use to replace the current expression. Select **Random | nextRandomRealNumberInRange ???, ??? | Other Real Number... | 2.0**. The **Enter custom real number** dialog box will appear. Enter **-2.0** and click **OK**.

10. Click on the **more...** drop-down menu button that appears at the right-hand side of the recently dropped statement. Click on `duration` and then on `10.0`. Click on the new **more...** drop-down menu that appears. Click on `asSeenBy` and then on `this.cow`. The following code includes the expression that generates a real random number to pass it as a parameter:

    ```
    this.cow.move(FORWARD, nextRandomRealNumberInRange(-2.0, 2.0),
    duration: 10.0, asSeenBy: this.cow)
    ```

11. Drag the **do in order** statement, located at the top, and drop it as a new statement within the `do together` block. The `do in order` statement will display a **drop statement here** placeholder.

12. Drag the **count** statement, located at the top, and drop it on the **drop statement here** area located within the recently added `do in order` block. Select 3 from the context menu that appears. The `count up to 3` statement will display a drop statement here placeholder.

13. Select `part: Body_BackBody_Tail01` in the drop-down list located at the right-hand side of the chosen instance.

14. Activate the **Procedures** tab.

15. Drag the **roll** procedure and drop it in the **drop statement here** area within the `count up to 3` block. A list with all the predefined direction values to pass to the first parameter will appear. Click on `LEFT` and then on `0.25` in the cascade menu that appears. Click on the **more...** drop-down menu button that appears at the right-hand side of the statement, on **duration** and then on `1.0`. The following line of code will appear:

    ```
    this.cow.getPart(Body_BackBody_Tail01).roll(LEFT, 0.25, duration:
    1.0)
    ```

16. Drag the **roll** procedure and drop it in below the previously dropped statement within the `count up to 3` block. A list with all the predefined direction values to pass to the first parameter will appear. Click on `RIGHT` and then on `0.25` in the cascade menu that appears. Click on the **more...** drop-down menu button that appears at the right-hand side of the statement, on **duration** and then on `2.0`. The following line of code will appear:

    ```
    this.cow.getPart(Body_BackBody_Tail01).roll(RIGHT, 0.25, duration:
    2.0)
    ```

17. Select `chicken` in the instance drop-down list located at the left-hand side of the main window, below the small scene preview. Make sure that `part: none` is selected in the drop-down list located at the right-hand side of the chosen instance.

18. Drag the **move** procedure and drop it below the `do in order` block, within the `do together` block. Select `FORWARD` and then `1.0`.

19. Now click on the down arrow that appears with a gray background at the right-hand side of `1.0` on the previously defined statement, after **move**. A drop-down menu will display different options to use to replace the current expression. Select **Random | nextRandomRealNumberInRange ???, ??? | Other Real Number... | 1.0**. The **Enter custom real number** dialog box will appear. Enter **-1.0** and click **OK**.

20. Click on the **more...** drop-down menu button that appears at the right-hand side of the recently dropped statement. Click on `duration` and then on `10.0`. Click on the new **more...** drop-down menu that appears. Click on `asSeenBy` and then on `this. chicken`. The following code includes the expression that generates a real random number to pass it as a parameter:

    ```
    this.chicken.move(FORWARD, nextRandomRealNumberInRange(-1.0, 1.0),
    duration: 10.0, asSeenBy: this.chicken)
    ```

21. Select `rabbit` in the instance drop-down list located at the left-hand side of the main window, below the small scene preview. Make sure that `part: none` is selected in the drop-down list located at the right-hand side of the chosen instance.

22. Drag the **move** procedure and drop it below the previously dropped statement, within the `do together` block. Select **FORWARD** and then **1.0**.

23. Now click on the down arrow that appears with a gray background at the right-hand side of `1.0` on the previously defined statement, after **move**. A drop-down menu will display different options to use to replace the current expression. Select **Random | nextRandomRealNumberInRange ???, ??? | Other Real Number... | 1.0**. The **Enter custom real number** dialog box will appear. Enter `-2.0` and click **OK**.

24. Click on the **more...** drop-down menu button that appears at the right-hand side of the recently dropped statement. Click on `duration` and then on `10.0`. Click on the new **more...** drop-down menu that appears. Click on `asSeenBy` and then on `this.rabbit`. The following code includes the expression that generates a real random number to pass it as a parameter:

    ```
    this.rabbit.move(FORWARD, nextRandomRealNumberInRange(-2.0, 1.0),
    duration: 10.0, asSeenBy: this.rabbit)
    ```

25. Select **horse** in the instance drop-down list located at the left-hand side of the main window, below the small scene preview. Make sure that `part: none` is selected in the drop-down list located at the right-hand side of the chosen instance.

26. Drag the **turn** procedure and drop it below the `do together` block, within the `count up to 20` block. Select `RIGHT` for the first parameter and then click on **Other Angle....** The **Enter Custom Other Angle** dialog box will appear. Enter **0.05** and click **OK**. Click on the **more...** drop-down menu button that appears, on `duration` and then on `1.0` in the cascade menu that appears. The following code will appear as a new statement, as shown in the next screenshot:

```
this.horse.turn(RIGHT, 0.05, duration: 1.0)
```

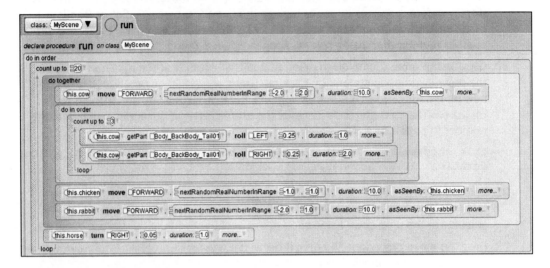

How it works...

We added a `count up to 20` statement that allowed us to create a block of code that will be repeated `20` times. The `run` procedure will perform the following visible actions at the same time `20` times because we included the statements in a `do together` block.

1. The `cow` moves forward or backward a random number of units. Because the random number is between `-2.0` and `2.0`, the `cow` can move backward when the random number is negative. The movement takes `10` seconds.

2. The `cow` rolls its tail (`Body_BackBody_Tail01`) three times while it moves.

3. The `chicken` moves forward or backward a random number of units. The random number is between `-1.0` and `1.0`. The movement takes `10` seconds.

4. The `rabbit` moves forward or backward a random number of units. The random number is between `-2.0` and `1.0`. The movement takes `10` seconds.

Once the `do together` block has completed is execution, the `horse` takes `1` second to turn to his right, and the loop starts again until its count reaches `20`.

The following screenshot shows one of the rendered frames with the animals in different positions:

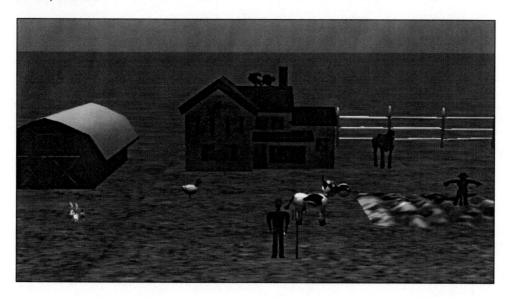

10
Customizing the Output

In this chapter, we will cover:

- ► Controlling the output to get different views
- ► Setting the camera's initial position
- ► Exporting a video
- ► Sharing a video
- ► Working with multiple camera markers
- ► Providing different points of view for a 3D world
- ► Following characters with the camera

Introduction

Alice 3 allows you to move, rotate, and set properties for the camera that defines the visible viewport of the 3D world. When you want to create dazzling real-time scenes, you must animate the camera at the same time that you animate the actors. This chapter provides many tasks that will allow us to control cameras and the output produced by the real-time rendering process that transforms a viewport of the 3D world into a 2D frame.

We will change the properties that define the active viewport and we will animate the camera while the actors move. We will generate a video and we will share it on YouTube. In addition, we will use shortcut keys to switch between multiple cameras and we will use different cameras to follow characters while they change their position in the 3D world.

Controlling the output to get different views

In this recipe, we will animate the camera to get different views while an actor moves his body. We will add blocks of code that run many statements at the same time. Alice will render the actor's animation from different points of view because the camera will change its position many times.

Getting ready

We will use an existing project that has a child from the Looking Glass Characters. This child interacts with a palm tree and a skateboard.

1. Open the project saved in the *Interacting with the environment* recipe, in *Chapter 7, Working with People*.

2. Click on **Edit Code**, at the lower-right corner of the big scene preview. Alice will show a smaller preview of the scene and will display the **Code Editor** on a panel located at the right-hand side of the main window.

3. Click on the **class: MyScene** drop-down list and the list of classes that are part of the scene will appear.

4. Select **MyScene | Edit run**.

How to do it...

Follow these steps to move the camera to a new position while the child moves his body and interacts with a palm tree and a skateboard:

1. Drag the **do together** statement, located at the top, and drop it above the first statement. Alice will display a green line indicating the position in which this new statement will be inserted. The do together statement will display a **drop statement here** placeholder.

2. Place the mouse pointer over the light shade at the left-hand side of the statement that calls the this.trevor.walkTo procedure, below the do together block. The mouse pointer will appear as a link select hand.

3. Drag the statement and drop it in the **drop statement here** area located within the do together block.

4. Select camera in the instance drop-down list located at the left-hand side of the main window, below the small scene preview.

5. Activate the **Procedures** tab. Alice will display the procedures for camera.

6. Drag the **getGoodLookAt** procedure and drop it as the first statement within the do together block. A list with all the possible instances to pass to the target parameter will appear. Click on this.trevor. Then click on the **more...** drop-down menu button that appears. Click on duration, select **Other Real Number...** and the **Enter custom real number** dialog box will appear. Enter **5** and click **OK**. The following code will appear as the two statements within the do together block:

```
do together
    this.camera.getGoodLookAt(this.trevor, duration: 5.0)
    this.trevor.walkTo(this.trevorsSkateboard, spatialRelation:
    IN_FRONT_OF)
```

7. Drag the **do together** statement, located at the top, and drop it below the previously dropped do together block. Alice will display a green line indicating the position in which this new statement will be inserted. The do together statement will display a **drop statement here** placeholder.

8. Place the mouse pointer over the light shade at the left-hand side of the statement that calls the this.trevor.sitOn procedure, below the second do together block. The mouse pointer will appear as a link select hand.

9. Drag the statement and drop it in the **drop statement here** area located within the second do together block.

10. Drag the **getGoodLookAt** procedure from the camera's procedures and drop it as the first statement within the do together block. A list with all the possible instances to pass to the target parameter will appear. Click on this.trevor. Then click on the **more...** drop-down menu button that appears. Click on duration, select **Other Real Number...** and the **Enter custom real number** dialog box will appear. Enter **4** and click **OK**. Click on the new **more...** drop-down menu that appears. Click on asSeenBy and then on this.sunLight. The following code will appear as the two statements within the do together block:

```
do together
    this.camera.getGoodLookAt(this.trevor, duration: 4.0, asSeenBy:
    this.sunLight)
    this.trevor.sitOn(this.trevorsSkateboard)
```

11. Drag a new **do together** statement, located at the top, and drop it below the previously dropped do together block. Alice will display a green line indicating the position in which this new statement will be inserted. The do together statement will display a **drop statement here** placeholder.

12. Place the mouse pointer over the light shade at the left-hand side of the statement that calls the this.trevor.lookAt procedure, below the third do together block. The mouse pointer will appear as a link select hand.

13. Drag the statement and drop it in the **drop statement here** area located within the second do together block.

14. Drag a new **getGoodLookAt** procedure from the `camera`'s procedures and drop it as the second statement within the `do together` block. A list with all the possible instances to pass to the `target` parameter will appear. Click on `this.palmtree`. Then click on the **more...** drop-down menu button that appears. Click on `duration`, select **Other Real Number...** and the **Enter custom real number** dialog box will appear. Enter **4** and click **OK**. Click on the new **more...** drop-down menu that appears. Click on `asSeenBy` and then on `this.sunLight`. The following code will appear as the two statements within the `do together` block, as shown in the next screenshot:

```
do together
    this.trevor.lookAt(this.palmtree.getPart(Leave04))
    this.camera.getGoodLookAt(this.palmtree, duration: 4.0,
    asSeenBy: this.sunLight)
```

15. Select **File | Save as...** from Alice's main menu and give a new name to the project. Then you can make changes to the project according to your needs.

How it works...

The output shows `trevor`'s movements and the `camera`'s animation:

▶ While `trevor` walks to his skateboard, the camera changes its position to get a good look at `trevor`

▶ When `trevor` sits on the `stakeboard`, the camera changes its position to get a good look at `trevor`, as seen by `sunLight`

▶ Finally, while `trevor` looks at one of the palm tree's leaves, the camera changes its position to get a good look at `palmtree`, as seen by `sunLight`

The kid, `trevor`, shows realistic movements for each action and the camera's animation provides different points of view, as shown in the following three screenshots of the rendered frames:

We added three `do together` statements that allowed us to create three blocks of code that run two statements at the same time. Each `do together` block runs the statement that animates `trevor`'s body at the same time that we move the `camera` to a new position.

> In a 3D scene, the active camera defines an eye for the models, and therefore when this scene is rendered in a 2D screen, we can see a part of the entire 3D world through the camera's lens. The camera changes the perspective for the 3D models that compose the 3D world. In order to show the 3D scene in a 2D screen, a rendering process must create a 2D image in a specific resolution that shows the portion of the whole 3D world seen by the lens of an active camera. Alice's output window displays the resulting 2D images that represent each rendered frame.

When rendering 3D scenes in a 2D screen, a camera represents a vantage point. The easiest way to understand how a camera component works is comparing it with a video camera's behavior.

If you watch a real life scene through a video camera, you will not be able to see the entire 3D world in which you are located. You will see a part of the whole 3D world rendered in the video camera's 2D LCD screen. You can move the video camera in many ways by using your hands. In addition, you can walk while recording the video and rotate the video camera by using your hands.

You can decide to zoom in to get closer to a look-at point or zoom out to move further away from it. The part of the whole 3D world rendered in the video camera's 2D LCD screen will change as you translate and rotate the video camera in the 3D space, zoom in or zoom out.

The same happens when using the `camera` instance to render Alice's virtual 3D world in a 2D screen. You can perform nearly the same operations than you can do with a real video camera. However, you will be performing these operations by calling procedures or changing the values of many properties for the `camera` instance instead of moving the camera with your hand.

Alice provides a default camera for a scene (camera), an instance of MyCamera. The MyCamera class is a subclass of SymmetricPerspectiveCamera. We called the getGoodLookAt procedure for camera to move and orient the camera to a specific look-at point. This procedure requires a target instance as a parameter. We also specified a value for the optional duration parameter to make the camera's translation and rotation last for a certain number of seconds. We passed this.sunLight to the optional asSeenBy parameter to define the partial view of the models with a specific look-at point as seen by the current location of the sunLight instance.

See also

▶   *Interacting with the environment*, in this chapter

Setting the camera's initial position

In this task, we will set the initial position of the camera and we will change one of the camera's properties. We will use the different views provided by Alice's scene editor. One of the different views will allow us to visualize the first frame preview as seen by the camera.

Getting ready

We will use an existing project that moves the camera while an actor performs actions.

1.   Open the project saved in the *Controlling the output to get different views* recipe.

2.   Click on **Edit Scene**, at the lower-right corner of the scene preview. Alice will show a bigger preview of the scene and will display the **Model Gallery** at the bottom.

How to do it...

Follow these steps to set the camera's initial position near the child and to change one of the camera's properties before animating the camera:

1.   Select Layout Scene View in the in the drop-down list located at the top of the big scene preview. You will see the three instances (trevor, trevorsSkateboard and palmtree) on the sandy ground and how the camera is looking at them. Select the camera instance. The next screenshot shows the aforementioned view and you can see the camera with a circle around it because it is selected:

2. Move the camera to point at `trevor` and to get a closer look at him. Follow the steps explained in the *Setting initial properties for an actor* recipe, in *Chapter 2: Working with Actors*. A red line from the `camera`'s lens will indicate you the viewport's center while you drag the `camera` to its new position. Make sure that the red line crosses `trevor`'s body, as shown in the next screenshot:

3. Now select `Starting Camera View` in the drop-down list located at the top of the big scene preview. Alice will render the scene as seen by the new `camera`'s position. The next picture shows the first frame that will be rendered when you run the project. `trevor` seems to be alone because `trevorsSkateboard` and `pamltree` aren't visible with the new `camera`'s position.

4. Click on **Edit Code**, at the lower-right corner of the big scene preview. Alice will show a smaller preview of the scene and will display the **Code Editor** on a panel located at the right-hand side of the main window.

5. Click on the **class: MyScene** drop-down list and the list of classes that are part of the scene will appear.

6. Select **MyScene | Edit run**.

7. Select `camera` in the instance drop-down list located at the left-hand side of the main window, below the small scene preview.

8. Activate the **Properties** tab. Alice will display the properties for `camera`.

9. Drag the **FarClippingPlaneDistance** assignment statement and drop it as the first statement within the first `do together` block. The **FarClippingPlaneDistance** assignment statement contains the **this.camera** and **FarClippingPlaneDistance** labels followed by an arrow and three question marks **???**. Select **1.0**, the desired `RealNumber` to assign to the property.

10. Drag the **FarClippingPlaneDistance** property and drop it on **1.0**, at the right-hand side of the assignment operator ← of the recently added statement. A black rectangle will surround the **1.0** value when you start dragging the **FarClippingPlaneDistance** property. The **FarClippingPlaneDistance** property contains the **this.camera** and **FarClippingPlaneDistance** labels with a yellow background.

11. Now click on **this.camera.FarClippingPlaneDistance**, at the right-hand side of the assignment operator ←. A drop-down menu will display different options to replace the current expression. Select **Math | this.camera.FarClippingPlaneDistance / ??? | Other Real Number...** in the cascade menus that appear.

12. The **Enter custom real number** dialog box will appear. Enter 50 and click **OK**. The following code will be displayed as the first statement within the first do together block, as shown in the next screenshot:

```
this.camera.FarClippingPlaneDistance ← (this.camera.
FarClippingPlaneDistance / 50.0)
```

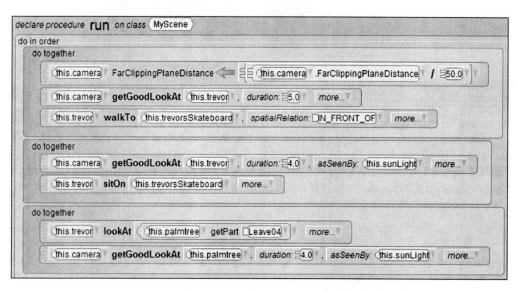

13. Select **File | Save as...** from Alice's main menu and give a new name to the project. Then you can make changes to the project according to your needs.

How it works...

We switched from the starting camera view to the layout scene view. The latter allowed us to change the initial position, size, and rotation of the camera that defines the viewport for the output. We changed the camera's initial position and then we switched to the starting camera view to visualize the first frame preview as seen by the camera.

We added a new statement that sets a new value for the `camera.`
`FarClippingPlaneDistance` property. We divided the current value for this
property by `50` and we assigned the result of this mathematic operation to `camera.`
`FarClippingPlaneDistance`. The blue sky becomes larger because the visibility
for the `camera` has been reduced to a nearer clipping plane.

There's more...

The values for the **clipping planes** determine how close to or far away from the camera a
3D model can get before it disappears from the rendered view. The part of the 3D world
that is going to be rendered can be represented as a four-sided frustum, generated by the
perspective field of view, the **near clipping plane** and the **far clipping plane**. The following
diagram shows a 2D representation of the near clipping plane and the far clipping plane that
define the boundaries for a perspective camera's frustum:

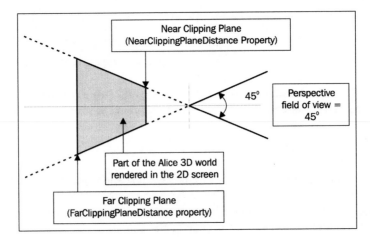

The line that crosses the center of the frustum determines the **look at point**. The perspective field of view for the camera defines the angle for the perspective camera's lens. We change the near clipping plane by setting a new value for the `camera.NearClippingPlaneDistance` property.

The 3D region which is visible on Alice's output screen is formed by a clipped pyramid, called frustum. The near clipping plane (`camera.NearClippingPlaneDistance`) and the far clipping plane (`camera.FarClippingPlaneDistance`), determine the clips. The 3D representation and its relation with the perspective field of view is shown in the following diagram:

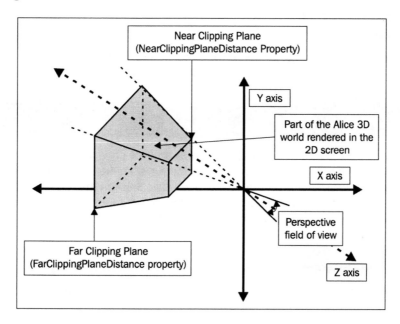

The **near clipping plane** controls the position of the plane that slices the top of the pyramid and determines the nearest part of the 3D world that the camera is going to render in the 2D screen. We can change the near clipping plane to define the frustum to render by setting a new value to the `camera.NearClippingPlaneDistance` property.

The **far clipping plane** controls the position of the plane that slices the back of the pyramid and determines the more distant part of the 3D world that the camera is going to render in the 2D screen. We can change the far clipping plane to define the frustum to render by setting a new value to the `camera.FarClippingPlaneDistance` property.

The camera's position, rotation, and size in the 3D world and its transformations will determine the final effects of these values. As aforementioned, these values can affect whether a model is visible or not in the rendered view. Sometimes, we cannot see a model rendered in a frame because these values create a frustum that does not include the models in the rendered view. Therefore, it is very important to understand all the parameters related to the `camera`. The 3D world is more complex than the simple 2D screen.

See also

▶ *Controlling the output to get different views*, in this chapter

▶ *Setting initial properties for an actor*, in *Chapter 2, Working with Actors*

Exporting a video

In this recipe, we will record the output generated by an Alice project and we will save the resulting video file. Alice will render all the frames for our animation and will encode these frames in an Apple QuickTime Movie video file. Once Alice finishes the rendering and encoding processes, we will be able to play the video in any device that reproduces Apple QuickTime Movie video files without requiring the Alice environment.

Getting ready

We will use an existing project that animates both a child and the camera that renders the output. This child interacts with a palm tree and a skateboard.

1. Open the project saved in the *Setting the camera's initial position* recipe.

2. Click on **Edit Scene**, at the lower-right corner of the scene preview. Alice will show a bigger preview of the scene and will display the **Model Gallery** at the bottom.

How to do it...

Follow these steps to export the output as a video file:

1. Select **File | Export Video / Upload to YouTube™...** in the main menu. The **Export Video** dialog box will display a small preview of the first frame, as shown in the next screenshot:

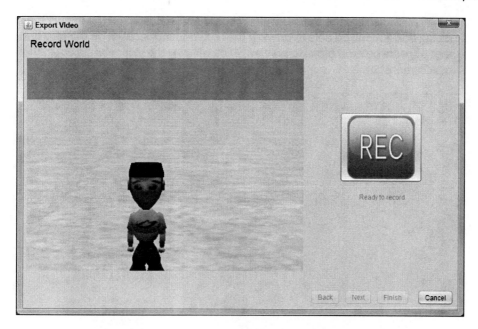

2. Click on the red **REC** button. Alice will start rendering the frames and will update the small preview. The dialog box will display the frame number that Alice is recording below the **STOP** button, as shown in the next screenshot:

3. When Alice displays the **Successfully recorded movie!** label on the **Export Video** dialog box, you will be able to preview the recorded movie. Click on the play button that appears below the movie preview. Alice will play the video, as shown in the next screenshot:

4. Click on the **Save Movie to File** button and give a name to the video. Then you can reproduce the video with an external video player or use video editing software to enhance the output.

How it works...

Alice renders the frames and encodes an Apple QuickTime Movie video file with the `.MOV` extension. The resulting video shows `trevor`'s movements and the `camera`'s animation.

Once we have exported a video, we can reproduce it with our favorite video player software that supports Apple QuickTime Movie video file. In addition, we can use specialized software to convert the video file to another format.

There's more...

We can open the Apple QuickTime Movie video file exported by Alice with VideoLAN VLC media player (www.videolan.org/vlc). We can download and install this free and open source software in all the operating systems that run Alice.

Select **Media | Open File...** from VLC media player's main menu and then choose the video file exported by Alice. The video player software will display a toolbar at the bottom of the window. This toolbar allows you to control the video playback, as shown in the next screenshot:

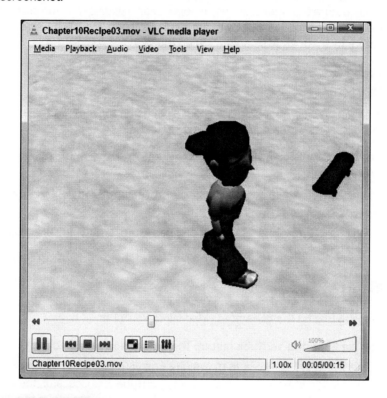

See also

▸ *Setting the camera's initial position*, in this chapter

Sharing a video

In this task, we will upload a video the output generated by an Alice project to YouTube. Alice provides a special feature that makes it easy to login to an existing YouTube account and upload the rendered and encoded video without having to open your Web Browser. We will use this feature to share an Alice animation on the Web.

Getting ready

We will use an existing project that animates both a child and the camera that renders the output. This child interacts with a palm tree and a skateboard.

1. If you haven't generated a video, follow the steps explained in the *Exporting a video* recipe.

2. Make sure that Alice displays the **Successfully recorded movie!** label on the **Export Video** dialog box.

3. If you don't have a YouTube username and password, create a new account at www.youtube.com.

How to do it...

Follow these steps to upload the generated video file to YouTube:

1. Click on the **Export to YouTube** button. The **Upload to YouTube** dialog box will appear.

2. Enter your YouTube username in **Username** and your password in **Password**. Then click on the **Login** button. If the login to your YouTube is successful, the **Logged in as:** label followed with your YouTube username will appear at the top of the dialog box.

3. Enter **Trevor's day**, in **Title**. This string is the desired title for the new video.

4. Enter **Trevor finds his skate under a palmtree**, in **Description**. This string is the desired description for the new video.

5. Enter **trevor alice alice3**, in **Tags**. This string indicates the desired tags for the new video.

6. Select **Film & Animation** in **Category**.

7. If you want to share the video without restrictions, make sure that the **Is Private** checkbox is deactivated, as shown in the next screenshot:

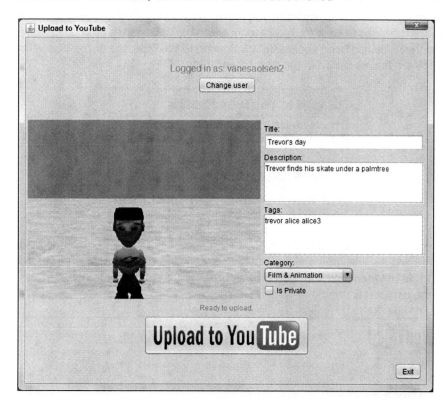

8. Click on the **Upload to YouTube** button. Alice will display the **Uploading Status** dialog box that will show the upload progress with ten small bubbles from Alice's icon to YouTube's icon. The following snapshot shows the Uploading Status dialog box with two filled bubbles, indicating that 20% of the upload process is completed:

How it works...

Alice uses the username and password you provided to log in into your YouTube account. Then Alice uploads the video to your YouTube account with the information you completed for each field. Once the video has been successfully uploaded to YouTube, the dialog box will display the link to this video, as shown in the next screenshot:

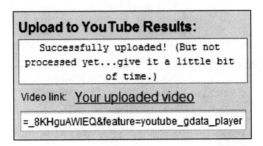

However, you have to wait until YouTube finishes processing the recently uploaded video before accessing the link. Wait a few minutes and then click on **Your uploaded video**, at the right-hand side of **Video link**. Your default web browser will play the video on YouTube, as shown in the next screenshot:

If you use third-party images, sounds, or 3D models, remember to check licenses and copyright issues before uploading a video to YouTube.

Working with multiple camera markers

In this recipe, we will use two different markers to simulate the existence of two cameras to render the output. Each camera marker will define a different point of view for our 3D world. We will add the necessary code to move the camera to the desired camera marker.

Getting ready

We will use an existing project that has `Trevor` from the Looking Glass Characters. This child interacts with a palm tree and a skateboard.

1. Open the project saved in the *Interacting with the environment* recipe, in *Chapter 7, Working with People*.

2. Click on **Edit Scene**, at the lower-right corner of the scene preview. Alice will show a bigger preview of the scene and will display the **Model Gallery** at the bottom.

How to do it...

Follow these steps to create two camera markers and move the camera towards them:

1. Select `TOP` in the drop-down list located at the top of the big scene preview. You will see the three instances (`trevor`, `trevorsSkateboard`, and `palmtree`) on the grassy ground and how the camera is looking at them.

2. Click on the **Create camera marker here...** button, located on the panel at the right-hand side of the big scene preview. A new camera marker named `cameraMarker_Red` will appear in the **Camera Markers** list. Click on this item and it will appear with a blue background, as shown in the next screenshot:

3. Move the red camera icon that represents `cameraMarker_Red` to point at `trevor` and to get a closer look at him. Follow the steps explained in the *Setting initial properties for an actor* recipe, in *Chapter 2, Working with Actors*. A red line from the red camera's lens will indicate you the viewport's center while you drag the `camera` to its new position. The initial red camera's position will be the same than the `camera`'s position:

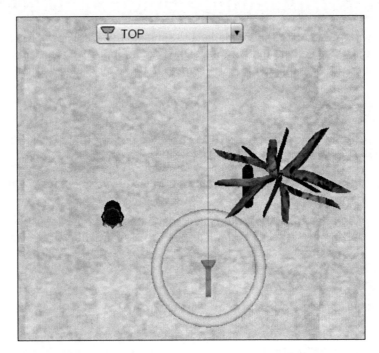

4. Move the red camera closer to `trevor`'s body. Then rotate the red camera to the left-hand side until the red line crosses `trevor`'s body.

5. Select `Layout Scene View` in the in the drop-down list located at the top of the big scene preview.

6. Click on the **Create camera marker here...** button, located on the panel at the right-hand side of the big scene preview. A new camera marker named `cameraMarker_Green` will appear in the **Camera Markers** list. Click on this item and it will appear with a blue background, as shown in the next screenshot:

7. Click on **Edit Code**, at the lower-right corner of the big scene preview. Alice will show a smaller preview of the scene and will display the **Code Editor** on a panel located at the right-hand side of the main window.

8. Click on the **class: MyScene** drop-down list and the list of classes that are part of the scene will appear.

9. Select **MyScene | Edit run**.

10. Select `camera` in the instance drop-down list located at the left-hand side of the main window, below the small scene preview.

11. Activate the **Procedures** tab. Alice will display the procedures for `camera`.

12. Drag the **moveTo** procedure and drop it as the first statement within the `run` procedure. A list with all the possible instances to pass to the `target` parameter will appear. Click on `this.cameraMarker_Red`. The following code will be added as the first statement:

    ```
    this.camera.moveTo(this.cameraMarker_Red)
    ```

13. Drag the **moveTo** procedure and drop it as the third statement within the `run` procedure, below the statement that calls the `this.trevor.walkTo` procedure. Alice will display a green line indicating the position in which this new statement will be inserted. A list with all the possible instances to pass to the `target` parameter will appear. Click on `this.cameraMarker_Green`. The following code will be added as the third statement, as shown in the next screenshot:

```
this.camera.moveTo(this.cameraMarker_Green)
```

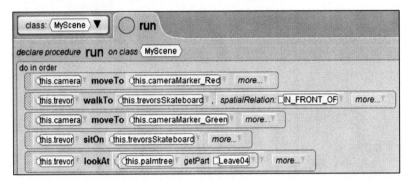

14. Select **File | Save as...** from Alice's main menu and give a new name to the project. Then you can make changes to the project according to your needs.

How it works...

The output shows `trevor`'s as seen by two different cameras:

▶ Before `trevor` walks to his skateboard, the camera changes its position to `cameraMarker_Red`

▶ Before `trevor` sits on the `stakeboard`, the camera changes its position to `cameraMarker_Green`

▶ Finally, `trevor` looks at one of the palm tree's leaves, with the camera located at `cameraMarker_Green`

The kid shows realistic movements for each action and two cameras markers define two different points of view, as shown in the following two screenshots of the rendered frames:

We added two camera markers, `cameraMarker_Red` and `cameraMarker_Green`. These camera markers allowed us to define different points for view for the 3D world.

We called the `moveTo` procedure for `camera` to move and orient the camera to one of the defined camera makers. This procedure requires a `target` instance as a parameter. Each camera marker is an instance of `BookmarkCameraMarker` and appears as a property of the `MyScene` class.

See also

▶ *Interacting with the environment*, in *Chapter 2, Working with People*

▶ *Setting initial properties for an actor*, in *Chapter 2, Working with Actors*

Providing different points of view for a 3D world

In this task, we will allow the user to switch between two cameras by pressing shortcut keys. Each camera will provide a different point of view for our 3D world. We will add the necessary code to switch to the desired point of view when the user presses a specific key.

Getting ready

We will use an existing project that moves the camera while an actor performs actions.

1. Open the project saved in the *Working with multiple camera markers* recipe.
2. Click on **Edit Code**, at the lower-right corner of the big scene preview. Alice will show a smaller preview of the scene and will display the **Code Editor** on a panel located at the right-hand side of the main window.
3. Click on the **class: MyScene** drop-down list and the list of classes that are part of the scene will appear.
4. Select **MyScene | Edit run**.
5. Delete the two statements that call the `this.camera.moveTo` procedure.

How to do it...

Follow these steps to switch cameras when the user clicks certain keys:

1. Select **camera** in the instance drop-down list located at the left-hand side of the main window, below the small scene preview.
2. Activate the **Procedures** tab. Alice will display the procedures for `camera`.

3. Drag the **addKeyListener** procedure and drop it as the first statement, inside the **run** tab. The `addKeyListener` procedure will add a `keyPressed` procedure declaration with a **drop statement here** placeholder.

4. Drag the **if _** statement, located at the top, and drop it on the **drop statement here** placeholder within the `keyPressed` procedure for the `camera` key listener. Click on **true** and two **drop statement here** placeholders will appear.

5. Click on the last down arrow that appears with a gray background at the right-hand side of the previously defined expression for the `if` block, before **is true then**. A drop-down menu will display different options to use to replace the current expression.

6. Select **e.IsKey ??? | digits (0-9) | DIGIT_1** in the cascade menus that appear.

7. Drag the **moveTo** procedure and drop it on the first **drop statement here** area located within the `if` block. A list with all the possible instances to pass to the `target` parameter will appear. Click on `this.cameraMarker_Red`.

8. Drag another **if _** statement, located at the top, and drop it below the `else` keyword, within the previously dropped `if` block. Click on **true** and two **drop statement here** placeholders will appear.

9. Click on the last down arrow that appears with a gray background at the right-hand side of the previously defined expression for the `if` block, before **is true then**. A drop-down menu will display different options to use to replace the current expression.

10. Select **e.IsKey ??? | digits (0-9) | DIGIT_2** in the cascade menus that appear.

11. Drag the **moveTo** procedure and drop it on the first **drop statement here** area located within the recently added `if` block. A list with all the possible instances to pass to the `target` parameter will appear. Click on `this.cameraMarker_Green`. The following screenshot shows the code that defines the two conditional `if` blocks within the new key listener:

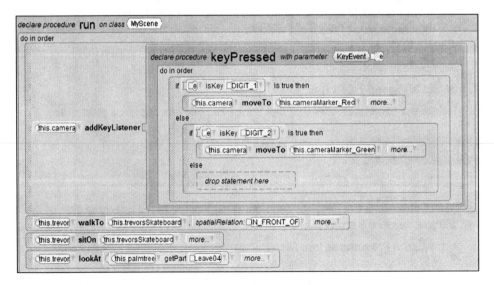

12. Select **File | Save as...** from Alice's main menu and give a new name to the project. Then you can make changes to the project according to your needs.

How it works...

When we run the project, we can press the following two keys to switch between the two available points of view for the 3D world:

- ▶ *1*: Moves the camera to `cameraMarker_Red`.
- ▶ *2*: Moves the camera to `cameraMarker_Green`.

When we press any key, Alice executes the `keyPressed` procedure because we added a key listener for `camera`. The `keyPressed` procedure for the `camera`'s key listener uses two chained `if` blocks to perform actions according to the key that the user pressed.

See also

- ▶ *Working with multiple camera markers*, in this chapter

Following characters with the camera

In this recipe, we will allow the user to select the actor that the camera has to follow by pressing shortcut keys. We will add the necessary code to instruct the camera to follow a specific instance when the user presses certain key. The camera will continuously change its position to get a good look at the desired instance as Alice renders the animation.

Getting ready

We will use a project that makes two robots dance when the user clicks on the scene:

1. Open the project saved in the *Defining a mouse button listener* recipe, in *Chapter 8, Working with Keyboard and Mouse Input*.

2. Click on **Edit Code**, at the lower right corner of the big scene preview. Alice will show a smaller preview of the scene and will display the **Code Editor** on a panel located at the right-hand side of the main window.

3. Click on the **class: MyScene** drop-down list and the list of classes that are part of the scene will appear.

4. Select **MyScene | Edit run**.

How to do it...

Follow these steps to follow different actors when the user presses certain keys:

1. Select `camera` in the instance drop-down list located at the left-hand side of the main window, below the small scene preview.

2. Activate the **Procedures** tab. Alice will display the procedures for `camera`.

3. Drag the **addKeyListener** procedure and drop it as the first statement, inside the **run** tab. The `addKeyListener` procedure will add a `keyPressed` procedure declaration with a **drop statement here** placeholder.

4. Drag the **if _** statement, located at the top, and drop it on the **drop statement here** placeholder within the `keyPressed` procedure for the `camera` key listener. Click on **true** and two **drop statement here** placeholders will appear.

5. Click on the last down arrow that appears with a gray background at the right-hand side of the previously defined expression for the `if` block, before **is true then**. A drop-down menu will display different options to use to replace the current expression.

6. Select **e.IsKey ??? | digits (0-9) | DIGIT_1** in the cascade menus that appear.

7. Activate the **Properties** tab. Alice will display the properties for `camera`.

8. Drag the **Vehicle** assignment statement and drop it on the first **drop statement here** area located within the `if` block. A list with all the possible instances to set as the value for this property will appear. Click on `this.gina`.

9. Drag another **if _** statement, located at the top, and drop it below the `else` keyword, within the previously dropped `if` block. Click on **true** and two **drop statement here** placeholders will appear.

10. Click on the last down arrow that appears with a gray background at the right-hand side of the previously defined expression for the `if` block, before **is true then**. A drop-down menu will display different options to use to replace the current expression.

11. Select **e.IsKey ??? | digits (0-9) | DIGIT_2** in the cascade menus that appear.

12. Drag the **Vehicle** assignment statement and drop it on the first **drop statement here** area located within the recently added `if` block. A list with all the possible instances to set as the value for this property will appear. Click on **this.biff**. The following picture shows the code that defines the two conditional `if` blocks within the new key listener. The key listener is the first block of code for the `run` procedure:

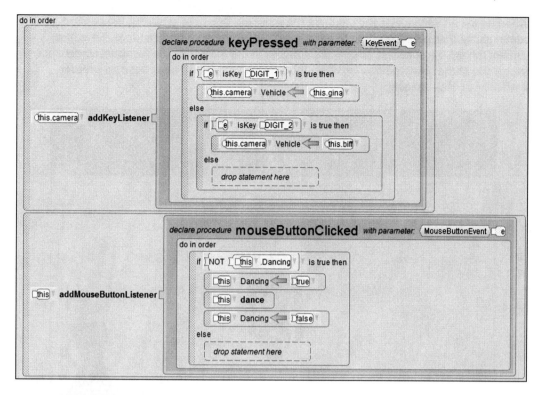

How it works...

When we run the project, we can press the following two keys to make the camera follow two different actors in the scene:

▸ *1*: Makes the camera follow `gina`.

▸ *2*: Makes the camera follow `biff`.

When we press any key, Alice executes the `keyPressed` procedure because we added a key listener for `camera`. The `keyPressed` procedure for the `camera`'s key listener uses two chained `if` blocks to change the value for `camera.Vehicle` according to the key that the user pressed.

When we set an instance as the value for the `camera.Vehicle` property, the camera continuously changes its position to get a good look at the specified instance. Thus, the camera follows the specified actor while it moves in the 3D world. The following screenshot shows one of the rendered frames when the camera follows `biff` because we pressed **2** while `biff` was dancing:

See also

▶ *Defining a mouse button listener*, in Chapter 8, *Working with Keyboard and Mouse Input*

Index

Thank you for buying
Alice 3 Cookbook

About Packt Publishing

Packt, pronounced 'packed', published its first book "*Mastering phpMyAdmin for Effective MySQL Management*" in April 2004 and subsequently continued to specialize in publishing highly focused books on specific technologies and solutions.

Our books and publications share the experiences of your fellow IT professionals in adapting and customizing today's systems, applications, and frameworks. Our solution based books give you the knowledge and power to customize the software and technologies you're using to get the job done. Packt books are more specific and less general than the IT books you have seen in the past. Our unique business model allows us to bring you more focused information, giving you more of what you need to know, and less of what you don't.

Packt is a modern, yet unique publishing company, which focuses on producing quality, cutting-edge books for communities of developers, administrators, and newbies alike. For more information, please visit our website: www.packtpub.com.

About Packt Open Source

In 2010, Packt launched two new brands, Packt Open Source and Packt Enterprise, in order to continue its focus on specialization. This book is part of the Packt Open Source brand, home to books published on software built around Open Source licences, and offering information to anybody from advanced developers to budding web designers. The Open Source brand also runs Packt's Open Source Royalty Scheme, by which Packt gives a royalty to each Open Source project about whose software a book is sold.

Writing for Packt

We welcome all inquiries from people who are interested in authoring. Book proposals should be sent to author@packtpub.com. If your book idea is still at an early stage and you would like to discuss it first before writing a formal book proposal, contact us; one of our commissioning editors will get in touch with you.

We're not just looking for published authors; if you have strong technical skills but no writing experience, our experienced editors can help you develop a writing career, or simply get some additional reward for your expertise.

Blender 3D Architecture, Buildings, and Scenery

ISBN: 978-1-847193-67-4   Paperback: 332 pages

Create photorealistic 3D architectural visualizations of buildings, interiors, and environmental scenery

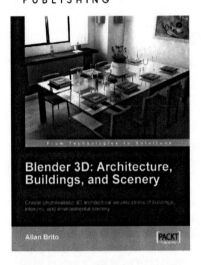

1. Turn your architectural plans into a model

2. Study modeling, materials, textures, and light basics in Blender

3. Create photo-realistic images in detail

4. Create realistic virtual tours of buildings and scenes

Blender 2.49 Scripting

ISBN: 978-1-849510-40-0   Paperback: 292 pages

Extend the power and flexibility of Blender with the help of the high-level, easy-to-learn scripting language, Python

1. Gain control of all aspects of Blender using the powerful Python language

2. Create complex meshes programmatically and apply materials and textures

3. Automate the rendering process and extend Blender's image manipulation capabilities

4. Extend Blender's built-in editor

Please check **www.PacktPub.com** for information on our titles

Papervision3D Essentials

ISBN: 978-1-847195-72-2   Paperback: 428 pages

Create interactive Papervision 3D applications with stunning effects and powerful animations

1. Build stunning, interactive Papervision3D applications from scratch

2. Export and import 3D models from Autodesk 3ds Max, SketchUp and Blender to Papervision3D

3. In-depth coverage of important 3D concepts with demo applications, screenshots and example code.

4. Step-by-step guide for beginners and professionals with tips and tricks based on the authors' practical experience

Blender 2.5 Lighting and Rendering

ISBN: 978-1-847199-88-1   Paperback: 252 pages

Bring your 3D world to life with lighting, compositing, and rendering

1. Render spectacular scenes with realistic lighting in any 3D application using interior and exterior lighting techniques

2. Give an amazing look to 3D scenes by applying light rigs and shadow effects

3. Apply color effects to your scene by changing the World and Lamp color values

Please check **www.PacktPub.com** for information on our titles

Lightning Source UK Ltd.
Milton Keynes UK

172140UK00001B/20/P